# Kern County Fair
# 1871-1952

# Kern County Fair

# 1871-1952

### Racing, Rodeos, Giant Pumpkins

### Lop-Eared Rabbits

### and Big Tops

by Gilbert Peter Gia

For Ramona Forquera Gia
who made it happen

and for

Jennifer Gia Page
who pushed it over the top.


Thank you to Kern County Historical Society members
Jerry Ludeke and Kitty DeArmond for their guidance
and generous help.

# Contents

# Style and Documentation

The styles used in this book are my own. Bracketed, italicized words in quotations I added for explanation. Brackets in the references section highlight sources. I silently corrected obvious typesetting errors; otherwise, quoted text, such as "Sixteenth street", reflects exact spelling, capitalization, and punctuation. For that reason some quotations have an outside, appended punctuation mark. Example: The number of exhibits inside the building was "simply enormous".

In the 1930s the Bakersfield Californian stopped spelling numerated streets and instead wrote them as numbers. About that time it also began capitalizing the words avenue, street, and county: Truxtun avenue became Truxtun Avenue, Sixteenth street became 16th Street, and Kern county became Kern County.

Kern County newspapers frequently interchanged the words Fair Association and Fifteenth Agricultural District even though they were not the same organizations. Today the California Department of Food & Agriculture oversees the Fifteenth Agricultural District, and the Fifteenth Agricultural District oversees the Kern County Fair Association.

Most endnotes do not have associated page numbers. Page numbers may be found via newspaper search engines, e.g., newspapers.com.

Dollar amounts in parentheses represent 2023 purchasing power.

The newspaper abbreviations are BC for Bakersfield Californian, DC for Bakersfield Daily Californian, and ME for Bakersfield Morning Echo.

This book was formatted with Word 2010. Line spacing is 1.5, multiple 1.35 kerning, while endnotes are multiple 1.25 kerning. The font is 10 point Bienetresocial Bold, 9 point in Endnotes. French typographer Claude Pelletier gave Bienetresocial to the public in 2003.

# Beginnings 1871-1890

Agricultural Society— Horses
Bad Press—Recession—Land Grabs
Mechanics Institutes—Fire

California became a state in 1850, and in 1866 Kern County was formed out of parts of Tulare, Los Angeles, and San Bernardino counties.[1] A Bakersfield newspaper wrote of that early year, "When we came here in 1866, there were, if we remember, only twelve voters in this precinct, and they were a majority of the male inhabitants of the valley of the Kern River. There were ten families, and the entire population did not, perhaps, exceed one hundred, counting all between the mountains from Fort Tejon to White River."[2] Kern's late start as a county was only one of the reasons its first fair was not held until 1892.

## Agricultural Society

In 1870, Kern County had five public schools, 12 general stores, and a population of 2000 clustered around Linn's Valley, Kernville, Havilah, Walker Basin, Tehachapi, and Bakersfield. Bakersfield represented 40 percent of the population.[3]

A.D. Jones who owned and published the Kern County Weekly Courier wrote articles to promote settlement.[4] "Rumor says that our population is put down at about three thousand, which, perhaps, is as near correct as under the circumstances it was possible to make it. Imagine this population scattered, as it is, over an area of not less than eight thousand square miles, and anyone can see how next to impossible it is to enumerate it accurately."

"Imagine a quarter section, with a post-and-rail fence along part of one side, brush enough to carry it out in the next ravine, with a slough for a barrier along the remainder, little patches of corn, and beans, and potatoes, and alfalfa, and pumpkins, and onions, and sweet potatoes, and the like occupying nooks and corners here and there, where most convenient to cultivate. Such are a majority of our farms in their present condition. A few years more and we will get things straightened out and be able to give a better account of ourselves. Our population is regularly increasing and our means still more rapidly. Our future is not only hopeful, but certain."[5]

In 1871 Col. Thomas Baker, George B. Chester, Julius Chester, John T. Collins, Andrew R. Jackson, Solomon Jewett, Augustus D. Jones, R.D. Kennedy, Edward Tibbet, C.D. White, and A.D. Jones founded an agricultural society. In the same year, rancher Philo Jewett bought 100 purebred Spanish Marino sheep in Vermont and shipped them by rail to San Francisco. He sold some at the Bay district fair and sent the rest by steamer to Los Angeles for the Southern Agricultural District Fair. Although his sheep were weakened by travel, Jewett received two medals. He sent the rest overland to his Rio Bravo Ranch at Kern Canyon and a year later showed them at the Santa Clara fair.[6]

## Horse Racing

Bakersfield had an excellent half-mile track in 1871, and at one of the races when betting rose to $225 ($5000), owners demanded jockeys of exactly

16

equal weight. In the same year, at another Bakersfield track, gambling winnings amounted to $1500 ($34,000). In 1875 there was a half-mile track just south of today's Kern County Metro Justice Building (1215 Truxtun Avenue).[7] The Weekly Courier wrote, "It will revive the interest in the sport and enable us to challenge Visalia and the South Fork on our own ground. It is proposed to extend the track a full mile during the spring."[8] The track was not only used for racing. That summer a bull fight was held, followed by an itinerant Mexican circus.[9]

In 1876 Dan S. Lightner built a track at his hot-springs resort near today's Lake Isabella and in the summer hosted a dance that attracted 200 visitors. Those from Bakersfield stayed overnight for the races. A week later, in Bakersfield, an Oregon horse surprised everyone by beating a local favorite. The news was print-worthy because the winnings and losses were $30,000 ($836,000).

In 1883 a local newspaper wrote, "When the race-track was established on the road to Sumner, few persons believed that much interest would be taken in racing, or that it would result according to the anticipation of the party who made the investment. But it has turned out differently. There proves to be plenty of fine horses in the county upon which their owners and others are willing to risk their money, and the races, from week to week, have been growing in interest." [10] That year "fairground track" located midway between Bakersfield and Sumner was also a site for foot races and baseball games.[11] Decades later, a vacant space between Sonora and Sumner Street by the railroad tracks was called the Circus Grounds. In 1950, Clyde Beatty Circus was the last to set up there.[12]

## Fairs Delayed

Historical events slowed Kern County's development. State newspapers portrayed Bakersfield as a rude, vice-ridden town, but its own newspapers contributed to the bad press. In 1876 a Reverend Leard came here "dispensing the charities of the gospel...with a sprinkling of school teaching."[13] Two years later, when he left town, the Southern Californian observed, "It is a noted fact that it is impossible for any preacher to make a success here; but, give us a circus or a horse race, and 'you bet' we are 'thar.'"[14]

In 1884 this account appeared in the Bakersfield Daily Evening Gazette: "At one time a stranger stopped here and expressed his fear at remaining during the night. He was told that there was scarcely danger in his remaining, and the porter was instructed to conduct him to room No. 1. "But," said the porter, "that dead man has not been taken from there yet. ...Well, take him to No. 2. The man that died there has been taken out." "'Yes," said the porter, "but there is another sick man in there, and the doctor thinks he will die tonight." The stranger paid his supper bill and concluded not to stay all night." [15] Six years later, California newspapers condemned Bakersfield because of a tar-and-feathering on Reeder's Hill, which was once just south of downtown.[16]

Recessions helped put the first fair on hold. In the early 1870s the Central Pacific Railroad was laying track south toward Bakersfield, and the residents, "Americans and Europeans, 1450; Mexicans, 600; and Chinese, 250", envisioned prosperity coming. To put an end to indiscriminate garbage dumping, horse racing, and wide-open prostitution on the streets, Bakersfield incorporated and enacted restrictive ordinances.

In the fall of 1873 an Eastern railroad went into receivership, Wall Street reeled, and the United States slipped into recession. The Panic of 1873 damaged Bakersfield business, and work on the rail lines halted 30 miles north at Delano. In January 1876, just 20 months after the town became a city, it disincorporated. In the second half of 1876 the economy rebounded, and in the decade, the population grew from 5600 to 9800, although less robust than counties to the north.[17]

Also delaying the first Kern County fair were the massive acquisitions of acreage by wealthy individuals. In the summer of 1870, A. R. Jackson, B. Brundage, C. G. Jackson, John Howlett, H. A. Cross, Solomon Jewett, L.G. Barnes, Col. Thomas Baker, and the firm of Chester & Livermore filed a petition under the Montgomery Act on 28,000 acres between Bakersfield and Kern Lake (now dry). Three years later, John H. Redington settled the affairs of Chester & Livermore, incorporated as Redington & Livermore, and sold its holdings to tycoon James Ben Ali Haggin. Haggin went on to acquire the 10,000-acre Buena Vista Ranch, the 17,700-acre Rancho San Emigdio, and many, many other ranches.

The Central Pacific Railroad acquired massive acreage granted to it under the Pacific Railroad Act, which in California was 10 square miles for each mile of track laid, but bailment requirements in the act required the railroads to eventually return the land to the public. The rails were built, and by the mid-1870s Kern County agricultural products were sold in San

Francisco markets, and when refrigerated rail cars came into use, Kern products were sold in New York City. By the 1890s Kern products were in British markets.

The Central Pacific Railroad had 4700 square miles of land in the San Joaquin Valley, and in the late 1880s it put some on the market. Isaac E. Gates of New York bought a large swath south and west of Bakersfield and subsequently sold it to James Ben Ali Haggin. Eventually, Haggin accumulated 400,000 acres (625 square miles) in the San Joaquin Valley.[18]

Two individuals north of Kern owned 85 square miles each, but the largest land owner, Miller & Lux, had more than 1000 square miles. Unlike Haggin's land ownership, Miller & Lux's did not stifle development. In 1882 the Fresno Fair Grounds Association had a fairgrounds, grandstand, and a pavilion valued at $20,000 ($538,000). Between 1880 and 1886, the populations of Tulare and Fresno County grew 66 and 89 percent respectively, while equally-well-irrigated Kern County declined one percent.[19]

In the mid-1870s, Haggin and Miller were in court over water rights, and for the next 10 years Kern's growth suffered. As the case moved to a conclusion, Haggin's business goals changed, and in 1886 his Los Angeles representatives were selling 20-acre parcels in the Mountain View and Lerdo colonies of Kern County. Three years later, Haggin's vast holdings in the United States and Republic of Mexico, worth $10,000,000 ($3 Billion), incorporated as the Kern County Land Company. By then Haggin's 2000-acre Rosedale Colony, with graded roads and private canals, was home to dozens of families. The company built a commodious hotel for prospective buyers and encouraged the settlers to build churches and schools.[20]

## Mechanics Institute

In the mid-1880s, Haggin's name at state fairs was better known than Kern County, but that, too, was changing. The Mechanics Institute of San Francisco invited Kern County to show at its 1887 exhibition, and Celsus Brower, Alonzo Coons, Herman Hirshfeld, Richard Hudnut, and Elisha M. Roberts urged local merchants and farmers, including the Haggin ranches, to join in the show. "We most respectfully and earnestly request all who have the interest of Kern county at heart to cordially cooperate with us in making this exhibit of Kern county one which will reflect lasting credit and honor on the citizens thereof."[21]

The Kern County Board of Trade sponsored a booth, and Col. L.W. Burr and Mrs. Dr. L.S. (Doris) Rogers managed the displays of grapes, peaches, pears, watermelons, almonds, cheese, honey, potatoes, onions, corn, sorghum, hops, ramie, wool, antimony, limestone, and building stone. Fifteen farmers attended, and all resided in Kern County except James Ben Ali Haggin.[22]

Dozens of photographs in the center of the booth attracted keen interest. Commissioned by Haggin and photographed by Carlton Watkins, they spotlighted Kern's vast countryside, impressive canal system, and the massive ranches of Haggin & Carr, Houghton & Stetson, and Miller & Lux. Everything in the booth was interesting and praiseworthy, and although the competition was fierce, Kern received the Special Grand Silver Medal for a display of apples and $10 ($300) for an artful arrangement of peaches. J.S. Drury's exhibit of ramie fabric was awarded a bronze medal, and, and W.J. Dougherty received $15 ($450) for his display of honey.[23]

In 1889 the Kern Board of Trade sent county produce to the institute's 24th exhibition, and Mrs. Doris Rogers and Manager S.N. Reed "ably attended" the apples, prunes, pomegranates, strawberries, squash, pumpkins, and canned fruit, all "surpassed by none." [24] Notable were the Bartlett pears, each weighing more than a pound and Orange Cling and George's Late Peaches measuring 13 to 17 inches around.[25] S.N. Reed recalled, "The finest prize was the grand gold medal and $250 offered for the best, most extensive and varied exhibit of farm products (outside of livestock) by any County in the State, and this being awarded to our own Kern County, we only felt it was a fitting tribute to the best County in our glorious State."[26]

Success at San Francisco encouraged Hugh A. Blodget, Celsus Brower, William B. Carr, Herman Hirschfield, William E. Houghton, Henry A. Jastro, Charles A. Maude, Hudson C. Park, and Alphonse Weill to plan a Kern County exhibit for the 1893 World Columbian Exposition in Chicago. It was an ambitious project for a county of 7500 residents.[27]

In the late 1880s the Fifteenth Agricultural District encompassed Kern, Tulare, and Santa Barbara counties. In 1889 Californian Governor Robert Waterman appointed Bakersfield residents Herbert H. Fish and Hugh A. Blodget to the board, and in fall, Kern's agricultural bounty presented well at the Visalia fair. Talk was now about holding the next fifteenth district fair in Bakersfield. State support for agricultural district was slim, county funding was insufficient, and Bakersfield Board of Trade turned to the public to help in the fair project. But disaster struck.

## Fire

The fire of July 7, 1889 destroyed 15 city blocks, 30 major business houses, many homes, and losses ranged from $890,500 to $1,250,000 ($29M—$41M). California cities offered to help, but Henry A. Jastro who was secretary of the disaster committee assured them that although Bakersfield was grateful, it needed no help. Bakersfield rebuilt in brick,[28] and when the German Saving Bank of San Francisco offered nine-percent loans, the Californian observed, "This is the first time in the history of Bakersfield that savings or other city banks ever were willing to loan money upon town property."[29] No fair was held here in 1889.

When a Bakersfield newspaper ridiculed holding a fair here, the Daily Californian sharpened its satirical pen and wrote, "It is good to live in Kern county. It is an isolated region which nothing ever comes near enough to bother. Among other things, it is mercifully spared from the occurrence of those dangerous educators known as County Fairs. If people will agree not to stir up this matter of its great productiveness and will avail themselves of the great chances to do nothing that so courageously offer themselves, never hold a County Fair, nor sprinkle the streets; never spread any gravel upon a roadbed and carefully avoid all internal improvements, there remains the reasonable assurance that at any future time the returning Rip Van Winkle will find the old place just as he left it, and probably be very sorry that he had the spunk to return."[30]

# Chapter 1, 1890-1893

## Fairgrounds Association
## Racetrack—Fair of 1892

In 1890, J.M. Reuck who owned the Daily Californian wrote, "That Kern county needs a fair grounds and a race track no one will deny. That they can be had, by united effort is a certain fact."[31] Reuck had been secretary of the Fresno Fair Grounds Association, and now, as proprietor of the Daily Bakersfield Californian, he championed a Kern County fairgrounds association. "The advantages which would accrue to Kern county from such an institution are of a character to merit the support of every citizen in the county who is interested in the rapid development of the county, its institutions, the enhancement of its values, and its identity with progress and enterprise."[32]

By this date Kern County Land Company was in transition. The Kern County Californian noted, "Work upon the race track and fair grounds, north of the railroad, has been temporarily suspended, the men and teams being employed upon some necessary road and levee work in the vicinity of the river. The general belief is that Mr. Haggin intends to make this a complete piece of work of the kind, well enclosed and with all the sheds, stables, buildings, etc., necessary. With his own stock that he has here, and the products of his own farms, he could have frequent and most creditable exhibitions without the assistance, that would be sure to be afforded by other people desiring to exhibit, or show the speed of their horses, and it would afford powerful aid in his work of colonization. When all his lands are sold, if not pressed too hard with the growth of the city and made valuable for building lots, unquestionably a large and rich Agricultural Fair Association will stand ready to buy it."[33]

The Eighth Annual Fair of the Fifteenth District Agricultural Association "comprising Kern and Tulare County" opened in Visalia in the second week of October 1890. It had stock shows, community exhibits, and five days of horse racing offering purses of $6000 ($200,000).[34]On one of the days it rained, but the fair was otherwise well-attended.

In 1891 the Fifteenth District fair again was held in Visalia. The Daily Californian advised, "Kern county must not be behind in the contest. Every resident can assist in some way. Whoever has fruits, minerals, handiwork or any other object of interest to show the resources of the County can add to the display." [35] But that required effort. There was no direct rail line between Bakersfield and Visalia, and the trip by buggy took two days.

As fair time drew near, enthusiasm faded. "It is not likely that Kern county will send much of an agricultural exhibit to Visalia, although by a little concerted action it might do so to its own credit, but it requires that peculiar human possession called

26

enthusiasm to be harnessed right down to the work. Big pumpkins, royal loaves of bread, and the daintiest needle-work are somehow exceedingly local and it requires a great deal of aggressive magnanimity to gather together such as these and enthuse over them." [36] Two weeks later the Californian scolded, "Kern county people are directly interested and should not forget that they are united with our sister county of Tulare in this enterprise; that it is their duty to support it in every way and that its success brings credit to both counties alike, as its failure if such a thing is possible – which it is not – would throw just as much discredit upon the people of Kern as of Tulare."[37]

The next fair was also in Visalia and was also well attended, but the association had been unprofitable, and despite five days of spirited horse racing, it once again wound up in the red. Two facts were insurmountable: The Visalia fairgrounds did not have direct railway service, and it regularly lost customers to the much-larger Twenty-First District Fair at Fresno.

On March 15, 1891, the Kern County Fair Grounds Association incorporated, and its directors were prominent and wealthy men: H.A. Blodget, S.W. Fergusson (director of the Kern County Land Company), H.A. Jastro, Solomon Jewett, Louise V. Olcese, W.H. Scribner, J.R. Simmons, and S.W. Wible. Four hundred shares of stock were offered at $25 par ($850), the public bought nearly 200 shares, and that encouraged the corporation to start looking for land.[38] Herbert H. Fish & Company offered 80 acres one mile south of Bakersfield for $160,000 ($490,000), but Kern County Land Company offered its refurbished racetrack and 90 acres "embellished by nature with oak trees and shrubbery" for $130,500 ($415,000). The land company said it was ready to complete the deal immediately.[39]

Kern County Fair Grounds Association embraced agricultural education, industrial growth, and the development of county resources. Newspaper owner Reuck wrote, "It also extends to the talents of our people in music, art and literature. However, to be plain, we will state that the fair is to be held under the supervision of the Fifteenth Agricultural District, which comprise the counties of Tulare and Kern. The fair itself will be given under the auspices of the Kern County Fair Grounds Association, which will receive the state appropriation for premiums, etc., through the directors of the Fifteenth Agricultural District."[40] When a reader suggested the association would favor Kern exhibitors over those from Tulare County, Reuck responded, "The affairs of the Kern County Fair Grounds Association are being conducted on business principles, with a fair field and no favors."[41]

Even though Reuck emphasized "music, art and literature" and "the talents of our people", he reacted sourly when the public asked for a more inclusive fair, one that did not favor horse racing. Reuck wrote, "We regret very much that western America is the only country in the world that cannot have a race without going to the expense of holding a fair. People there *[in the East]* turn out to see the races and do not hesitate to say so. But here people would hold up their hands in holy horror at anything that contemplated racing and nothing else. They must have a fair, with big pumpkins, patchwork quilts and cross-eyed poodle dogs embroidered in worsted."[42]

More money was needed, and association issued 2000 shares of stock at $25 par ($725). Members bought 1400 shares, most in lots of one, two, and three but a few in lots of eight. H.A. Blodget, S.W. Fergusson, John C. Morrison, W.H. Scribner, Solomon Jewett, and J.M. Reuck bought 10 shares each ($7250), Henry Miller, 25 ($18,125), and Director of the Kern County Land Company S.W. Fergusson, 50 ($36,250). The remaining shares were set aside for the public, and they sold so well that 500 more were issued. Funds accumulated and when added to the expected state contribution of $2500 ($75,000) the total came to $7500 ($225,000), which was considered enough to buy a fairgrounds.[43]

Weeks later the state told the association that it would not send the money until the treasurer of the fairgrounds association sat on the Fifteenth District Agricultural Association board. The solution was easy done because several association members already were on the agricultural board. A a shifting of seats took place: H.A. Blodget, H.A. Jastro, L.V. Olcese, J.R. Simmons, and S.W. Wible joined the association, and J. C. Morrison, J.J. Mack, and W.H. Scribner became members at large.[44]

The land company's offer of its old racetrack and acreage was still on the table, but the association advertised anyway "for the purpose of a racetrack, etc."[45] In May of 1892 when the board met at Reuck's office, the biggest issue was the high cost of land. When a bank loan was proposed, Reuck insisted that the buy "be done on a cash basis or let it be dropped altogether."[46]

The board turned to well-wishers who had promised to buy shares but had not yet done so, and. Reuck admonished his readers. "The building of a race course and erection of exhibition buildings must be pursued with dispatch, to an early completion. Every public-spirited resident of Kern county should subscribe for at least one share of this stock.—J.M. Reuck Sec'y Kern Co. Fair Grounds Ass'n."[47] Days later he wrote, "Bakersfield should have as good a race track as does any other city in the state. Local premiums are already coming in on subscriptions for a Kern county fair."[48] Reuck advised, "The pavilion should always be held in town, and not at the race track, for the reason that the people who patronize that portion of the show do not, in a general way, fancy horse-racing."[49]

## Racetrack

In the summer of 1892, Kern County Land Company Director William Saunders Tevis and Kern Fair Grounds Association President Solomon Jewett signed a lease on the old racetrack and its 90 acres, and the paperwork included an option to buy the property for $10,964 ($352,000). When that news went public, Kern Driving Club asked for a sublease and permission to build a clubhouse.[50]

Reuck thanked the land company for its civic mindedness. "The Kern County Land Company, always under the present management ready to encourage enterprise for the good of the county and to add to the prosperity of her people, very generously accorded the plot of 100 acres to the association on an option of five years with the privilege of purchase at $100 per acre *[$3375]* and to pay a nominal interest at six percent per annum during the interim. It is a good thing that a stable base of operations has at length been reached, for a fair grounds and an agricultural park are greatly needed right at this very time."[51] A week later a reporter wrote, "The site the directors have selected is a beautiful one that nature has endowed with many natural advantages, which with the artificial improvements in contemplation will make it a magnificent and popular resort for turfites generally."[52] Today that vast acreage encompasses the Kern County Museum, Pioneer Village, Lori Brock Discovery Center, Stramler Park, Sam Lynn Ballpark, Metro Recreation fields, and the U.S. Army Reserve Center.

## Fair of 1892

The Visalia fairgrounds association allowed its lease to expire, and the grounds were plowed under and sown to grain. At a meeting of the Fifteenth District Agricultural Association, which by then represented only Kern and Tulare counties, Bakersfield became the permanent location for the fair.[53]

Over the next several months the association spent $6000 ($202,000) for improvements[54] Contractor H.E. Fairman provided men with six teams to grade a 60-foot-wide track, cap it with clay, and construct a 50 by 75-foot grandstand—which was a duplicate of Fresno's but built higher to provide space for a lunch room, bar, and betting area. Also built were stables and a double-decker observation stand, the upper level for judges and the ground level for timers and reporters.[55]

The racetrack was ready for racing, but the surrounding grounds lacked driveways, sidewalks, and landscaping, the association explaining that everything was in "as good condition as the time would possibly allow". It added that there was no

31

pavilion because "something more than an ordinary shed" was desired.[56] In fact, the association had run out of money.

Weeks before the fair, the Women's Christian Temperance Union criticized the sale of alcohol at the fair. "Now let this sentiment take shape in absolutely refusing to grant to the liquor trade permission to continue its nefarious business in a place which belongs so much to the general public as the fair ground. -W.C.T.U." [57] The fair association turned a blind eye.

Niederauer Hall at Nineteenth and K was the preferred location for the pavilion, but the association settled on the two-story, public school house on Railroad Avenue—presently the site of Kern County Metro Justice Building at 1215 Truxtun Avenue.

Reuck devised a five-dollar ($30) cash prize for the winning student essay on fruit culture, but his influence over the fair went much farther than that: His Daily Californian was official voice of the fair association. He wrote, "As the coming agricultural fair is in some respects a new institution here, a few words explanatory of the objects and benefits to be derived therefrom may not be out of place or uninteresting. In the first place, it is not intended to be simply an advertising display gotten up to attract outsiders, although its influence in that direction will be good. It is not to be a display of abnormal or unusual products, although it will call forth many things which arouse curiosity and excite interest. Its prime object is to call forth the actual results of practical work and an instructing display of natural resources. It should be an illustrated convention of miners, mechanics, farmers, merchants, and artists. The actual comparison of ordinary results, methods and products

32

will certainly be of inestimable value. Because he *[a citizen]* has nothing of exceptional or unusual merit in any department should not deter anyone from exhibiting the best he has in the line of production in which he is most interested. Every progressive producer owes it to his community to give them the result of his progress, nor can he afford to lose an opportunity to profit by the experiences of his neighbors. Whenever a department fails of suitable representation it will not be because of lack of attention by the management, but because of carelessness of producers for that department. If the fast horse department receives more attention than cattle or hogs or something else it will be because the breeders of the former are alive to their own interests, and the latter are not. If the woman's department outranks all others, it will not be because the association is partial to the women, but because the women are early in the field and enthusiastic in their efforts. If the people of Kern and Tulare counties will remember these things, and if every man, woman, and child will consider himself or herself personally responsible for the success of that department in which he or she may be interested, the fair will be a great success, and, best of all, there can be no grumblers."[58]

Two weeks later he announced, "The agricultural and horticultural department will be fully represented, and as the fame of the county and that of the whole district has never exceeded the reality, the display of produce will be grand. The art department promises to be something worth seeing, and will present the ideal and real as photographed by the brush and pencil in the hands of home artists."[59]

## Fair and Pavilion

The fair was well managed. The president of the association, Solomon Jewett, reviewed applications for the bar, wheel-of-fortune, and lunch counter and sent invitations to 20 private stables to take part in the racing. Premiums of $1500 ($228,000) were as good as any fair in the state, and during the last few days before the opening, 60 top-quality thoroughbred trotters and runners were training at the track. Richard Hudnut's Sumner Standard blared, "Eleven More Days to the County Fair. Track To Get Finishing Touch This Week."[60]

The Tenth Annual Fair of the Fifteenth Agricultural District opened for its five-day run on October 25, 1892.[61] Tickets to the pavilion were 25 cents ($2.50) for adults and 15 cents for children or "two of the dear little things for a quarter." The special three-dollar ticket ($30) admitted families to both the pavilion and the racetrack.[62]

The Sumner Standard described the commotion. "Never before in the history of Bakersfield has there been such bustle and excitement. Walking along Nineteenth Street in the business quarter you encounter he who runs the shooting gallery, the street fakir, the patent medicine man, the organ grinder and his monkey– all of the same inclinations, as are the rest of us, striving for the mighty dollar. The tin-horn gambler with his paste sparklers [costume jewelry] and checker-board trousers is seen on the corners buttonholing his confiding, good-natured friend from the mountains, and giving him a tip on the right horses. Lodging houses are overcrowded, and enterprising hotel keepers are making hay while the sun shines, and turning all possible space into remunerative use, charging therefore their most exorbitant prices. Some of our visitors tell of being compelled to walk the streets all night. The hobo, too, reports business booming. Columbus Day came and went and is entirely forgotten in the more interesting attractions of the fair. Everything is heart and soul the county fair."[63]

It was cloudy and cold on the first morning, but several hundred race fans came early and shivered in the gloom. Even though the bar, food-service, and sure-thing games were open, it was generally too cold for much enthusiasm. The next day was perfect, and a sizable and lively crowd watched the afternoon races.[64] Hudnut wrote, "The bright, clashing colors of the fair maids and matrons with their beaming countenances made the grandstand a thing of beauty. Many stylish equipages are seen, as are also some exceedingly seedy-looking rattletraps of delivery stableman turning their laid-by vehicles into use. The racing as yet amounts to level or nothing; pool selling [gambling] that makes team and bookmakers all quiet. A sandstorm swept over the grounds Wednesday afternoon followed by a slight sprinkle of rain, which threatened to suspend today's program. After a short time though it had spent itself, and the clouds rolled by."[65]

Pavilion manager Mrs. Dr. L.S. Rogers welcomed exhibitors delivering items "indicative of their industry and talents": paintings, photographs, fancy work, school work, flowers, fresh fruit, and jars of pickles and jellies.[66] The Californian wrote, "Those who love the pretty, charming things of life, and admire the beautiful in form and color, should visit the pavilion and feast their eyes upon the many lovely things that one may see collected there. There is everything almost that one can imagine in the beautiful, the charming, the weird, the peculiar and the useful."[67] Glass globes and prisms filled with jellies of various colors and shades had been artfully arranged on a wire framework. It was a miniature of the California Jelly Palace then showing at the World Columbian Exposition in Chicago.[68]

With the help of Mrs. S.S. Hunter, Mrs. F.A. Langdon, and Mr. W.E. Houghton, Mrs. Dr. Rogers managed the pavilion with "characteristic energy and executive ability."[69] The Californian noted the friendly rivalry between Kern and Tulare exhibitors and added, "Everyone seemed to take pride in presenting some feature of his industry, and this ambition made the pavilion so attractive that it made the race track a secondary attraction to all except horse fanciers." [70]

The school-house door opened, visitors filed in, and Taylor's Military Band played. Just inside was a bedroom display of exquisite handiwork. "Very neatly-crocheted bedspreads covered the bed, with dainty pillow shams to show to advantage the pale green coloring of the furniture. Here you also will see ... a marvel of the finest needlework coming from the deft fingers of Mrs. Robichaux in the shape of a child's white dress of the finest white mull with a deep border of Spanish drawn work interlaced with baby ribbon. It shows patient, skillful labor on the part of the worker."[71]

"You now undertake to ascend the wide, old staircase amid the tuneful strains of the band seated in the hallway and find yourself confronting the display of woodwork of A.J. McLeod. Turning to the right you enter the room wherein you find on the walls the praiseworthy efforts of our "wielders of the lavish." The most notable feature here is the unique and original exhibition of Leet and Lang *[liquor distributors]*. On and around a high circular railing forming an enclosure about eight feet in diameter are arranged ... bottles of good, refreshing Buffalo Beer, which the genial Ben Leet and his jolly partner dispense with their usual good cheer to the thirsty. The public schools of the county had one side of the room occupied with all exhibitions of the penmanship and drawing of the rising generation of Kern county. By the way, I saw some very fine work by the Sumner school."[72]

"In the next room ... the first work you see is that of H. Corday, the leading tailor of Bakersfield. Here you will find as fine a display of material for gentlemen's wearing apparel as can be found anywhere in the state. Judging from this exhibit of Mr. Corday's, it is entirely unnecessary for any of our citizens to send away for their attire. Nelson also has a very agreeable display of the art of photography."[73] "Separated from the other exhibits by rich, heavy curtains was an elegantly-appointed table spread with beautiful dishes painted by Mrs. George Carr. Mrs. John C. Moore's heavy silverware added to the richness, and all glimmered under the soft glow of various colored fairy lamps."[74] Quilts and sewing shared space with school work, bottles of beer, and peach brandy. In the next room were boxes of fresh, dried, and canned fruit from Kern County Land Company. Nearby was Mrs. George W. Wear's black-satin, finely-embroidered banner of peaches and leaves that she made for Charlie Maul, whose prize peaches were going to the World Columbian Exposition.

Here, too, Miss Jesse Shottenkirk and Miss Myrtle Walker displayed their fine lace.[75] The Sumner Standard enthused, "These charming young ladies will show you the richly embroidered shawl worn by a maid of honor at the coronation of Mary, Queen of Scots. Here also are exhibited a set of white satin royalties [sashes] painted by the Duchess of Teck. All these beautiful things, together with a magnificent Goldenberg-spread [lace bedspread] are in the possession of Mrs. G.A. Kapper. They are indeed a treat to the sight of all lovers of fancy work."[76]

A diversity of farm products filled the next room. "Here are seen some extremely large potatoes, natural salt, fine wheat, barley and oats. In the center of this room is a large pyramid of built-up sacks of flour ranging from the ordinary size to the salt-bag size from the Kern River Mills. On the north side, George Tou & Co, our Japanese merchants, have installed themselves with a gorgeous exhibition from the Orient. A very novel contrivance is suspended from the ceiling which revolves around and around. With its sea green light and pretty gold fish it presents quite an attraction."[77] "Mr. Maul has on exhibition a bamboo fence, fastened by means of wire, that is a cheap and most durable structure and which commands itself to the fruit grower as absolutely stock proof [animal resistant]."[78]

An old gentleman was overheard to say, "Well, I do declare. You are returning to the old style of county fairs. This is wonderful." [79] Had he noticed the "chattering damsels and their attractive swains" mingling under the tented, flower-adorned water fountain? [80] Last-day attendance doubled what was expected, and the association added an extra day so everybody could see "the many pretty things collected there."[81]

A Fresno visitor wrote, "The superintendent is a woman, Mrs. Dr. Rogers, who has much executive ability as half a dozen ordinary men combined. Kern county has a class of people who, if they were living on an oasis two miles square in the midst of Sahara, would manage to advertise to the world that the whole desert was a veritable garden of Eden, and that the only way to live long and to be rich and happy would be to settle among them. No obstacles seem to daunt them."[82]

The Californian praised the organizers: Chairman H.A. Jastro, whose "executive ability is equal to any such occasion"; W.H. Scribner, "who has been exceptionally energetic in making the fair one of the best"; and Solomon Jewett for his "energy expended and the wisdom he has displayed in selecting his subordinates."[83] Days later the newspaper added, "The people of Kern county and of the district generally can congratulate themselves that they have now in progress one of the most successful fairs that has ever been held in any district in the state."[84]

# Chapter 2, 1893

Boom—Bust
Recovery and Fairs of 1900 and 1902
Central Fair Association
Auto-Buggies—Race of July 4, 1912

In the spring of 1893 the Californian wrote, "A quarter of a million *[$8,500,000]* in expended improvements in one year, and yet there is not an empty store, an empty house and hardly an empty room in the town! There are now projected buildings that will vastly outdo this list in cost, and it is probable that the building boom of the next twelve months will double that of the past."[85]

Joining in the Fourth of July Parade was the National Guard Band, Kern Driving Club, mounted riders and carriages and callithumpians, which how the Californian described the boisterous participants. The parade's line of march was east on Nineteenth Street, counter-march to Chester, and from there on to the fairgrounds, where prizes were awarded in foot racing, bicycle racing, a "fat-man race", a wheel-barrow race, and donkey races. A prize was given to the most-graceful woman bicycle rider and to the winner in the ladies' horse race. The Californian did describe the vaqueros' race, but it noted that in the butcher-cart race the drivers wore white aprons.[86]

H.A. Jastro, E.M. Roberts, W.S. Tevis, S.W. Fergusson, S.W. Wible, H.A. Blodget, J.R. Simmons, and G. Daggett, who were directors of the Fairgrounds Association, scheduled the 1893 Fifteenth District Agricultural Fair in late October to avoid overlap with nearby county fairs. Days before the grand opening, county prisoners cut weeds along Chester Avenue and filled in chuckholes. "By this means," wrote the Californian, "There will be a fine driveway from town to the race track."[87] The association now had a first-class racing operation: The racetrack, grandstand, judging stand, and stables. Opening day of the fair at Agricultural Park—as it was then called—started with horse racing, of course. The pavilion was held in town at Reich's Opera House, which opened onto the alley between 18th and 19th and Chester and K. The profusion of exhibits inside was "simply enormous". Next door on a vacant lot that also faced Opera Alley stood several gleaming farming "machines".[88]

## Bust

In August 1894 a harness-racing club put on a three-day meet at the fairgrounds that included a purse of $750 ($24,000). Weeks later, La Fiesta "Wild West Cowboy Tournament" came to Bakersfield by train and set up at Base Ball Park at 19th and Union. It was much like a fair with a "Grand Street Parade", bull fighting, sharp shooting, trick bicycle riding, chariot racing, rodeo, dancing, barbecue, and a midway that included muscle men and Turkish dancers.[89]

Bakersfield was La Fiesta's last last stop on its six-month tour of California, and at that late date it is likely it was not meeting expenses. In the fall of 1894, California was feeling the national recession, and in November, the Fifteenth Agricultural District wrote to the State Board of Agriculture, "Gentlemen: No fair was held this year, for two reasons: First, the depressing influence of the hard financial times made the people of this district feel unable to assume the expenses that would accrue; and second, the State appropriation was exhausted."[90]

In the spring of 1895 the British Club held a day of racing at the racetrack. It started with a five-mile bicycle race that was won by J.C. May on a Waverly—his time was 20 minutes, 4-4/5 seconds (15 mph). Horse racing took up the rest of the day, although the last race was a tandem-bicycle competition.[91]

Kern's economy improved, but feeble business conditions caused the fair association shy away from holding a fair. On the other hand, business was not depressed in all of California. On April 22, a Los Angeles excursion train reported to be carrying more than 100 members of the San Francisco Half-Million Club was on its way to Bakersfield to assess business conditions. With only hours of advance warning, a welcoming committee made plans to receive the visitors. The main floor of the land company's new building on Nineteenth Street was hurriedly decorated with flowers, fruits, grains, vegetables, and basement tables stacked with mineral samples. The Daily Californian called the palm fronds and sweet-scented orange blossoms "a picture that could scarcely be excelled."[92]

Shortly before the train arrived, the committee learned that no more than 110 members had boarded at Los Angeles, and because the train had made so many stops along the way, it was impossible to know exactly how many would arrive. About 10 a.m., 20 stepped off the train, and they were taken on a brief buggy tour of Bellevue and Stockdale ranches. An hour later they lunched at the Southern Hotel, and in the short time remaining, a few toured the land company building.[93]

In 1895, Pacific Coast Pony and Steeple Chase Racing Association invited the Stockdale British Club—also called the Country Club—to take part in its summer races at Monterey. Horse racing continued at the land company's racetrack, and Kern Driving Club got a lease and sold track privileges.

In the spring of 1896, the club held a "Pony Race Meeting" that attracted Solomon Jewett, Col. Shafter, Mr. and Mrs. Tevis, Mrs. McKittrick, General and Mrs. Mason, and R.A. Fergusson, who was Director of the Kern County Land Company. [94] The weather was excellent but the races less so, as noted in the Californian. "The racing, though good, was not of a very exciting nature, nearly all the races being matches *[equal competitions]*." [95] Later that year the Gun Club was allowed to build a club house and hold Blue Rock Shoots, which meant the targets were Lincolnshire Blue Rock Pigeons.[96]

During the brief but acute depression of 1896, the fairgrounds association stopped paying its lease on the land company's track, and racing meets there ended. The land company itself was also feeling economic strain, and it stopped paying the space rent for Kern County's booth at the State Board of Trade in San Francisco. The spot was so important to Kern business, however, that county supervisors and the League of Progress paid the fee. The exhibit received raves, and the Daily Californian projected that business "may look forward with confidence to good results therefrom."[97]

Kern County Board of Trade sent an agricultural exhibit to the Fresno Citrus Fair, but there was no Fifteenth District Fair in 1896 or 1897. In the summer of 1898, downtown Bakersfield suffered a massive fire.[98] No county fair was held.

Business was generally depressed through the 1890s; nevertheless, Kern's population grew 35 percent, mostly owing to the discovery of oil on the Kern River and the land company's sale of its properties. In 1897, Kings, Tulare, Fresno, and Kern County combined agricultural resources and formed the Central California Development Association for the promotion of dried fruit in Eastern states. The joint venture foreshadowed the tri-county cooperative fairs of 1906-1909.

## Recovery and Fairs of 1900 and 1902

Tulare County was now its own agricultural district, and that left Kern County as the sole representative of the Fifteenth Agricultural District. In 1899 the Daily Californian wrote, "Kern county forms the Fifteenth Agricultural District, but it has been some years since any attempt was made to hold a fair. But the last legislature, however, provided for a $1500 [$49,500] appropriation for the district, and the governor has given it a new life by appointing an excellent board of directors."[99]

Those named suggested that a comprehensive Kern County fair was on the way: P.A. Baer of

Buttonwillow, N.P. Peterson of Kernville, and J.M. Shaffer of Kern City (East Bakersfield). Others appointed were locally prominent in business, ranching, and mining: L. M. Dinkelspiel, H.A. Jastro, S.N. Reed, E.M. Roberts, and the recently-appointed director of the Kern County Land Company, W.S. Tevis.[100]

In June the Californian wrote approvingly of the coming fair, "A good agricultural exhibit will interest the farming classes, a display of our mineral resources will attract the desert population; in fact each of the county's industries must receive recognition in order that interest in the fair shall be general. Kern county is attracting much attention just now by reason of the oil development, and anything that tends to advertise her resources is of great value." [101] Its enthusiasm, however, was premature. Two months later it wrote, "It is probable that no agricultural fair will be held here this year, not enough funds being available. Next year, though, there will be $1400 [$46,200] on hand which is enough to get up a creditable fair."[102]

In 1900, Kern's population was 13,000, money flowed, and horse racing was more popular than ever. H.A. Baer, L.M. Dinkelspiel, H.A. Jastro, S.S. Reed, E.M. Roberts, and W.S. Tevis led the new fairgrounds association and scheduled a fair for early November, two weeks before the Twenty-Fourth Agricultural District Fair in Tulare. [103] The Californian wrote, "There will be a number of valuable purses offered at the track, and in addition to the races an agricultural exhibit will be arranged."[104]

In a letter to the Californian in fall of 1900, a Mrs. E.M. Coe described a blueprint for future fairs. "In the program of the coming fair to be held here the first three days of November there has been no important mention of anything except races. Now, it is nothing but fair that other subjects should be given their due notice. Races are alright in their place, but a miscellaneous exhibit should be arranged that we may see what we have in our own county. The farmer's wife with her nice thoroughbred poultry, the Belgian hare fancier, the grower of fruits, grains, vegetables should be induced to exhibit their product in best form. No doubt, there should be a splendid poultry show department, and many of us would be greatly surprised to know what fine birds we have amongst us. Fine songsters with the interesting parrot would add their entertainment. There is a large cattle industry here, which calls forth much interest: fine cattle, horses, hogs and etc. should all be on display. We have fine dogs and pet stock here that would not let outsiders carry off many prizes. A floral display would be appreciated by all who attend. Machinery display should not be overlooked as it is of great importance. It would be nice to see some oil rigs at work, and by the way, they might strike oil."

"Some years ago, when a child, I remember attending our county fair. Among points of interest to women was the baby show, prizes being offered for the prettiest, largest, and healthiest baby under one year old. The fancywork show was something beautiful: crazy-patch work, quilting, painting, embroidering and crochet work were on display. The $5 prize offered for the best loaf of light bread made and baked by any young miss of from eleven to seventeen years was the cause of much good bread on exhibition. And no one can help but see the great inspiration that would be created in encouraging the girls to learn to make excellent bread. The various creameries should have a chance at a prize, as the milk, butter and cheese should be put to the front, for there is no place in the state better adapted to such industries. Fruit should be a splendid attraction as it is a prominent item of our products and exports. Dried, preserved, pickled and canned fruits and jellies and etc. should be included. Divide up the premiums and let it be known all over the country that the best of everything is wanted in displays. A fair should be an educational affair and the grounds should be filled to overflowing with the good goods of the land. - Mrs. E.M. Coe"[105]

The racetrack was in "the very pink of condition" on opening day. Beer and "cold temperance drinks" were sold on the grandstand, and a pigeon shoot and stock show were underway[106] In downtown Bakersfield, under the shade of a tent at Nineteenth and Chester, goods from Roberts & Graves store and produce from the land company's packing sheds were on display: Persimmons, lemons, oranges, prunes, pears, peaches, quinces, two-pound Ben Davis apples, dried, jarred, and trayed grapes, and pumpkins, including one that weighed 125 pounds. Arranged nearby were vases overflowing with ostrich plumes, sunflowers and Japanese chrysanthemums, cages of doves, ducks, geese, varicolored pigeons and several fine-looking chickens from the Stockdale Ranch. A delicate glass display case containing curiosities from the Spanish-American War attracted viewers, while others visitors flocked around Mrs. H.W. Klipstein's

Battenberg and Belgian lace and Misses Mildred and Mattie Klipstein's embroidery.[107]

Kern County was becoming prosperous, more citizens had disposable income, and bicycle and motorcycle shops were making sales. In January an unusual fairgrounds race was advertised in the Californian. "Agricultural Park. Sunday, Jan. 6th, 2 P.M. The Event of the Season. World's Champion Middle Distance Bicycle Rider with his Motor Tandem Cycle vs. Four Horses, a different horse each mile. Distance four miles."[108] The motor-tandem won, and there was talk of building a velodrome for winter racing.[109]

Success of the 1900 fair prompted the Californian to ask why Kern was not sending an exhibit to the 1901 New York World's Fair. "Bakersfield is known all over the United States, by reason of the oil fields, and an exhibit of the resources of the county would be most timely and effective. What does Kern county intend to do about it?"[110] An exhibit was hastily assembled, and it was a popular attraction at the six-month Buffalo exhibition.

Bakersfield newspapers between June 1901 and December 1901 are missing. Hanford newspapers suggest that no agricultural fair was held in Kern, although its oil products showed well at the Hanford fair, and Bakersfield was "well billed."[111]

The Hanford Daily Journal wrote, "The bonds of sociability and business interests which linked the pioneers of Tulare and Fresno and Kern counties in the days of the early settlement of this part of the San Joaquin valley have been woven closer by a mutuality of esteem and by business interests, and today each county rejoices in the prosperity and progress of the other, as is evidenced by the sentiments voiced in the press of the several counties."[112]

## Carnival and Fair

Louis W. Buckley, Fred Gunther, John M. Jameson, Al Lindley, Thomas J. Packard, Frank W. Smith, Tim Spellacy, and Joseph Yancey made plans for a downtown carnival, and a San Francisco newspaper wrote, "It is believed this city *[Bakersfield]* will never have seen so many strangers as will come and go during carnival week." [113] The day before carnival, Pullman cars pulled into Santa Fe Station, and 100 San Franciscans stepped out to assess Bakersfield's economic pulse. The next evening the lights on Chester Avenue between Wall Street Alley and Hughes Drug Store came on for the crowd that had come out to hear President Theodore Roosevelt's wired congratulations to Bakersfield for its ambitious street carnival. Booths and displays then opened on Nineteenth Street between Chester and K, and a "free, refined vaudeville show" from San Francisco began.

The carnival was a useful warm-up for the fair which would be held for three or four days in October. The Hanford Journal wrote, "Bakersfield is one of the liveliest towns on the Pacific Slope, is in the center of the oil belt and is a thriving, booming place. The Bakersfield Fair will be a hummer."[114]

On a Saturday in June, fair association directors Thomas Fogarty, Henry Jastro, and Elisha Roberts made the rounds of downtown businesses, put the bite on every owner and before lunch collected $1050 ($33,300). The amount was only a third of what was needed for a fair, but it was felt that the rest could be easily managed, and they were right. The California State Fair Commission gave the Fifteenth District $2500 ($80,000), Bakersfield Driving Club gave an equal amount, and local business contributed $2000 ($63,000).[115]

The fair opened on Wednesday October 8, 1902. The clay track awaited, the weather was perfect, and the $4500 ($143,000) purse attracted gamblers early, and by mid-morning 2000 people crowed the fairgrounds. A band played as California Governor Henry Gage appeared and greeted his Democratic supporters, foremost of whom was the fair's General Secretary, Henry A. Jastro.[116] The friendship between the two went back 35 years to Wilmington Harbor where they cowboyed for Phineas Banning's stock business. But Jastro was more than an old friend. He was also a head ranch manager for the Kern County Land Company, president of the Californian State Agricultural Society, and a Kern County supervisor serving in his tenth term. It is possible that Gage already knew that Jastro soon would be appointed general manager over all of Kern County Land Company's properties in the West.[117]

Corrals and pens by the race track held Jersey bulls and cows, thoroughbred mares, Southdown and Persian sheep, an Icelandic pony, and swine— Berkshire, Poland, and China—one that "weighed in the neighborhood of 300 pounds."[118] The pavilion was in town at Armory Hall, where Professor Newman and his orchestra set up on the sidewalk and played selections from La Traviata. As visitors entered the building they beheld American flags lining the three walls and an enormous, unfurled Stars and Stripes on

51

the stage. The flag was a gift from patriotic citizens in celebration of the end of the Philippine-American War.

Harry Jastro (son of Henry A. Jastro) supervised the Armory show. On display were kitchen stoves from Weill's, a fine two-seat surrey from C.M. Stoll's, a functioning Fairbanks-Morse gasoline engine, and a wheeled, small-scale pipe cannon. Among locally-manufactured goods were kitchen cabinets, marble tombstones, sacks of Kern River Mills Flour, and a pier of bricks from Kern County Brick & Concrete Company.[119] Stacked next to them were boxes of bacon and hams, trays of fruit and vegetables: Grapes, dates, figs, corn, chilies, beans, butter, and giant pumpkins. Bales of alfalfa and several potted plants were stacked against a far wall alongside cages of pigeons, cackling chickens, turkeys, a three-legged duck, and "a large Philippine game cock, that looks as if he could fight anything of his class."[120]

The second floor was "devoted to the ladies for the exhibition of the products of the distinctly feminine genius and ability." [121] Here were biscuits, breads, cookies, cakes, candies, canned vegetables, embroidery, quilting, paintings, drawings, and decorated shopping bags, all evoking the fair of 1892. Displayed, too, was hobby photography, pyrography (wood burning), and a collection of Confederate money. Everything was interesting and exemplary, but the premiums, $2000 ($7400), were scarcely half of those awarded at the fairgrounds.[122]

## Central California Fair Association

Kern's recovery from the 1896 recession paced that of the nation. In 1902 the Southern Hotel Corporation designed a fourth floor for the Southern Hotel, and the Kern County Board of Trade prepared a county exhibit for the St. Louis World's Fair. The Board of Trade asked county supervisors to impose a county-wide tax to fund the show, but the answer was no. Unfazed, the board partnered with Fresno, Tulare, and San Joaquin counties in a joint showing at St. Louis.[123]

The California State Fair, as well as larger district fairs, drew thousands of visitors. National manufactures spent lavishly for displays and advertising, but they avoided the smaller district fairs for cost vs. payback reasons. The smaller districts lost space rent and visitors. Consequently, Fresno, Kings, Tulare and Kern districts formed the Central California Fair Association, held a joint fair in Hanford in 1904, and named each day of the fair for one of the counties. On Kern County Day, 2000 Kern citizens rode train to Hanford. The four-county, cooperative fairs were repeated in 1905 and 1906.[124]

## Auto-Buggies

The Los Angeles Breeders Association delivered two dozen champion harness and running horses to the Fresno race track in 1905. Two automobile races were held when the horse races ended, and "two handsome solid silver cups" were awarded.[125] Interest in automobiles was growing, and eight weeks after that, in Bakersfield, a Frank S. Snell took delivery of an "auto-buggy". The Californian wrote, "It resembles a buggy in every way and has ordinary buggy running gear and is certainly an innovation in the automobile line."[126] Snell's vehicle was probably utilitarian, but race cars in 1905 could hit 30 mph.

On April 18, 1906 a massive earthquake hit San Francisco, and E.D. Buss of Bakersfield organized a rescue committee here in town. Substantial donations came in from Truxtun Beale, Alfred Harrell, and Henry Jastro, and more from Chinatown, the Japanese Association, "The Mexican Colony," schools, ranches, and citizens from Onyx, Weldon, Randsburg, and Tehachapi. All in all, $12,730 ($420,000) was collected, and when the San Francisco relief trains carrying survivors stopped off at Bakersfield, warm food and clothing awaited.[127] The need eased, and two weeks later the committee disbanded, but the disaster had other fallout, and that had no immediate relief. London underwriters paid massive insurance claims, the world's economy contracted, and the U.S. fell into a brief but severe recession. Just how bad it was in Kern County is unclear, but supervisors waited until August to pay the $1000 fee ($33,000) to reserve Kern's place in the 1906 joint fair at Hanford.[128]

Owens River Automobile Transportation Company ran a 196-mile service between Mojave and Bishop, and in 1907 it replaced its horse-drawn coaches with motorized vehicles. Automobiles and railroads vied for customers. In 1907, Hills Brothers Coffee representatives G.W. Linder and H.G. Parrish arrived to Bakersfield by car, and Parrish remarked "not for worlds would he go back to the old style of traveling by train, and waiting by day or night in a dingy, dilapidated country station for hours, perhaps, for a belated Southern Pacific or Santa Fe local."[129] In 1907, too, J.A. Hughes and Clem Wilson set out from

Buttonwillow in a four-cylinder Mitchell Runabout and one hour later arrived in Bakersfield—an average speed of 25 mph.[130]

In 1910, counties in the state levied fees on automobile owners. Taft historian Edith Dane wrote, "Up to this time it had been truly the heyday for automobile owners, as anyone with the money to buy a car could do so and run it where and how he pleased, there being no state license, no drivers' license, no restrictions of any sort upon driving except those passed by various cities and counties for their own protection, such as the ordinance in the incorporated city of Taft requiring them to be lighted before and after dark."[131]

The rough condition of roads tested new automobiles. On Washington's Birthday 1911, Bakersfield automobile dealer "Spider" Campbell organized a Bakersfield to Fresno round-circuit race, which was financed by Kern's automobile trade. Some of the funds had to be used to fix the notoriously-bad spots on the 224-mile circuit. Winner of the race was A.H. Dixon in his Cadillac. His time was 7 hours, 16 minutes, an average speed of 31 mph.[132]

For three nights in the spring of 1911, Bakersfield Armory, at 1917 H Street, hosted an auto show, and visitors crowded to see the popular models: Cadillac, Apperson, Ford, Velie, Pope-Harford, Thomas Flyer, Winton, Peerless, White, Moon, Midland, Sterling, Marlon, Overland, Premier, and Hupmobile. National Guard Troop A recently had been enlarged to 60 members, each of whom had to have room for their firearms, dress and service uniforms, and other such items. It made the Armory less useful for large shows and mass meetings.[133]

# Race of July 4, 1912

A high point in Bakersfield's Fourth of July celebration of 1912 was the cross-county automobile race. On the day before it started, visitors arrived by horse, wagon, and train to see the cars roar out of town and catch the mid-morning parade. On the Fourth, too, a baseball game was planned between the Bakersfield Electrics and the Coalinga Colts followed by a water-fight between local fire companies. At sundown, fireworks would light the sky.

The road race, approved by the American Automobile Association, started 7 a.m. for the smaller cars at Jewett Lane and Thirtieth Street and one half hour later for the heavy cars, although engine displacement for both was limited to 303 cu.in. Drivers crossed the Kern River at Jewett Lane Bridge (now gone), bore west to North Chester Avenue, and turned east on China Grade Loop. Three miles farther along they crossed over Gordon's Ferry Bridge, negotiated China Grade, and at the top gunned their machines down to Union Avenue. Just past Bakersfield Brewery they turned west on today's Espee Street and paralleled the railroad tracks for three blocks to the judging stand. None stopped there because that was only one lap in the 150-mile spin.[134]

There were a few accidents. J.J. Jefferies "turned turtle" in his Buick at the Jewett Lane Bridge and was thrown clear, but mechanic Frank Davis was pinned under the heavy machine, and "Those who saw the car turn over expected to lift Davis out a corpse".[135] His injuries were not severe. Even though thousands lined the route, that mishap was the only life-threatening accident of the day. Harvey Herrick in his blue National Motor won the $1000 ($31,000) prize and silver Tevis Cup, but he was not allowed to keep the trophy; the Tevis boys, Lloyd, Will, Gordon and Lansing, said he had to win it three years in a row to keep it.[136]

The prize offered by Pioneer Mercantile owner Gus Schamblin offered may have been a gentle poke at the Tevis trophy. The Californian wrote, "The light-car driver who came in dead last would win a "wonderfully complete kit of tools, which would be welcomed by any auto driver. The tools are now on display in the I-Street establishment of the donor."[137]

The next road race was on Washington's Birthday 1912, organized by the Kern County Automobile Racing Association and financed by 100 Maricopa, Taft, and Bakersfield businessmen. Major supporters were Thomas E. Klipstein, $250 ($8000) and Fred Tegeler, $100 ($3200), the balance of the contributions ranging from $2 to $10 ($65-$320). The planned route was Bakersfield, Maricopa, Taft, McKittrick, Buttonwillow, Rio Bravo, Rosedale, and back to Bakersfield.

For several days before the race, drivers tested the route. Some hit 50 mph through Maricopa, and the town immediately demanded that they limit their speeds to 10 mph. On February 22, 1912, the morning of the race, thousands watched 14 drivers roar off the starting line, and for the next several hours, county roads and towns along the way were closed to public traffic. Five hours, 44 minutes later, Jack Bayse in Stutz No. 19 was awarded the $1000 ($32,000) cash prize. His average speed was 37 mph.[138]

As car ownership increased, it began losing its novelty. In spring 1912, 100 county supervisors from across California came to Bakersfield for a convention, and 200 automobile owners offered the use of their cars to hospitality chairman W.E. Drury.[139] In 1913 the Kernville Stage switched from horses to motor-carriage service, and about that same time, stage service between Caliente and Kernville was switched to motor-vehicle service. In the spring of 1913 Kern County Sheriff Tom Baker's cousin was in town for an automobile-financing company. The Californian noted, "The banks frown on financing such sales or purchases as they think it encourages extravagance." [140] How expensive was a new car? Ford's Model T touring model cost $600, which equals about $18,500 today.

Factories were making faster and better cars. In 1913, Henry Klipstein, Jr., 33, wagered $150 ($4000) with friends that he could reach downtown Los Angeles in his Kissel Kar in under 12 hours. Klipstein, who was a bachelor, did it in 11 hours, 54 minutes, and that included the blowout. Did his friends know he had to catch the early train to El Paso to get married?[141]

# Chapter 3 Hudnut Park

Driving Association—Sequential Fairs
Balloons—Agricultural Association
Fair of 1908—Eagles Picnic—Fair of 1909
Golden Flyer—School Farm

Richard Hudnut (1828-1903) soldiered in the Mexican-American War, mined for gold in Kern County, and joined the New York 25th Cavalry during the Civil War. He returned to Kern County, sold his mining interests, and in 1868 bought 25 acres from Col. Thomas Baker "near the waters of Kern River immediately north of the Town of Bakersfield". Today that area may be generally described as L to P Street and 26th north to the railroad tracks.[142]

Hudnut worked in newspapers. In 1870 he edited the Kern County Weekly Courier, owned it in 1873, and sold it in 1875. From 1881 to 1892, he edited both the Kern County Californian and the Kern County Gazette, and in 1893 he was editor and part owner of the Kern City Standard. In 1897, he was part owner of the Bakersfield Morning Echo.[143]

Hudnut's property was in hay and grazing, but in the mid-1880s, as Bakersfield's population closed in on 10,000, he built a racetrack, subdivided 50 residential lots, and in 1889 built a two-story, family home on the hilly rise once at today's 26th and M. After his death, two full-blown agricultural fairs were held on the property.[144]

59

## Driving Association

Sulky and trotters were locally popular in the 1890s, and in 1906, harness-racing enthusiasts Ham Farris, Thomas H. Fogarty, Fred Gunther, T.E. Klipstein, M.A. Lindburg, W.J. Lutz, and Joseph Yancey organized the Kern County Driving Club. and tried to interest Bakersfield Power, Transit & Light Company (BPT&L) in building a track at Recreation Park—just east of today's 18th and Union. BPT&L was not interested.

In the summer of 1906 Richard Hudnut's widow sold the family acreage to the Kern County Driving Club for $1000 ($30,000) down and a promissory note of $7000 ($210,000). The club incorporated as the Hudnut Park Driving Association and issued 20,000 shares of stock equal to about $620,000 today.[145] Its bylaws stated, "The purpose of the association is to promote and encourage all kinds of racing and driving of horses, to promote and encourage all kinds of field and athletic sports, and to carry on all kinds of business in which natural persons may lawfully engage."[146] The association made plans to affiliate with Southern California racing clubs.[147] In the fall of 1906 the Californian wrote, "The driving association not only intends to build the race track and grandstand, but the grounds will be improved and planted in lawns and trees so as to have an ideal spot for the holding of county fairs and exhibitions of different sorts."[148]

## Sequential Fairs

In 1906, Fresno, Kings, and Tulare County agricultural districts agreed to hold fairs in sequence, one following the other. When Kern County did not sign on, the Hanford Sentinel wrote, "Kern county should, and perhaps would, come in on the circuit, and with four fairs going a "continuous performance," by one following the other, exhibitors would come in much large numbers from abroad; with agricultural implements, poultry, livestock and racing stock, and the agricultural fairs of the lower San Joaquin valley would receive a state, and perhaps a national fame, which little Kings county, or one of the larger counties adjacent to it, could not secure alone and unaided." [149]

Business was good, and state government was on solid financial ground. Senator E.O. Miller introduced a bill at Sacramento that would provide $16,000 ($470,000) for the agricultural districts, and with that promise, Kern signed on to the continuous-performance plan, which now required the districts to share and share alike their state appropriations.

In February 1907 the districts sent a unified, four-county exhibit to the Sacramento State Fair, and Kern's fruit, flour, honey, vinegar, crude oil, asphaltum, and minerals received high acclaim. Plans were made for the exhibit to be shown at each sequential fair. [150]

On March 22, 1907 Bakersfield's Cosmopolitan Block on 19th between L and M went up in flames, but business remained robust, and merchants recovered, but when Hudnut Park Driving Association asked the fair association to help building a new racetrack, it demurred.[151]

The association preferred a standard one-mile track, but its property was uneven and hummocky, which meant 10,000 cubic yards of earth would have to be shifted, which was why a half-miler was built instead. Contractor J.B. Frye bid $885 ($26,000), and work started immediately. The sweeping turns were ideal, and although the straightaways were shorter than standard, that did not matter to the racing crowd. After the first meet, the land company donated an old grandstand to the association, and once the association built stalls, installed fencing, and enlarged the grandstand, Hudnut Park would equal most professional racetracks in California.[152]

The southland racing circuit welcomed the Hudnut Park Driving Association, in the summer of 1907 it affiliated with the Los Angeles Driving Club, and accredited racing began. Kern County thoroughbreds were well known in the racing world, particularly the four-year-old stallion named Richard B., owned and raced by Kern County veterinary surgeon C. H. Sears. Richard B. ran the mile in 2 minutes 10 seconds, which was so astonishingly fast that gamblers expected racing clubs to create a new category.[153]

The association planned to have racing, stock shows, and agricultural exhibits for the 1907 Fifteenth District Agricultural Fair. Interest mounted, and the Daily Californian wrote, "Secretary Fogarty of the Bakersfield Driving Club has received a large list of classy entries for the Bakersfield trot and the Bakersfield pace, to be run here on the occasion of the fair meeting, the first week in October, and a large field of starters seems assured. There will be four days of the fair in Bakersfield and five races will be run each afternoon, both harness and running horses being represented. A very classy string of animals is expected to follow the circuit of the four counties, as the meeting will commence immediately following the state fair in Sacramento, and later most of the horses can be taken to the Los Angeles County Fair, the second week in October. They will be the first high-class events which have taken place in Bakersfield for many years, and it is expected that they will do much to revive racing interests in the county. The new half-mile track, on the Hudnut Tract, is now practically complete and is a fine piece of work. All of the sandy soil from the north side of the track has been taken out, and its place has been taken by earth which will pack hard. A well packed and springy track is the result".[154]

A day of varied racing was held in July. "One of the finest race meetings ever held will take place at the new Hudnut Driving Park. The program is a very long one, consisting of motorcycle races, auto races, mule races, and running and trotting races." [155] Winners in the harness dashes and half-mile and five-eighths-mile races received $700 ($21,000), and for the Bakersfield Trot—the featured race—it was $1000 ($29,000).[156]

Planning for the fair continued. Driving association president W.J. Lutz was buoyant, although one of his comments raised eyebrows: "What we want to do now is merely to secure the cooperation and good will of the Board of Trade, and there is no doubt but that they will give it to us. The fair will certainly be held."[157]

Senator E.O. Miller's bill to fund agricultural districts did not pass, which meant the association would have to dip into ticket sales and entry fees to build its racing fund. Tulare, Kings, and Fresno county had awarded their fairs $1000 ($30,500), $1500 ($46,000), and $2000 ($68,000) respectively, and Lutz hoped Kern County supervisors would do the same. He forged on, creating premium lists for beef, dairy, sheep, poultry, "and all other branches of a well conducted county fair". A 100 by 200-foot tent was rented from Los Angeles.[158]

County supervisors were expected to award funds for the fair at their tax hearing on September 12, but when that day came, Lutz was absent.[159] Some days earlier he learned that supervisors had given the county's special-exhibit money to the Eagles for their convention, and when he asked about the fair, they replied that Hudnut Park lacked essential buildings and "necessaries" (toilets) for a fair.[160] By then it was too late to reach out to business, and on September 17th the association's secretary, T.E. Klipstein, announced that the fair was cancelled, explaining that finances were "unpropitious" and that the fees would be reimbursed.[161]

Tulare's district fair opened in October, and Kern products were there. The Bakersfield Morning Echo wrote, "Great regret was expressed that Kern was not going to have a fair, and a very cordial invitation is extended to the people here to come up to Tulare. No one will regret having accepted the invitation, for there is much information and entertainment to be had each day."[162] Cancellation of the Fifteenth District fair did not dampen interest horse racing. In November, stalls at Hudnut Park were full, professional and private trainers worked their horses, and on Thanksgiving Day, the association put on six races.[163]

In 1908 the park was well established with a 500-seat grandstand, new baseball field inside the racetrack, and a picnic grove. In January, Hudnut Park hosted a high school field day, and a week after that, Los Angeles horses ran at the park. Heavy use continued. In the summer, horse races included racing butcher-carts entered by Opera Market, Bakersfield Market, City Market, California Market, and Estribou's in Kern City. That afternoon, two automobile trophies were awarded for Dr. West's Rio and A.H. Dixon's Tourist and other trophies to winning motorcycle riders. [164]

## Balloons

It was stifling on the Fourth of July 1908. Visitors arrived early from Porterville, Tehachapi and Randsburg to see the big downtown parade and horse racing and a hot-air balloon ascension at Hudnut Park.[165]

Balloons had been attraction here for at least 15 years, but they still drew crowds. In 1891, aeronaut Charles Howard lifted off from Athletic Park (between Truxtun and 19th, east of Union) and at some great height parachuted off, the Morning Echo observing that it looked like an "easy thing". [166] Days later Howard repeated the show at Tehachapi and collected $100 ($3000). In 1894, City Brewery patrons paid 25 cents ($2.25) each to watch Hagal the "Prince of Parachute Jumpers" lift off from City Brewery Gardens at the northwest corner of 20th and M—present site of the Downtown School.[167] In 1900 at the land company's racetrack north of town, "the strongest man on earth" showed his prowess, horse racing followed, and later that afternoon there was a "Grand Balloon Ascension." [168] Four years later, J.C. Mars lifted off from the vacant Fish Block on 19th Street, rose 5000 feet, jumped, and floated to earth.[169] On the Fourth of July 1907, an aeronaut named Smith was here to fulfill a $300 ($9000) contract between Bakersfield's Fourth of July Committee and the Archie Levy Amusement Bureau of San Francisco. Smith lifted off near the courthouse but when he reached altitude was unable to cut the safety tether, and he and the balloon came down in Bakersfield cemetery, then a block east of Chester Avenue on today's Terrace Way. Smith tried it again hours later, but this time he and the balloon were blown out of sight, and when he got back to town he insisted he had made the jump. Director of the Fourth of July Committee M.H. Wangenheim did not buy it. He was a "show me" Missourian, and had to have seen it with his own eyes. By then it was too late for another try, and the committee wired the Levy group for refund of its $100 ($3000) good-faith money. Nevertheless, the committee gave Smith $25 ($750) for risking his life for the show.[170]

## Agricultural Association

In 1908 two key individuals, Kern County Supervisor Henry Jastro and E.M. Roberts, were instrumental in helping the driving association put on its first fair. Roberts was Fifth District Kern County Supervisor from 1887 to 1892, and when he spoke before county supervisors they paid close attention as he described his vision for a week-long fair at Hudnut Park that would bring together horse racing, stock, agricultural exhibits, dancing in the cool of the evening, and a "good fireworks display".[171] Supervisor Jastro nodded in assent, and the other supervisors fell in line.

Mr. Jastro and Col. Roberts brought complementary strengths to the project—Jastro's political savvy and business acumen and Roberts' bluster and local sway. At a planning meeting in Jastro's land company office, W.G. Lutz agreed to inform other agricultural districts that Kern would hold the Fifteenth District Fair in three months, and it would be at Hudnut Park. Joseph Redlick, Fred Gunther, and Wasco farmer A.E. Beckes took over the planning, and Kern County Board of Trade members W.J. Doherty, James Curran, and J.G. Stahl said they would look into the cost of shading the grandstand, adding pens and sheds, and building a permanent pavilion. The findings were brought to the next meeting, and the committee agreed that $8000 ($240,000) was almost enough for capital improvements and hold a five-day fair.[172]

Twenty thousand stock certificates denominated at one-dollar ($30) each were offered to the public, but they only sold well for the first few days. Roberts collared a Daily Californian reporter and told him that even though the association had a big grandstand, 100 stalls, and the two-story, eight-room Hudnut house, it did not mean there was enough money for a fair, and he cautioned that unless the public bought more shares, there would be no fair.[173] He added, "The businessmen of the county have been generous in furthering the affairs of the association, and if the ranchers and stockmen show the same liberality, there will be no question of the success of the fair."[174]

Kern's economy was healthy, the county treasury was flush, and Supervisor Jastro remarked that Kern could build a new courthouse and hall of records without raising taxes. After Roberts' warning, the public stepped up, business bought 2400 shares

($72,000), and by mid-September the association had a comfortable reserve of $3500 ($105,000). That flash of green built livestock pens and 40 more stalls.[175]

In September 1908, Kern County Judge J.W. Mahon approved the association's request to change its name to Kern County Agricultural Association, saying it had provided "sufficient reasons". The reasons were in the bylaws: "To encourage the cultivation of the soil and the general development of all agricultural resources of the county and the improvement and development of all kinds of livestock; to foster every branch of mechanical and household arts calculated to increase the comforts of life; to extend and facilitate the various branches of mining and mining interests."[176]

## Fair of 1908

A reporter visited the park in July. "Looking over the track from the grandstand the view is already pleasing. Behind the park fence, and the railroad which passes just the other side, are Chinese gardens, stacks of hay and big cottonwood trees, and in back of that are the Kern bluffs and a portion of the Kern river oil fields."[177] Just behind the reporter, lumber was being unloaded and footings constructed for new buildings.

Present were four midway consultants: Steve Woods of Oakland, known as "the greatest show-man on earth since the demise of P.T. Barnum" and A.W. MacRae, G. Lute, and Ed Fussel of Fresno.[178] The four were experts and did not have to prove their ability, but the fledgling Kern County Agricultural Association had yet to show it could stage a successful fair.[179]

The Californian wrote, "The program consists of an automobile race, two motorcycle races, several bicycle and novelty races, a tug of war, three boxing matches, and a wrestling match. The Union Band of nineteen pieces will be on hand during the afternoon to disburse inspiring music to the sprinters and in the evening will play for the dance, which will be held on a special platform in front of the grandstand."[180] The article did not mention that there also would be a track meet. Days later, the newspaper noted, "The Santa Fe is to have a special round-trip rate for the fair for all stations between Johannesburg and Fresno to Bakersfield, and return. The SP might follow with the same offer."[181]

The Fresno district fair opened September 28, and when it ended, owners sent their horses on to Hanford, which was not having a fair but offered rich harness and running purses. The last fair on the circuit was Hudnut Park, but as opening day drew near, the association was still squeezed for time. The electrical lighting was not finished, and although smaller tents were up, the three big ones from Los Angeles were still in boxes on the Southern Pacific platform and could not be delivered until space was made. Meanwhile, trainers conditioned their horses, and carpenters built stalls for more expected from the northern counties.[182]

The quantity of livestock and horses was the largest seen in this part of the valley. Eight rail-cars arrived on September 11, and in the following days so many horses were on the grounds that the association had to build more stalls. The race track, however, was ready, in first-class condition, and fast times were expected.[183]

Adult tickets were 50 cents ($14), 25 cents for children, and the little ones under eight were admitted free "when accompanied by parents or guardian". The fair officially opened at 8 p.m. on Monday October 12, 1908. [184] A modest-sized crowd saw E.M. Roberts introduce Fifth District Supervisor Henry A. Jastro, who congratulated the committee for the good work it had done in such a short time and expressed grand prospects for the next fair. [185] Jastro recalled Kern County of 1871, mentioned past fairs held under the state subsidy system, and urged the association to continue its good work "whether or not aid is secured from the state."[186] Jastro was well aware of economic cycles of bust and boom, but this was not a time for gloom. The ceremony ended, the Sixth Regimental Band played, and dancers filled the grandstand platform.[187]

Attendance the first full day was massive. One tent held poultry and livestock, and another held pumps from Weed Pump and Engine Company of Porterville, Morton Gas Engine Company of Fresno, and Fairbanks-Morse gasoline engines. Farmers crowded around them because the new technology was making thousands of acres profitable which only a few years earlier had been nearly worthless. Occupying a small section of the same tent were modest displays of quilts, "fancy work", paintings, photographs, and hand-decorated china.[188] Outside was the tent of the Women's Christian Temperance Union, which had rocking chairs, mirrors, and plenty of pure water.[189]

Another tent was partitioned into several eight-by-ten-foot sections. In one, Manager W.A. Eardley of Kern River Flour Mill operated a miniature electric machine that ground wheat into flour, which he mixed, kneaded, and baked into bread. In another

70

section were trays of "monster" pears from J.W. Lovejoy's Tehachapi ranch and flowers, fruit, and small bunches of bananas from the San Emigdio Ranch. Local business brought sewing machines, pianos, bottled spirits, saddles, and harnesses, while the remainder of the spaces were occupied by Shredded Wheat Company, National Cash Register, and the Chamberlain Canning Company of Kern City.[190]

Blue-ribbon livestock that had taken honors on the cooperative fair circuit was present, notably the huge Percheron (draft horse) that astonished visitors. Dairy, which was already a profitable local industry, was represented, the association offering attractive premiums for top butter-fat-producing animals. Proud little boys displayed their pigeons, and earnest adults vied for premiums in 100 divisions of sheep, goats, swine, and poultry. Mrs. William Tracy of Buttonwillow showed two fully-grown, difficult-to-handle ostriches from the Tracy Stock Farm and demonstrated the preparation of ostrich feathers for market. It was a new industry for Kern.[191]

The cacophony between the ticket booth and the grandstand came from the Snow-Woods Carnival, which the Californian said had all the "side shows of a modern circus":—snake charmers, knife-throwers, palmists, "coon shouters", and Salome dancers. It also had marksmanship booths, ring and dirk games, a merry-go-round, a Ferris Wheel, wrestling matches, "Loretta the Armless Wonder," and other "high class attractions".[192] (The Salomé dance was infamous for its near-naked attire. Coon shouters were white women, singing songs disparaging of Black Americans.) Aerial acts, tumbling, and Slide for Life drew crowds, and tickets to the Lions' Den sold briskly. Madam Schell and her lions were not yet there, but whenever showed up, Madam Schell would join a yet-to-be-named couple in matrimony.[193]

Professor Virgil Moore from the Chutes in San Francisco offered balloon ascensions, and Ted Richards was back with his balloon but this time not as a parachute jumper. For one dollar ($30), he hoisted intrepid spirits 1000 feet into the air for a bird's-eye view of the countryside.[194]

Automobile racing was held each day, the grandstand seating sold fast, and Manager F.B. Fussell and assistant W.G. Lutz regularly announced only a few tickets left. Prior to each race, the drivers paraded their cars around the track, and the machines attracted "no little attention, as interest in the gasoline vehicle is steadily growing in Bakersfield."[195]

The half-mile oval was fine for horses and motorcycles, not so good for automobiles. The association had banked the turns for higher speeds, but auto technology had evolved so fast that race cars were capable of 70 mph. The Californian wrote, "It is not probable that an auto race will be arranged to take place at Hudnut Park as the auto drivers do not look upon the track as a good auto race course. The turns are said to be too sharp and the drivers say they would be somewhat wary in taking them at a high rate of speed."[196] The association understood the danger but made no improvements.

Bakersfield City Recorder W.H. Thomas, who held credentials from the National trotting Association, was official starter in the bicycle, car, and motorcycle races. Tilton's Sixth Regiment Band played during racing, but prior to one of the motorcycle competition, it had to lay the instruments aside for fully 20 minutes as riders roared around the track waiting for Thomas to fire his starting gun. In the automobile races, the headline show was the 80-mile double-circuit run between Hudnut Park and Famosa. The winning car was a factory-model 40-hp Chalmers rated at 60 mph.[197]

The fair's track and field awards sound odd today. In the 50-yard dash it was a pair of shoes, and in the 100-yard dash it was a case of beer. In the 50-yard dash for boys under 16, the prize was an eight-day clock, and in the 40-yard dash for boys eight to 12, it was a sheep. Winner of the women's 50-yard dash got a silk shirtwaist (a functional blouse), and the winner in the newspaper-men's contest got a bottle of whiskey. The prize for the Kid Jackson/Fred Mercer boxing match was a $5 ($150) sweater, and prize in the wrestling match between Charles Mitchell of Los Angeles and Eddie Fitzgerald of Denver was a suitcase.[198]

Madam Wanda and her trained dogs were a popular attraction. "Among the tricks was a three round boxing contest between two of the dogs. The dogs were fitted with boxing gloves and stood on their hind feet and cuffed each other very cleverly."[199] Each night, a roller-skating daredevil sped down the Slide for Life and crashed through a burning wall of fire. Ticket-sales ended at 9, and Tilton's Band played on for dancing until midnight. All the hustle and bustle suggested the fair would be profitable. The final attendance count was 12,000, boosted by 2250 free tickets given away to schools, and $2500 ($83,000) collected at the gate, but concessions made no money at all, and the fair was only marginally successful.[200]

Motor racing continued into November, and late that month the association held an unusual race. "For the motorcycle event, riders will stop at the end of each lap, dismount their machines, eat a half a pie, and then ride on for another lap. The race will be for two miles, which will mean the consumption of two pies per rider." [201]

In 1909 the association was an ailing investment struggling to pay its bills. The park's half-mile oval was dangerous for fast automobiles, and the city's expansion around the park added more problems. The Panama Slough which once meandered through town was filled in 1901, but its northerly part next to the Hudnut property was not. Richard Hudnut petitioned city trustees to take down the Hudnut Road Bridge and fill in the rest of the slough, but the city took down just the bridge, dammed the slough at that point, and left the part next to Hudnut's property uncovered. The abandoned section became a worse garbage-dumping nuisance than ever.[202]

Auto enthusiasts were scouting for a new track. [203] In an article entitled "Auto Track For Bakersfield" the San Francisco Call wrote, "This winter an effort may be made to organize an automobile club ... which we auto men down here should have by all means. ... A few of us who have taken an active interest in the forming of an automobile club have learned that we can obtain sufficient land not far from the city which offers splendid facilities for a first class racecourse. The price asked for this land is a very reasonable one. More than 150 automobile owners in the county may be counted upon for moral and financial support in such an undertaking."[204]

The state highway that was then building south toward Bakersfield would enter town by way of Roberts Lane and continue south past the land company's old race course facing Chester Avenue. [205] Who would have guessed that the property soon would become a state-wide destination for high-speed automobile racing?

## Eagles Picnic

In 1909 the Eagles' Fourth of July Picnic took place at Oak Street Park. and very much resembled a county fair with its foot races, food booths, band concerts, dancing, and midway, which the Californian called a pike, plaisance, pay-streak, "Do'em-All Row", or "whatever name may seem most fitting." [206] A reporter wrote, "Two charming and beautiful local ladies will examine palms at 10 cents [$3] a throw. A second visit, it is announced, will cost a dollar [$30]."

H.A. Jastro remarked that Hudnut Park needed trolley service, but so did Oak Street Park. When the Eagles' picnic broke up, pedestrians crowded sidewalks and spilled out onto streets as they made their way to Hudnut Park to see horse racing, automobile racing, and a balloon ascension.

The Californian reported the speed of the cars in horse racing terms: fastest five miles, 31 minutes, 56 1-5 (9 mph); fastest half-mile loop, 2:49 (12 mph). [207]

Charles P. Fox who was editor and owner of Bakersfield Oil World was attempting to take aerial photographs of the Kern River Oil Field. He had mounted a string-tripped camera to a weather balloon, filled it with illuminating gas at Power, Light &

Transit's plant at 16th and P Street, and towed it to the bluffs. Fox got one shot, but on his second try the wind swept this balloon away. Ted Richards, who had parachuted in the Fourth of July celebration of 1906 and hoisted intrepid spirits aloft in the fair of 1908, was back for the Eagles Picnic. He met with Fox and offered to go up in a balloon and take the shots—if Fox supplied the balloon. Nothing shows a deal was made.[208]

Richards arrived early at Hudnut Park. "A deep hole was dug in an open space half-way between the ticket gate and the dancing pavilion, and fuel was carried to the spot. Two uprights from which ropes were run through pulleys supported the top of the balloon."[209] He was uneasy because some days earlier flames had spread to the balloon, and it was ruined. Friends chipped in for a replacement, and a certain Mr. Engle who was planning a trip to Los Angeles said he would "look up a balloon which Richards thinks he can buy from Chute's Park."[210]

As the last few drops of fuel filled the trench, Richards paused, struck a match, and "with zealous care" watched smoke and flames arise.[211] The bag expanded, and the emblazoned words Eagles Aerie No. 92 appeared. Richards was soon in the air.

## Fair of 1909

The Kern County Agricultural Association needed more money. Shares were sold, and the county's contributed of $700 ($24,000) sweetened the pot to $2000 ($67,000), but it still was not enough for a fair. Meanwhile, the public criticized the association for not making more improvements, and it demanded to see the new premium book.

The association's failures were apparent: It had underestimated building costs and overestimated the public's willingness to buy shares. Moreover, all board members were volunteers, and their first responsibilities were to their own livelihoods.[212]

By August the association had sold $5000 ($167,000) of shares, but it had tapered off. Bakersfield Booster Club was called, and weeks later it presented the association with $1700 ($57,000). Things were now looking up. The association received $1400 ($47,000) from the Royal Arch Masons and $1000 ($33,000) more from Kern County supervisors, but all told that still was not enough for a fair. A look at the books indicated that last-year's ticket sales were $3000 ($100,000), and that and the fact that this year the fair would encompass Labor Day and Admission Day suggested a gate of $5000 ($167,000). [213] The association forged on.

Fences, corrals, and cattle sheds were built, and a dance platform installed in front of the grandstand. Association member William J. Doherty, who was a contractor, drew plans for two exhibition buildings: a 50 by 112-foot, two-story machinery building and a 50 by 100-foot exhibit hall, both aligned so at some future date they could be joined together as one large structure. Such detailed planning and measured progress suggested that the "Second Annual Fair" would be a money maker.[214]

Its theme was Progress and Growth, and the association invited the public to submit essays to win cash prizes. The topics were "Best original plans for increasing the consumption of oil, be it a mechanical device, plan for transportation, or any plan which renders it cheaper, better or more accessible"; "Best original plan, process or mechanical device for

cheapening the cost of placing fruit on the market";
"Best original plan, process, or mechanical device for
cheapening the cost of placing dairy products on the
market."[215]

The Morning Echo wrote, "The fair grounds are
taking on an appearance of stability and beauty that
should make every citizen of the county feel proud
that he has an interest in it. Our improvements this
year have not been as complete as we plan later on,
but we intend to see that all our exhibitors are given
the best treatment; that they will be satisfied in every
detail and will go home to return again next year and
bring others with them. In another year or two we
should have the best fair grounds in the valley." [216]

Livestock arrived from Stockton, Chico, Tulare,
and Los Angeles. The association created six premium
classes for cattle and four for sheep and swine. Bee-
culture and poultry remained unchanged at one
premium class each, but an extra class was added for
horses.[217] Among the other classes and awards were
"Best rooster any age or breed, $2.50 [$75]. Green
fruits: First and second best varieties of each of the
following varieties of apples will be granted diplomas:
Arkansas Black, Ben Davis, Baldwin, Spitzenburg,
Rome Beauty, White Winter Peiris, Wine Sap, Newton,
20-ounce Pippin, and Bellflower."[218]

The Exhibition Hall held industrial machinery
and poultry, the latter an up-and-coming Kern
industry. Wholesale and retail exhibits filled the lower
floor of the old Hudnut house, while the second floor
was reserved for domestic work and "fine quarters for
the lady exhibitors." [219] Plans were also made to
convert the entire Hudnut House into a "spacious
resting room for women."[220] Association member W.J.
Doherty pronounced, "We intend to see that all our

exhibitors are given the best of treatment; that they will be satisfied in every detail and will go home to return again next year and bring others with them."[221]

Hudnut Park's track was sprinkled and rolled and in "sufficient condition to assure some of the valley circuit records being smashed to bits."[222] City Recorder W.H. Thomas was back again but this time shared judging responsibilities with T.E. Klipstein, E.W. Roberts, and attorneys Rollin Laird and Rowen Irwin.

This year the double-run automobile race between Hudnut Park and Famosa was two competitions, one for the light cars and one for heavy ones.[223] The Morning Echo wrote, "The automobile enthusiasts of Los Angeles and Southern California will be afforded an opportunity to see the greatest automobile racing teams in the world in action during the winter season, as a racing team of the Buick Motor company will bring his team to the coast this winter."[224]

The Hudnut Park fair had a haunted house, a dog-monkey-goat show, Norris' troupe of trained dogs and baboons, and the Ocean Wave, described as an electrically-driven, brilliantly-lighted elliptical contraption, "a cross between a Ferris wheel and a merry go-round."[225] The elephant act from the Seattle Fair had not arrived, but President Lutz was satisfied with what already had been done and was pleased to announce that next year he would have the "Human Roulette Wheel that proved to be a scream in San Francisco."[226]

Ted Richards offered long-distance balloon flights on The American. "The big balloon will make a long trip, and if you desire a long trip in the air make your reservation now. Ted Richards states that on the Sunday following the fair, with a party of four or five persons, he proposes to take an aerial trip of several hours duration. The American is now at The Chutes Park, Los Angeles."[227]

The American was actually a second hand balloon. Six months earlier, aeronaut Dick Ferris and passengers were forced down on Strawberry Peak in the San Gabriel Mountains, and the American lay snagged there for weeks until pack mules hauled it down to Chutes Park.[228]

Opening day at Hudnut Park had been crowded, but each successive day had fewer and fewer visitors. The Californian predicted failure, but when the fair ended, the association came close to breaking even. The Californian criticized management for not working more closely with the newspapers of Randsburg, Tehachapi, Maricopa, and Delano, all of which lacked staff to dig up news about the fair, but days later it conceded that the association itself lacked workers. It wrote, "The public generally regrets that the fair was not a success; it should have been as should every county fair, for these annual local expositions can be made of the greatest value to the county, and to its very interest. In repeating the commonly expressed view as to the failure of the fair, the Californian does not feel that the blame rests directly with President Lutz and his fellow trustees, except in this: A fair cannot be arranged in a day, not a week not a month. Preparation must be made for it during the year, details being worked out from time to time; interest awakened among the farmers and others who have something to exhibit, and plans to formulate which, when fair time comes, will result in order instead of chaos. The directors of the agricultural association are all busy men with their own affairs to attend to. Obviously the time that they can give up to the business of the fair is limited, nor can they be expected to attend to details themselves. They should be able financially to have capable employees at their command whose effort in behalf of the fair would extend over a considerable period of time." [229]

Automobile racing had been financial tonic for Hudnut Park. Barney Oldfield, who recently set a world's speed record at Indianapolis, was riding the train to San Francisco in December 1909 when he stopped off at Bakersfield to test his 200-horsepower Lightning Benz on the park's half-mile dirt track. He hit 51 mph and set another world's record.[230]

Lively ticket sales and eye-popping racing fees suggested that the association was on solid financial ground, but it was not, and management struggled to meet expenses, a large chunk of which paid the Hudnut mortgage. When the association missed the December 1909 payment, Mrs. Hudnut went to court Disclosure revealed that the association was $2300 ($70,000) in debt and still had 5000 unsold shares. Mrs. Hudnut got her money, but that left the association in immediate need of cash for an upcoming aircraft show. The board discussed floating another loan.[231]

Despite the association's financial woes, Kern's economy was robust. Bakersfield boasted 22 blocks of paved streets, 10 miles of concrete sidewalks, a streetcar system, four banks, 140 brick business buildings, three theaters, several schools, a children's shelter, a park, library, well-equipped fire department, new sewer system, and "the best baseball park in the state." [232] Unmentioned was Hudnut Park, among the faster turfs on the San Joaquin Valley horse-racing circuit.

Ten years had passed since discovery of oil on the Kern River, eight years since hydro-electric power arrived from Kern Canyon, and two years since electricity came in from Big Creek Power Plant above Millerton Lake. In 1910 a new, natural-gas-fired steam plant on north Union Avenue produced electricity, and it strengthen Bakersfield's utility grid even more.

Oil made the county rich. In 1911, Kern County Board of Trade sent an oil exhibit to the San Francisco and Sacramento fairs, and the show was so well received that San Jose, Stockton, Fresno, and Hanford fairs asked for it. The new state highway through Bakersfield boosted the economy $100,000 ($3,000,000) a year, business thrived, and festivals flourished. Bakersfield was doing fine without a county fair.[233]

## Golden Flyer

In January 1910, five Glenn Curtiss biplanes were entered in the international airshow at Dominguez Field which was located 25 miles south of downtown Los Angeles. Records set in America's first-ever aviation meet: shortest distance before rising, 98 feet; greatest distance flown, 76 miles; peak altitude, 4165 feet; and fastest average speed, 50 mph.

The Kern County Agricultural Association contacted Curtiss's agent—the Frank H. Johnson Mercantile Company—to find out if it was possible for a Curtiss flight at Hudnut Park. It was possible, and the association went to work finding space for take-offs and landings. The oval track was 60 feet on the straightaways and 75 feet in the turns, which meant

82

its long dimension was within the range of the Curtiss factory's 100 and 300-foot runways. The deal was struck, and thousands of dollars of good-faith money was wired to reserve two flights of a Curtiss at Hudnut Park on January 30, 1910.

Two weeks after the Dominguez Field air show, the first-ever aviation meet in the San Joaquin Valley was held at Hudnut Park. The judging stand was moved 100 feet to the side, the fences were taken down, and the field carefully leveled—critical safety measure because the Curtiss' altitude-control rod that extended from front to back cleared the ground by only 2-1/2 inches.[234]

Pilot Charles K. Hamilton and mechanics Lotty and Pearson arrived by train the night before the show, wagoned the aircraft to Hudnut Park, and worked on it into the wee hours of morning. The engine, shipped separately, had not yet arrived.

The "Golden Flyer" was a bi-plane. It was 32 feet front to back, the same wingtip to wingtip, and its spruce-and-bamboo frame was braced with 1/8-inch wire cable and the wings skinned with double-layered rubberized silk. It was called a pusher because the propeller and eight-cylinder, 50-hp engine was located behind the pilot's seat. The aircraft weighed 575 pounds and needed to be rolling 40 mph for lift off.[235]

Days before the show so many visitors arrived in town that the hotels could not meet the demand. On Sunday January 30, 1910, long before sunrise, 100 automobiles circled the improvised airstrip, but the turnout was less than expected. Days before the show, the association visited every saloon in town and asked that they close their doors for two hours during the show. It was agreed, but later that the day the saloon association called an emergency meeting. Liquor wholesaler Fred Gunther argued that even if they briefly closed, prohibitionists would use that as fuel against them. The saloons stayed open. [236]

The aircraft engine arrived in the early hours of morning but was not bolted into place until noon. By then 8000 spectators, the greatest number in Hudnut Park history, filled the grandstand and overflowed onto the track. The show began without fanfare as Hamilton slowly strolled across the empty field and climbed up onto the seat. He waved to Lotty and Pearson, they rotated the propeller, the engine caught, and Hamilton revved the engine for two minutes.

The blocks were pulled, and the airship inched forward and gathered speed. [237] "For 100 yards the biplane sped along the ground. Then the governing plane in front of the machine was turned on an incline and as gracefully as a bird Hamilton left the ground and started into the air. Just as the machine left the ground 8,000 voices joined in a wild burst of applause. Automobile horns were blown, flags were waved and several hundred persons who were standing on the straightaway course leaped and shouted and cheered. The biplane sped on, gradually mounting higher until an altitude of about 500 feet had been reached. Then Hamilton circled around the east end of the park, went in the direction of the oil fields and circled back, gliding easily to the ground and landing in almost identically the same spot from which three minutes before he had started." [238]

At 3 p.m. Hamilton appeared on the field, inspected the cables, replaced some, and when satisfied climbed onto the seat. In less than a minute the Curtiss moved forward and gracefully lifted into the air. He rose 1000 feet, descended to 300, circled the grandstand twice and came in for touch down. The second the Curtiss touched the ground, it bounced, slammed down hard, and disappeared in a cloud of dust. Spectators swarmed the field. Its wheels were broken and the engine case shattered, but Hamilton was okay.[239]

Ted Richards was next in the show. In the past he had ignited oil in a trench to make hot air, but not today. Instead, he had an iron furnace, which 50 young men and boys placed under the folds of the deflated balloon. He ignited the fuel, the bag expanded, and the stenciled words "Bakersfield Californian" appeared.

Standing next to him was Bakersfield Californian reporter Dan McGregor in one of Richards' brilliantly-colored flight suits. The newspaperman was helped with a parachute and was shown how to perch on the trapeze and grip and pull the break-away rope. The wind was calm. The balloon strained at its tether. Richards waved to McGregor, McGregor waved back, the rope was cut, and the big balloon sailed skyward, "going up as serenely and smoothly as could be."[240]

Hours later at the newspaper office, McGregor wrote, "That gave me a rather exhilarating feeling. From where I was before I cut loose, I had a most magnificent view of the whole country side. It would have been still more extensive if the day had been clear, but there was a haze all over the country around the mountains. I was busily enjoying this view when I heard the pistol shots that were my signal to cut loose. I reached up for the cutaway, and pulled on it. No result. I pulled again. No result. So I reached my other hand through my wrist-hold and jerked as hard as I could with both hands. The next second the bottom of the heavens had dropped out, and I was going through."[241]

On Washington's Birthday 1910 the association hosted blue-blooded horse racing, motorcycle competition, a balloon ascension, a Junior Aero Club exhibition, and a fireworks show. Ted Richards announced he would jump from 2500 feet and describe the countryside via "wireless telephony" as he floated down, which would have been another first for Bakersfield, but just one day before the event, and "without any superfluous regrets or any courtesy, Radio-Wireless Electric Company notified Richards it would not send the equipment. [242] It was windy as hundreds watched Richards ascend to 1200 feet, jump, and fall for an alarmingly-long time before his parachute opened. He landed in a tree at Nineteenth and N.[243]

The association held a grammar-school field day in April that attracted parents and kin from all parts of the county, but the proceeds did little to help the association's bottom line, and some weeks later it was out looking for funds for another air show. But optimism prevailed; the fair was just six months away.[244]

In August, the Morning Echo wrote, "The old type of county fairs that were little more than racing meets and places for gamblers is almost a thing of the past. The modern county fair has its full share of amusements, but they are for the most part clean. A good horse race is enjoyed by every red-blooded farmer. A baseball game or balloon ascension adds to the enthusiasm, and opportunity is given to the farmer and his family to meet their friends from all parts of the country. The village and town people mingle with the farmers on equal basis, and all get better

86

acquainted. The best part of the fair, however, is the educational feature. What the county fair does for localities, the state and district fairs do for the larger territory."[245]

Harry Jastro, son of Henry Jastro and manager of Power, Light & Transit, advised the association that he could install a trolley line to Hudnut Park and have it ready by fair time. The construction had to have the blessings of Bakersfield City Council, which was always wary of financial strings, and it rejected the fine print. In the summer of 1910 a few baseball games were played at Hudnut Park, but that fall the park was gone.[246]

## School Farm

Kern County High School's agricultural program expanded at the turn of the century. In May 1910, Dr. Leroy Anderson of the University of California Farm School was commencement speaker at graduation, and the next day he met with the Kern County Board of Education. Some weeks later, high school principal Harkey M. Macomber spoke before county supervisors and asked them to buy acreage for a model-school farm.[247]

A.W. MacRae who was an investor in the Kern County Agricultural Association read about what Macomber said. MacRae "hit upon the idea" of selling Hudnut Park to the county, and took his idea to the association, and days later Kern County bought the 27-acre Hudnut Park for $16,000 ($520,000). Fences, sheds, and stalls were razed and salvageables sold, but the machinery pavilion was left standing for a future dairy. To preserve easy access between the acreage and town, the vacant lots facing M Street that had been for sale were taken off the market. Irrigation ditches were back filled and the racetrack leveled. An electrically-pumped well was installed and 10 acres disked and sown to barley. The property began to look like a town farm, and twelve students were enrolled in advanced agriculture, in late September, and given garden plots.

The high school had a farm, but racing fans no longer had a racetrack.[248] The Californian observed, "Hereafter Bakersfield horsemen will find no track nearer than Los Angeles to the southward, but there are good tracks at Hanford, Visalia and Fresno."[249]

In 1913 a student dormitory was built on the southwest corner of the school farm, and over the next 10 years there were other changes. In 1924, California Farm Bureau sent a motion-picture crew to record the activities of the Boys' Agricultural Club, and although the large-animal program was gone—owing to residential sprawl—the crew took 1000 feet of film, and for the next six months it screened at major California high schools.

In 1927 the Kern County Board of Education accepted a shipment of purebred Guernsey cows and heifers from Washington State. It reinstated the large-animal program and leased a 40-acre dairy farm in the Norris School District. Not long after the Great Depression hit Bakersfield, the town farm closed.[250]

In 1933, on a vote of four to one, Kern County supervisors, exchanged 10 acres of the school farm for E.H. Houchin's town lots just south of Kern County Jail—then at the northwest corner of Truxtun and Q Street. Attorney Alfred Siemon challenged the vote and filed charges of fraud against Kern County Auditor, Treasurer, and those council members who had voted for the exchange. Siemon argued that Houchin's lots were worth no more than $17,500 ($400,000), while the old school farm, which had 1500 feet on the state highway, was worth at least $50,000 ($1,400,000). In the fall of 1934 supervisors rescinded their vote, and a year later they issued the state a 30-year lease on the property.[251]

Traffic on Golden State Highway crossed over Kern River Bridge, rounded the Traffic Circle, and passed over what was once the high school farm. State and Federal New Deal programs of the 1930s built an elongated, red-tile adobe structure on Golden State Avenue between M and O. The State Division of Forestry moved in, California Highway Patrol used it next, and finally the Kern County Fire Department. Today the building is gone, replaced by the county's four-story Public Works building at 2700 M Street.[252]

# Chapter 4, 1911

Fourth of July—Development Company
Fair Association—Motordrome
Washington's Birthday—Panama-Pacific Race

In the Californian's review of the Fourth of July race of 1911 it wrote, "Thousands of guests were royally entertained for the day, the resident population passed a safe-and-sane Fourth with genuine enjoyment, and there was little to mar the pleasure of the 15,000 or 20,000 men, women and children who thronged the city and its environs during the forty hours given up to the celebration. When 10,000 people for eight continuous hours face the heat of a July day to see the occasional racing car dash on its way, and stay patiently in their places until the last wheel is stilled, there can be no question as to an auto race furnishing a feature that grips the people and holds their closest attention"[253] The popularity and economics of racing was not lost on investors, and some turned their attention to building a modern motordrome with comfort for spectators, security for racers, and profits for the investors.[254]

## Development Company

Bakersfield Development Company was incorporated in 1912 to find land for a modern motordrome. The 21-member board represented a pantheon of Kern leaders, whose names guaranteed success: Henry A. Jastro (president), C.A. Barlow, H.A. Blodget, D.L. Brown, J.L. Bruce, C.L. Claflin, Angus J. Crites, W.E. Drury, L.P. Geaster, F.L. Gribble, Fred Gunther, George Haberfelde, Alfred Harrell, Bud Harrington, W.H. Hill, Solomon Jewett, H.C. Katz, H.G. Parsons, G.J. Planz, A.E. Savole, Mel P. Smith, and N.R. Solomon. Stock certificates were issued, and board members bought all except 500, which were left for the general public, "not so much for the purpose of gaining money as to enlarge the interest in the organization."[255]

Open land was available around Edison and west of Bakersfield, but none had the same easy access as the land company's old racetrack just north of town. In April 1912, Kern County Land Company General Manager Henry A. Jastro sold the track and surrounding grounds to the development company, and it, in turn, leased the property to the recently-formed Kern County Automobile Racing Association. Plans were made for a mile-and-three-quarters motordrome.[256]

## Fair Association

Bakersfield Merchant Association incorporated the Kern County Fair Association and issued $50,000 ($1,500,000) of stock. The Californian wrote, "The movement to form a Kern County Fair Association should be supported by the citizens of the county, and the meeting tomorrow ought to be well attended. The holding of a county fair is a community event that not only interests the entire county but advances every material interest in it. There was genuine regret when the old association disbanded, and the interesting annual fairs ceased. To inaugurate them again will be a splendid work, and the Californian urges hearty cooperation with those who have set the present movement on foot."[257]

Fair director Angus Crites announced that work would start soon, even though that very day he had 50 men working on the new track. The Morning Echo noted, "The Fair Association plans to cover the whole field of activity of such organizations, and in addition to automobiles, motorcycle and other races held from time to time, an old-time county fair with everything from horse races to yellow pumpkins will be given in the fall."[258]

In April 1913, the Morning Echo named more than 200 people who already had bought stock, and it added they could expect a four-percent annual return—based on expected success. But it also encouraged potential buyers "to invest for other than mercenary reasons."[259] The Californian wrote of the project, "It has been pending for some time and is far and away the most important step in advancing the automobile racing game in Kern county ever taken here. It is years since the old fairgrounds was turned into a pasture, but the old mile-track is said to be in much better condition than would be supposed."[260]

# Motordrome

Three dozen men with 100 mules and horses relocated a sluggish stream that had meandered across the northern end of the hummocky grounds leaving pools of standing water.[261] The Morning Echo visited a month later and wrote, "The big tract of land is being fast transformed from a wilderness of spear grass, willows, holes and hummocks into one of the finest fair grounds and automobile racetracks in the state of California. The irrigation canal which used to run through the grounds has been moved to the north of the tract, and the high banks of the abandoned portion are being used to fill in low ground along the front of the tract next to Chester avenue. Between the race track building and Chester avenue is a roomy space which will be utilized for buildings and other purposes connected with the Kern county fairs."[262] The cost of labor, materials and fees, $50,000 ($1,400,000), put the corporation $100,000 ($2,800,000) over budget, which probably was why the mile-and-three-quarters track became a one-miler.

Money problems continued. Bakersfield City Council was scouting for park property in spring of 1913, and the Development Company offered the city one-third of its 200 acres, but the asking price was high, and Bakersfield would have to call a special bond election. No deal was made, but if was, this story would end here.[263]

Thirty-two-year-old John C. "Paul" Derkum who had made a name for himself in American and European motorcycle racing was hired as consultant in the construction of the motordrome, and he probably had a large say in its dimensions. It had 900-foot straightaways, and the wide, sweeping, banked turns were built up with earth taken from the hummocky areas of the grounds. A two-ton sheepsfoot roller compacted the surface, a 17-ton roller smoothed it, and scrapers covered it with six inches of gravel fines taken from the city's Panorama Heights gravel pit— then just west of today's Garces High School. Repeated sprinkling, tamping, and rolling produced a hard, dense surface. For the safety of spectators, the grandstand, booths, and private boxes were screened with wire netting, and lengths of railroad track were placed automobile-hub height and welded to 16-inch oil-well casings firmly anchored in the earth.[264]

## Washington's Birthday

Paul Derkum's first racing show was scheduled for the weekend of Washington's Birthday. Discount railway tickets attracted racing fans, and one day before the race, five Pullman cars called the "Howdy Special" stopped at the East Bakersfield station and 100 passengers stepped off.[265] Prize money of $35,000 ($96,000) had attracted nationally-recognized drivers George Hill, Felix Magone, Barney Oldfield, Teddy Tetzlaff, and Frank Verbeck, who brought with them the fastest race cars in America. In the preliminary races, two dozen drivers from Bakersfield, Delano, Visalia, Porterville, Lindsay, Fresno, San Jose, and Los Angeles competing for $1500 ($41,000) in various races, which included two "free-for-alls" for the fastest cars over a set distance.[266]

Frederick Eldridge and Pliny Horne from Seltagraph Films of Los Angeles set up motion-picture cameras on the western curve and captured 300 feet of spectacular skidding. Between races a 17-ton roller smoothed the gouges, and a water truck settled the dust.

Barney Oldfield's 100 hp front-wheel-drive Christie V-4 had an over-head camshaft, three-inch valves, displacement of 1237 cu. in. (20.3 liters), and it redlined at 1300 rpm. On day one, Oldfield hit 77.6 mph, missing the world speed record on a dirt-track by a second and a fifth. Teddy Tetzlaff in his Fiat Cyclone set a new five-mile record of 4 minutes, 19-2/5 seconds (69.4 mph), beating the Los Angeles Ascot Park record by an even second.[267]

Derkum's work at the Motordrome, now called "The Play Ground of Bakersfield", necessitated settling disputes between vendors and the association. The Echo reported, "The directors of the fair association registered a protest against the reported sale of programs at exorbitant prices and announced that under no circumstances should anyone pay more than ten cents [$3] for one. Derkum stated that nothing sold on the ground save cigars and cigarettes should be over 10 cents, and anything more than this is excess charges. Nothing but soft drinks are sold on the ground, and any person bringing anything stronger inside the fence will have the Fair Association to reckon with."[268]

On race day the Motordrome was packed. "Thousands of people from all over the state attracted by the big automobile races yesterday thronged the streets. From the north and south people hearing of the initial appearance of the fastest dirt track in the world and the great drivers who participated in the meet came to town by every available conveyance. Bakersfield has the name of having sportsman-like citizens, and this was proven to the many guests. In many cities when some big event is given as an attraction for the crowd, the restaurants and hotels put the prices higher than usual. This cannot be said of Bakersfield. In the afternoon anything that could ride was used to convey the people to the race track. The entire length of Chester avenue was lined with people walking and riding, so that the city had the appearance of some great metropolis."[269] After the last race, 600 automobiles left the parking lot at the same time. "Chester Avenue from the grounds into the center of the city was packed with a double line of machines for an hour or more." [270] Those traffic tangles were a harbinger of problems that plagued the fairgrounds for the next 39 years.

## Panama-Pacific Race

The Panama-California Exposition at Balboa Park in San Diego was still under construction when Southland auto enthusiasts organized a 455-mile road race to start in Los Angeles on July 4, 1913 and end many hours later at the Panama-Pacific World Fair in San Francisco. The grand prize, $25,000 ($660,000), was a compilation of fees paid by towns along the route to qualify them as check-in points. Bakersfield's part would be $5000 ($132,000) plus 40 percent of Motordrome sales. Bakersfield did not grouse about that because the race would attract crowds and benefit merchants during the town's Fourth of July celebrations. During negotiations with Southland organizers, it was revealed that the first cars would arrive here in the wee, dark hours of morning. Nevertheless, the contact must have been signed because about 4 am on July 4, the first race car appeared at the Motordrome.[271]

The Los Angeles Times described the route, "Out of Los Angeles the limit of speed is largely up to the car and the driver. At Newhall there will be a slowing down, and through the canyon it is mostly up to the driver. I would not say the battle will be fought in this canyon, but many a driver will get an awful jolt there. Beyond Elizabeth Lake there are treacherous places that may bring grief to more than one car. The bad part of this road is that it is apparently smooth ahead when sudden chuck holes appear across the road and it takes driving to get across safely. The Tejon Pass is about the same shape as usual. There are some fords and high centers, but with ordinary care a man should not have any trouble."[272]

On July Fourth at one minute past midnight, 51 race cars roared off from 11th and Figueroa in Los Angeles and headed out for the San Fernando and Santa Clarita valleys. Under feeble moonlight and dim head lamps, drivers faced rutted roads, 40 streams, and steep mountain passes.[273]

At the same moment the gates at Bakersfield, Motordrome were thrown open, and fans streamed onto the "recreation park of the Kern County Fair Association". [274] Telephones reported progress of the race and the placards were updated. By 2 a.m. most drivers had passed Saugus, and some were negotiating the 1600-foot San Francisquito Canyon Road. At Elizabeth Lake, drivers faced 23 twisting, dark miles

97

to Fort Tejon and from there the back-and-forth descent of Grapevine Canyon. Speeds of 40 mph were possible on the valley floor, but the finish line, recently changed to Sacramento, was still many grueling hours ahead.

At 4:20 a.m., lookouts spied fast-approaching headlights. The Cadillac was flagged around the streets of town to the Motordrome, where the machine, driver and mechanic were resupplied. The Cadillac made one lap of the track and disappeared into the night to the next check-in points: Famosa, Terra Bella, Porterville, Strathmore, Lindsay, Tulare, Goshen, Traver, Kingsburg, Malaga, and Fresno.[275]

By mid-morning all race cars had come and gone, and at 12:00 noon the Merchants' Association, Realty Board, and Kern County Board of Trade served 5000 ticket holders a deep-pit barbecue: pots of potatoes and pickles, 25 bull heads, and 25 quarters of beef, all "dressed in the real old fashioned Spanish style."[276]

The grandstand filled, and crews arranged the cars, some privately-owned but most from local dealerships. "Although the crowd numbering approximately 8000 people that assembled yesterday afternoon at the speedway saw no records broken, but exceptionally fast time was made in all the automobile and motorcycle races comprising the card of events. The meet was crowned with eminent success; it was, indeed, the most notable event of the kind ever held in Kern county."[277]

The first car across the finish line at Sacramento was a huge Fiat driven by Frank Verbeck assisted by mechanic Harry Ham. Their time, 11 hours, 1 minute, 16 seconds (39 mph), validated the

New York factory's claim that Fiats were reliable high-speed machines. Tenth crossing the line was Fresno's Eddie S. Waterman and mechanic Clifford Perry in an old, unmodified Buick Model 17. Waterman, who was a college student with some racing experience, bought the Buick with 70,000 miles on it from a Coalinga oilfield company for $50 ($1500).[278]

The third race meet was in September 1913, and this time it was a two-day event, with rodeo, that attracted 5000 spectators, many from Southern California. Barney Oldfield promised to race his 100-hp Christie against a monoplane, but several days before the show, track manager Frank W. Cameron said the deal with Oldfield had fallen through. But the rodeo, automobiles, and motorcycles were a hit. The 100-mile race was won by Earl Cooper in a Stutz in "1:46:06 4-5", equaling 58.2 mph. The automobile races were punctuated by three accidents, none fatal. The most alarming was when Fresno's Tim McKelvey swerved his Overland to avoid hitting Felix Magone's Stutz. "In a second, the car turned completely around, rolled over twice and disappeared from view over the embankment. By a miracle McKelvey escaped without injury, but his mechanician [mekə'niSH(ə)n] Bob Reed, sustained several minor injuries but was able to be around today."[279]

The wild-west rodeo part of the show had "thrills a plenty", including a bucking horse contest. "About a dozen riders entered the contest, among them a young woman from the Poso ranch. This young lady mounted a bucker on both Saturday and yesterday. She did not win a prize, but the management gave her a tidy sum of money for her daring." The Californian continued, "Not since the days of the old Miller & Lux rodeos way back in '75 has there been so much bronco "busting" crowded together into one afternoon."[280]

# Chapter 5, 1914

Homecoming
Association Gets Fairgrounds
Pure Foods Fair—Air Show
Spring Festival—Fourth Of July
Non-Profit Fair Association—Fair of 1916

In the spring of 1914 Bakersfield celebrated Homecoming. Harry W. Thomas who had grown up on the East Coast told Charles Barlow about how his old town had invited former residents to return to visit. Barlow shared the story with W. Grant Hudlow of the Merchants Association, and days later Hudlow announced, "I have talked with a number of people about the home coming week, and it appeals to me. I propose that it shall be discussed at our next meeting."[281]

The idea caught fire, and at the next merchants' meeting S.P. Wible and W.E. Benz organized a Homecoming committee with H.G Parsons, Captain Lucien Beer, W. R. Benz, C.F Johnson, and E. M. Roberts. Alfred Harrell of the Bakersfield Californian was the chair. Wible noted that Bakersfield had not enjoyed a big celebration for a long time, "and it was about time it held one."[282] Harrell suggested April as a good month because the wild flowers would be in bloom, and he suggested auto racing, a special day for lodges, and a day of horseracing.[283] Harrell wrote, "In the years between 1872 and 1913 thousands of people have lived in Bakersfield who now reside elsewhere but who still call Bakersfield home. Homecoming week will bring them back, and along with their relatives and friends. It is safe to prophesy that 20,000 visitors will be entertained in the city during the week designated. Bakersfield will play the host, and invitations will go out north and south and east and west to all who ever resided here to return and spend the week in their former home. And they will come, too, for no man or woman or child ever resided in Bakersfield or Kern county long, who have not a desire to return to visit old scenes and renew old acquaintances among the best people on earth."[284]

The committee arranged for a parade, rodeo, horse racing, an aircraft fly-in at the Motordrome, street dancing, and a concert.[285] The heading Home Coming appeared on official Kern County correspondence, and free promotional stickers were given out for mailing.

At 7 a.m. on April 21, 1914, steam whistles at the Southern Pacific overhaul shop on Kentucky Street blew for five full minutes heralding Homecoming. Under gray-morning skies, the two-mile-long parade that formed on 19th Street had bands, floats, hundreds of marchers, and many gaily-decorated automobiles from Tehachapi, Maricopa, Taft, McFarland and Delano. Ten thousand spectators lined the sidewalks, and after the parade they made their way over to the courthouse steps to watch a Miss Barbour crowned Queen of Homecoming Week.[286]

Bakersfield Band played at Beale Clock Tower where rodeo boss F.J. Griffin assembled 175 cowboys and cowgirls—all resplendent in "picturesque sombreros, high-heel boots, spurs and riding accessories of the Western plain—the type made so familiar by novelists and other writers of romance and fiction."[287] As the riders made their way along Chester

Avenue, applause regularly erupted from the sidewalks.[288]

The rodeo had bull riding, bulldogging, and trick and fancy roping. The Morning Echo also mentioned the Cowboy Tug of War and Roman Race, both of which are easily visualized, but less clear are the Romance Race and Potato Race. The rodeo also had a Wild Mule Race, described by the Echo like this: "A mule is about the best comedian on earth, and Griffin had a score of the best wild mules going through unscheduled performances which finally got most of the audience weak and sick from laughter. These marvelous animals, suspicious they were to be drawn and quartered or treated in some horrible and painful manner, barked, balked, kicked, pawed the air, bit, reared, and struck, in fact went through the whole category of mules tricks, and then some in an effort to convince Boss Griffin there would be no wild mule race."[289]

The Californian called the rodeo a return to the Old West, but local nostalgia for the cowboy past went back at least 40 years earlier when the Kern County Courier wrote, "A general rodeo has been going on in the southern part of the county over on the San Emidio side for the last week. Cattleman and their vaqueros from all parts are gathered there. This is a relic of the old times when the wealth of the ranchers was estimated not by the dollars that he possesses, but by the horses he counted. But the palmy days of the rodeo in California have departed forever."[290] Times indeed had changed. While Boss Griffin's show was happening, a Ford automobile outside the Motordrome was stolen. It was recovered the next day at Kingsburg, 90 miles away.[291]

103

Foley & Burke Carnival set up at 17th and K Street, bands played, a Chinese orchestra tuned up, and at 8 p.m. Caesar LaMonaca's 26 "superb" Italian musicians played on the courthouse steps for street dancing. Meanwhile, East Bakersfield Improvement Association told the manager of Walter J. Clarke Carnival Company of Prescott, Arizona that Bakersfield ordinance did not allow carnivals to set up on paved streets. The carnival had to move to the unpaved part of Baker Street between Fremont and Grove (East 18th and East 19th). The sprinkled street was still damp when the carnival lights went on for 12 acts and 30 concessions. Nearby, spectators marveled at Dr. Kellogg's Orange Acres Menagerie, which the Morning Echo wrote was an "avery, duckery, monkeys, alligator, etc." [292] In the same block was Shaw's Aerodome, East Bakersfield's open-roof movie house, where customers queued up for a show.

At the Motordrome the track was smoothed, sprinkled and rolled as spectators filled the grandstand to see 36 harness and running races, but minutes into the first race, misty rain began to fall and the races were called. The old saying again had come true: Fairs always got at least one day of rain.

Some airships in the Sonoma/Los Angeles fly-in already had touched down at Stockton and Dinuba but none yet had reached Bakersfield. Die-hards waiting in the drizzle were rewarded at 3 p.m. when a Curtiss-type biplane appeared from out of the low clouds and touched down easily on the speedway. It was Silas Christofferson, and his average speed in flight from Sonoma was 4 hours, 39 minutes (75 mph). Next landing was Harold Blakeley in his 100-hp Scott-Curtiss-type biplane. His average speed in flight was faster, 109 mph, but he was second because of a broken strut at Ducor.[293]

The grandstand was nearly dry when an airship trailing smoke came in low over the track. It was Arthur "Otto" Rybitsky, and he was looking for a place to land. But where? Five thousand people filled the grandstand, automobiles occupied the infield, and people and livestock surrounded the Motordrome. Rybitsky turned south and landed next to the railroad tracks.[294]

## Association Gets Fairgrounds

Late in 1913 the fair association built a 50-foot-wide, half-mile equestrian track inside the one-mile speedway, but part of it was so close to a pit-stop that a 3-1/2-foot protective board fence had to be built around the horse track. That cost and other expenses may have been factors in what happened next.

In January 1914, Bakersfield Development Company bought $3500 ($98,000) of fair association stock and then deeded the entire fairgrounds and Motordrome to the fair association. At first glance the transaction appeared one-sided, but it benefited both parties: Association stock doubled in value, and the fair association now had cash for improvements.[295]

Barney Oldfield promised to push his Fiat Cyclone to a new record at Homecoming, and that caused a problem for Angus J. Crites because his stop watches were no longer accepted as official time pieces, but on race day, Crites had an electrical timing device, and Oldfield set a five-mile world record of 76 mph. Afterward when the famous racer was interviewed, he peevishly remarked that he almost skipped Bakersfield altogether owing to its "inexperienced promoters".[296] The old speed king was posturing. He had known long in advance that he had to pay the racing fee like everyone else, and when he threatened to skip Bakersfield, the Californian replied "no tears shed" owing to his "excess ability compared to the local men who were racing."[297]

Dignitaries from San Diego, Los Angeles and Fresno arrived for Homecoming. "The visitors formed in line after breakfast at Harvey House [by Santa Fe Station], marched up F Street to Nineteen and on to the Southern *[Hotel]* corner. Here fifty autos with banners flying drew up in line and within a few minutes there as a long procession of cars en route to Stockdale."[298] The group returned by way of Kern River oilfields, Gordon's Ferry, and China Grade.

Bakersfield businessmen were enthused. Gus Schamblin who owned Pioneer Mercantile beamed, "It showed that Bakersfield can do things and do them on a large scale." Joseph Redlick of Redlick Brothers remarked, "Business was so stimulated that I think it would be well to make the event an annual one."[299] Homecoming attracted $18,000 ($490,000] of new money, and the many reports of out-of-town newspapers boosted Bakersfield's image.

Five years had passed since the last agricultural fair, and civic leaders felt it was time for another. Farming districts around McFarland, Delano, Wasco, and Weedpatch were just getting started, and all of them were eager to take part in a fair. In the fall of 1914, Kern County Fair Association called a meeting of 250 ranchers and farmers to sound-out their interest in a fair. It was strong, but there was doubt about how to pay for a fair. California Governor Hiram

W. Johnson recently had vetoed a financing bill for agricultural districts, but was a scaled-down Kern fair possible? The association asked Bakersfield Board of Trade for help, and it agreed, but one of its requirements went too far: The show could not include livestock. Ranchers balked, and planning collapsed.

The fair association made capital improvements but in the summer of 1914 ran out of money and had to assess the stockholders. No fair was held that fall, but Kern livestock and agricultural products showed well at the Fresno and Hanford fairs. When exhibitors complained about the distance, the Californian agreed with them. "It does not profit the farmers of Kern County that a fair is held in Fresno or in Sacramento. Such fairs to be of real service must be more or less local, and they must be held at points where the people interested can have access to them." [300]

## Pure Foods Fair

Hochheimer's general merchandise between 19th and 20th Street on Chester hosted a mini fair in 1914 that brought memories of the 1902 fair. The Californian wrote: "It will really be a county fair, for there will be domestic art displays, a Board of Trade display of local products from the exhibition now held by the Kern County Board of Trade, a domestic science demonstration, and exhibits from the Kern County high school." [301] It added, "The men's furnishing department with its many square feet of show windows will be filled with things of interest to the housewife or her lesser half."[302]

For five days in October, crowds filled Hochheimer's store. Kern River Mills demonstrated a miniature wheat-grinder, and Bakersfield Broom Factory showed a broom-making machine. Displayed were Toledo Cooker Company's fireless cooker; Panama Electric Lamp Company's tungsten lamp; Victor Manufacturing Company's wonder washing machine; and M.J. Brandenstein's M.J.B coffee and Tree Tea. H.J. Heinz Company of Pittsburgh, Pennsylvania served morsels of its baked beans, spaghetti, conserves, and 57 varieties of pickles. Three high school girls distributed candy, buttered biscuits, and nut-and-chocolate cookies, and a day later the Bakersfield Californian printed the complete recipes and full names and addresses of the young ladies.[303]

## Air Show

There were horse races and an air show a week later at the Motordrome. Admission was free, but a 50-cent ($15) ticket was needed to watch stunt-pilot Lincoln Beachey, the same Lincoln Beachey who had flown an aircraft through the 1000-foot Palace of Machinery in San Francisco and who made loops over the White House for President Woodrow Wilson.[304] The Californian wrote, "Here he will give exhibitions of air maneuvers and will drop bombs on a miniature battleship 150 feet long. Besides the flying, Beachey will race with a high-powered automobile." Beachey remarked, "I know as sure as fate that someday there will be a tiny flaw in a piece of steel, just a little speck, but it will not take longer than just a tick of a watch, and then it will be all over, that is if I stick to it forever. When I make a million dollars, I quit. The only science that ever appealed to me is the dull thud of the dollars as they bounce in the strong box. But I never cheat the spectator. I give the pumpkin-fair patrons just as much for their 'two-bits' as I give those who pay twenty-five dollars for boxes at the big city meets."[305]

Among Beachey's tricks were a breathtaking, high speed nose dives and a speed contest matching his seven-cylinder aircraft against a motorcycle and two race cars. Beachey's final stunt reminded those present that Europe was still at war. "Anchored in shoal water four hundred yards from the grand stand was a battle ship *[wood and cardboard]* on detached duty from the Swiss navy. With a few bombs, Beachey showed how the aviators attached to the Allies destroy battleships. Certainly, Beachey has skill, nerve and cleverness, and the best of all, modesty."[306]

## Spring Festival

The Kern County Board of Trade sent a wildflower exhibit to the 1915 San Diego County Fair and an agriculture/oil exhibit to the Panama–Pacific International Exposition in SanFrancisco, but the Kern County Fair Association, now two years old, had yet to hold an agricultural fair. The reason, perhaps, was money. In spite of Beachey's well-attended air show, the association once again had to assess its stockholders, and that continuing shortage of funds was probably why, in 1915, that it joined Homecoming and Hochheimer's Pure Food Show in the First Annual Spring Festival.[307]

The two days and nights of "Excitement and Frolic" began with a parade of 200 floral-decorated automobiles that were captured on film by a Los

Angeles motion-picture company. Fair Association President Angus J. Crites claimed the automobile, motorcycle, and horse racing would be the "greatest demonstration ever seen in this part of the state," and he was not exaggerating. Running and trotting races occupied the first day, and second was filled with motor racing. First Annual Spring Festival concluded with a street masque (a costume parade), concert, and a Mardi Gras/serpentine ball (dance).[308]

In the fall of 1915 Paul Derkum announced that on Washington's Birthday he would bring famous auto racers to the Motordrome, and with characteristic Derkum-gusto he added, "The meet held at that time will place Bakersfield permanently on the map of the racing world, and starters of international reputation will be here, drawn by purses big enough to get them. Motorcyclists will have their chance at the big meet, and local riders will compete in races the same as the big fellows, but whatever is promised will be delivered without any hitches."[309]

Derkum then lived in Los Angeles and commuted on an irregular basis to Bakersfield for his Motordrome work, and that may have been why his plans did not work out because the Elks Club rented the Motordrome and scheduled a 50-lap race open only to drivers and cars "known to belong in the county".[310] The Morning Echo approved. "These provisions are causing car owners with a bit of sporting blood to take more interest than they would take if some professional from Los Angeles or elsewhere could import a powerful car and play a cinch game."[311]

Fresno's agricultural fair of 1915 was stunning, and Bakersfield reporters showed up for the bull fighting, bronco-busting, gun fighting, historical reenactments and agricultural shows. Bakersfield's population was 10,000, and enough took the train to the Fresno fair to leave $33,400 ($860,000) there. The statistic must have caught the attention of the Kern County Board of Trade, Kern County Board of Supervisors, and Kern County Fair Association. [312]

## Fourth of July 1916

The friendships and organizational skills that grew out of the Fourth of July celebration of 1913 and the Home Comings of 1914 and 1915 benefited the Fourth of July celebration of 1916. The patriotic gaiety started on the third with a Mardi-Gras-like parade of "comical characters" and "queerly caparisoned individuals" and continued into the evening with concerts and late-night street dancing.[313] The next day, patriotic speeches were delivered from the court house steps, 10,000 people saw the downtown parade, and then made their way to the fairgrounds for automobile, motorcycle, bicycle, and horse racing.

One of the auto races was not a race at all. Verner Copeland entered his Chevrolet, but his was the only entry and after making a leisurely turn of the track, he was awarded first prize. Much more exciting were the motorcycle races, particularly the eight-valve, 1000cc, twin-cylinder Indian built by Hendee Manufacturing Company that in speed in five circuits of the track averaged 68 mph.

When the races ended, several spectators stayed to watch a public wedding, and after the tears, kisses and applause, most left for the courthouse to see California Assemblyman W.W. Harris speak on the significance of the Fourth of July and the soul of

America. America's gravest challenge, he said, was not foreign but home-grown—industrial and social. After those sobering words, music and street dancing started and continued into the late evening.[314]

## Non-Profit Association

In the spring of 1916 Charles Barlow addressed the Farm Bureau and urged the formation of a non-profit agricultural fair association. The Californian wrote, "A co-operative non-profit county fair association was suggested to a well-attended meeting of Kern County Farm Bureau directors on March 25 by President Barlow of the Kern County Board of Trade and was very favorably received. The proposition is that a county fair association be formed under the special law for that purpose, having for its directors one representative from each of the twelve local Farm Bureau centers, two more from each supervisorial districts, the Farm Adviser, the Horticultural Commissioner, the president of the Board of Trade, and Mr. Burke, who managed the Kern county exhibit which won the premium for best collected county exhibit at Panama Pacific Exposition. The old private Kern County Fair Assn. has 75 acres fenced and a pavilion, which could be leased by the new association."[315]

The special law Barlow mentioned was the 1916-1917 California Marketing Commission Act that called for the identification, analysis, and amelioration of agricultural-marketing problems. The act also required agricultural-district boards "to promote in the interest of the producer, the distributor, and consumer, economical and efficient distribution and marketing of all or any agricultural, fishery, dairy and farm

112

products produced, grown, raised, caught, manufactured or processed within the State of California."[316] The phrase "promote in the interest of" laid the way, and provided secure funding, for future agricultural fairs.

A non-profit fair association was formed. Sitting on the executive board were Charles A. Barlow, Thomas F. Burke, Charles L. Claflin, E.C. Clark, J.C. "Paul" Derkum, F. H. Hall, J.W. Jennings, and Louis V. Olcese. In farming and ranching were C.F. Cheney (Shafter); C.E. Clark (Muroc); O.C. Heck (Fellows); R.H. Hiett (Delano); Harry Hopkins (Taft); L.J. Kanstein (Tehachapi); Henry Klipstein (Maricopa); H. S. Knight (Rio Bravo); P.A. Lee (McFarland); L.F. Lavers and A.J. McCoombs (Wasco); T.H. Martin (Rio Bravo); Robert Neill (South Fork); A.B. Robinson (Panama); E.E. Rumbaugh (Willow Springs); H.R. Seat (Arvin); J. Waters (Rosedale); N.E. Van Dam (Shafter); and J.C. Working of Pond.[317] Forty division managers and scores and scores of sub-managers were also named. Paul Derkum was designated speedway manager.

## Fair of 1916

The for-profit fairgrounds association leased the fairgrounds to the newly-created non-profit association, and it began plans for a fair. Secretary T.F. Burke rented an office on 19th Street, installed a telephone, and hired two stenographers and a messenger boy.[318] Burke enthused, "We are beginning to realize that we have one of the most resourceful territories in the world right here in Kern county. It belongs to us. We take pride in its wealth and in its

113

greater wealth to be produced. We believe the coming fair is our great opportunity to let not only California, but the entire country know of the splendid opportunities Kern county offers for home building and successful farming." [319]

The executive board went to Ventura to see how its fair was going, and they came back with the disconcerting news that Kern's plans were insufficient. Ventura's fair at Seaside Park had livestock shows, agricultural and school exhibits, moving picture shows, a "native babes" (healthy-babies) show, concessions, carnival, automobile racing, chariot racing, and "The Most Thrilling Wild West Performance on Record." [320]

The fairgrounds at Bakersfield had twice the space of Seaside Park, but the non-profit association was planning for only half the attractions. And fixing that required money. Mark M. Lichtenstein, William E. Drury, and George M. Haberfelde invented a special-admission ticket that allowed bearers also to vote for future fair directors, and other funding was found. Planning advanced, and the association now anticipated 10,000 visitors a day. [321]

Stock and agricultural exhibits arrived from Kern's 11 farming districts and more arrived from Tulare, Kings, Fresno, and Ventura counties. Night lighting and tents were set up, extra show space made under the grandstand, and 10 acres of free parking laid out, with men "to direct the cars and look after them." [322]

The association added an information kiosk, free-use telephone, "chemical fire engines" (wheeled canisters from Bakersfield Fire Department), security patrols, and a resting room for women and children to be staffed by the Parent Teacher Association.[323] The Californian wrote, "No matter what you want, it's there somewhere, and there is someone at hand to tell you how to find it."[324]

Secretary Burke praised what had been accomplished: "Let us not be a day late in the final work. In closing I desire to thank all who have so generously volunteered in the great work. It promises such results that when the work is over, we will feel happy and satisfied in having again placed Kern county in the front ranks of wide-awake Californian communities."[325]

Mid-morning on Tuesday October 24, 1916, the downtown parade began with floats, bands, marching lodges, and elaborately-decorated automobiles, some which had come from as far as Muroc and Willow Springs. B.E. Lopez, Jr. and his crew from Pathe News had motion-picture cameras at strategic corners, and a week later, news of the parade showed in movie houses across the country.[326]

The gates swung open at noon for Farm Center Day, and B.E. Lopez was there to capture the flapping flags, blaring bands, and jumbled clamor of humanity. Inside the main gate were flashy side shows, games of chance, and a merry-go-round and Ferris wheel. Food booths sold hot dogs, lemonade, popcorn, and paper "grenades", which were hollowed-out eggs filled with brightly-colored confetti. Broken shells and colorful paper littered the grounds.

Sitting in front of an easel in a nearby booth was "Baron Scofield, eminent in his line" tracing marvelously-lifelike silhouettes. Very likely it was Captain F.N. Scofield, who was also Director of

Standard Oil's Westside Division and a member of the Kern County Chamber of Commerce.

The area for swine, rabbits, sheep and goats area was south of the main gate, and on the far opposite side of the fairgrounds horses and cattle still were being unloaded at the railway spur.[327]

Midway between the carnival and the grandstand stood two 102 by 218-foot rented tents from Los Angeles. The first held farming and industrial equipment, petroleum products, automotive parts, and new cars, which the Californian called "automobile machines." Sharing space with all those was Tracy Farms, whose colorful exhibit of plumes and ostrich feathers evoked memories of the 1908 fair.

The next tent was still closed for judging. Inside, Misses Lydia Siemon and Mae White managed the school manual-arts exhibits while others attended spaces for painted china, embroidery, crochet, lace, tatting, knitting, punch work, dolls, oil paintings, and amateur and professional photography. Judging was underway for jams, jellies, crystallized and canned fruit, breads, cakes, donuts, cookies, pies, pickles, and catsup, but exhibitors 12 and under had their own competition.[328]

North of the main gate was the speedway. There, on the field, J.W. Jennings of Tehachapi judged cows, calves, and mules. New agricultural equipment filled the speedway, including farm tractors, which the Californian called "traction engines."[329]

The Californian wrote about the horse races, "Many entries have also been received in the stallion classes ranging from Richard B, admittedly one of the handsomest small horses in the state, to a monster 2300-pound black Percheron. Altogether, the livestock

116

department of the fair promises to assume the proportions of a real horse show."[330]

On Tulare Day, C.L. Claflin supervised auto racing on the "fastest dirt track in the United States."[331] On Bakersfield and Oil Day, Mayor George Hay proclaimed, "I hereby request that all places of business be closed from 12 o'clock noon until 6 o'clock pm."[332] School Day was next, and 7000 pupils passed through the gates. Some had arrived by Pullman from Tehachapi.

On Automobile and Southern California Day, Paul Derkum promised "undoubtedly the best auto and motorcycles race ever staged on the local track", and this time he was right.[333] Ten thousand spectators saw San Francisco taxi driver William Bolden push his white "Chow Chow" to a 10-mile world-speed record: 8 minutes, 44 seconds (75 mph). The "Chow Chow" was a two-year-old, 4500-pound, H.C.S. (small-chassis) Stutz Bearcat with a 361-cubic-inch Duesenberg engine. Clifford Durant of Los Angeles, also driving a Stutz, won the 50 lap race in a time of 47 minutes, 38 seconds (63 mph).[334]

This fair had orators, solo singers, a "colored" Jubilee Quartet, and bands from Bakersfield and Taft. [335] A pay event was the Venice Diving Girls performing their "fancy exhibition" each night under floodlights. Each night ended with music and dancing. The last show on the last night of the fair was "Comeroni's daring Slide for Life from the top of the grandstand hanging by his teeth, lighting his way with a barking six shooter in either hand." [336] Visalia business-owner Robert Johnson remarked, "I've seen a lot of county fairs in my time, but this tops them all."[337]

117

Attendance was steady, but Secretary Burke worried about cash flow, and he veiledly hinted failure. "We have paid out $10,140 *[$260,000]* and the end is not yet". His unease was understandable because the non-profit association had yet to prove it could pay its own way. Burke urged those owing the association to pay up: "We will need all the money due for space, advertising, and from other sources for settling up the business." [338]

Checks trickled in, including one from the Kern County Board of Supervisors, but the Motordrome probably played the biggest part in turning the profit of $3185 ($80,500). Burke: "Through its scope, Kern county was put on the map as one of the leading agricultural, horticultural and mineral producing sections of the state."[339]

No story of the 1916 fair can be complete without mentioning W.R. Shreve, who at the moment was standing before Police Judge Bunnell and praying for a break: ""I came to town from Buttonwillow to see the fair," declared Shreve. "But I got drunk before I had a chance. Please, Judge, won't you turn, turn me loose so that I won't miss it." After Shreve promised to stay out of saloons, Judge Bunnell allowed him to go. "I think everyone ought to see the fair" he said as he smilingly left the court room.""[340]

The Bakersfield Californian praised civic-minded volunteers and the organizations that helped make the fair a success, and it stressed a truth that is valid today. "A good deal of the quasi-public work that is done in a given community falls upon the shoulders of the few. These few naturally ally themselves with the civic bodies, and on those bodies rest the responsibility of taking care of that part of the people's business, which is the business of everybody, but which would receive the attention of nobody were it not for a few active citizens."[341]

While the fair was underway, the for-profit association placed petitions at strategic corners urging the county to buy the fairgrounds.[342] Farming districts favored the idea and so did most Bakersfield merchants, including Alphonse Weill, Joseph Redlick, and Ira Hochheimer. The Californian wrote, "It is hoped that sometime a way will be found to permit the county to own a fair ground and erect the necessary buildings for the conduct of the annual fairs. That institution has come to stay; it has proved its worth both to the city and county, and the people would be unwilling to see it go out of existence. These things being true, the fair should have not only the county behind it but the county government as well."[343]

The Morning Echo was against public ownership of a traditionally private enterprise. "In view of the experience of other counties along that line, it would be well to act with due caution in investing public funds in a fairgrounds and race track. The fair will probably be a greater success as long as it is kept out of the realm of county politics."[344] But days later it acknowledged that even though any number of financial catastrophes could wipe out a privately-owned fair association, those would be insignificant to 50,000 taxpayers. It went on to declare that the fairgrounds was ideally located for a mammoth, publicly-controlled resort and would build community solidarity.[345]

The for-profit association now had owned the fairgrounds two years and already spent $50,000 ($1,400,000) on improvements. The investors held $30,000 ($815,000) in shares, and if past assessments were included added in, the fairgrounds was worth about $90,000 ($2,400,000). That sizable figure meant the county had to be sure that voters wanted it.[346] And that would take time.

# Chapter 6, 1917

War–1917 Fair—Cotton is King
Boys' Club Fairs—Deadly No. 99
1925 Fair—Armistice Day Remembrance

On April 6, 1917, the United States went to war, and a week later, 25,000 Kern citizens lined downtown streets for a patriotic parade. The Californian wrote, "The remnant of the Grand Army of the Republic, the vanishing heroes of our own titanic struggle of a half century ago, were there, few in number but stepping swiftly to the inspiring sound of fife and drum. Men who wore the Grey, followers of Lee and Jackson, were in the line, and there were women representing the allied patriotic orders, veterans of the Spanish war, the local militia, long lines of members of fraternal organizations, officials of the city and the county, white gowned nurses ready to follow the symbol of the Red Cross, teachers of the public schools, and men, white and black, of native and of foreign birth, and thousands and thousands of boys and girls, the men and women of tomorrow all of them come together for a common cause, inspired by a single sentiment, to show their loyalty to the nation in its hour of peril, to attest their fealty to the cause in which the nation is at war with one of the great powers of the earth."[347]

## 1917 Fair

Five months passed. In September, business and schools were closed, and children were admitted free to the fair. Bakersfield, Tehachapi and Wasco bands played on the grandstand field, and prayers were offered for the safety of the nation. Emerson School band played as Alma Forker of Kern County Union High School led 10,000 voices in singing "America", and against the backdrop of trees along the Kern River, pupils dressed in red, white, and blue formed an immense Stars and Stripes.[348]

The fair had auto, motorcycle and horse racing, trick-riding, stock and agriculture shows, carnival, home crafts, and mineral and industrial exhibits. Each night at sunset a Foley & Burke diver climbed to the top of a 110-foot ladder, drenched himself with gasoline, struck a match, and dove, his flaming body making hardly a splash in the tiny tank of water below.[349]

Kern County's population was 23,000, and 25,000 came to the fair. The Morning Echo wrote, "The success of the Kern county fair this year is remarkable in the face of the unsettled conditions on every hand."[350] A week later, Rio Bravo and Weed Patch farming districts held a community fair and encouraged Tehachapi, Edison, Fairfax, Kern Delta, Wasco, Delano, McFarland, Pond, and Shafter farming districts to do the same in 1918.[351]

In October, T.F. Burke spoke before the Kern County Automobile Dealers Association about the public's fascination with automobiles: "We must admit that Dobbin is too slow. Everybody has an automobile or contemplates buying one. We love horses, but we demand something with more pep and speed. In spite of the fact that the race horses gathered here at the fair were the best ever assembled on the coast, the people would not turn out to see them race, and your automobile day drew almost as much money as the best three days of the horse races."[352]

Burke turned to the expense of fairgrounds operation, particularly the high cost of tent rentals, which in 1917 cost $2000 ($46,000). He stated that the initial cost of building a $12,000 ($278,000) permanent pavilion was a lot but in the long run would be a savings and an advantage in case of wind and rain.

Burke's mention of unsettled weather at fair time was factual. Years later, in 1946, when Paul Derkum was asked why he was called "rainmaker of the fairgrounds", he replied, "About three percent of such shows ordinarily are stopped by rain, while fifty percent of my shows were held up."[353] Burke's support for a permanent pavilion was well received, and the Chamber of Commerce, Board of Trade, Farm Bureau, and Fifteenth District Agricultural Fair Association said they would explore it, but by this time America had been at war for six months, and planning for the pavilion was shelved.[354]

On September 1, 1918, Derkum held 10, 15 and 20-mile bicycle, motorcycle, and automobile races, and the prize money attracted competitors from Fresno and Los Angeles. The featured five-mile event, however, was between two locals: Eddie H. Tice and his eight-valve Indian V-Twin motorcycle against Al Wilson and his "tractor airplane"—meaning its cockpit was behind the engine. Tice beat Wilson by more than a mile.[355]

The flu came in the summer of 1918, infections rose, and in October, Kern County Council of Defense ordered churches, lodges, vaudeville and movie houses to close. Two weeks later, 2000 people came to the Motordrome grandstand to watch five military airplanes touch down on the speedway. The next day Dr. S.F. Smith of Kern County Health Department reported 1000 new cases of the flu. No fair was held in 1918.[356]

The Armistice was signed on November 11, 1918, and six months later Paul Derkum was busy staging Victory Celebration and Rodeo. As the parade made its way along Chester Avenue, Army personal from San Francisco were signing up recruits at 1409 Nineteenth Street.[357]

## Cotton is King

In fall of 1920, Fresno district fair featured a new, $250,000 ($3,420,000) speedway, stock and agricultural shows, community exhibits, music, dancing, bathing girls, carnival, bull fighting, bronco busting, Tom Mix's "horde of boisterous cowpunchers", and the "most wonderful trained horse in existence." [358] The fair was a moneymaker, and weeks later, Bakersfield Commercial Club, Farm Bureau, Kern County Chamber of Commerce, and the Fifteenth District association discussed holding a fair in Bakersfield, but a different plan evolved: Cotton is King Week.[359]

Cotton farming around Arvin, Shafter, and McFarland was profitable during the war, but in 1919, cotton prices fell, and the slump continued into 1920.

Nevertheless, Cotton is King prevailed, and on October 15, bunting and flags adorned downtown Bakersfield streets, and miniature cotton fields appeared in show windows. Grand Marshal and former Mayor of Bakersfield Fred Gribble led the parade from Emerson School on Truxtun to the breakup point at Chester and 26th Street. Twenty thousand people watched the parade, and Universal, Pathe, and Fox & Selig news services were there to film six bands, 50 floats, 500 festooned automobiles, mounted police, and 1200 paraders. When it ended, crowds headed to the fairgrounds to see the Hollywood celebrities promised by Grogg Amusement Company: Fatty Arbuckle, Wallace Beery, Hoot Gibson, Buster Keaton, Harold Lloyd, Tom Mix, Hedda Nova, Ben Turpin and more.[360]

Legends in automobile racing tested their skill and daring on the raceway, but the greater draw was Bert Barr's air show featuring a female wing-walker performing at 3000 feet. Cotton is King Week delivered everything promised, California newspapers covered it in great detail, and the free publicity burnished Kern County's image.[361]

## Boys' Club

Kern County Union High School's agricultural program grew under the direction of Professor Howard K. Dickson, and by 1921 there were 75 students enrolled in agricultural bookkeeping and the leasing, buying, and selling of land. That fall at the fairgrounds the Boys' Agricultural Club planned a modest stock show, and the Californian gave the details. "Everyone having stock is invited to exhibit his best. No charge is to be made for entering stock,

125

and there will be no concessions at the fair ground which might cause exhibitors and visitors to spend money." [362] Ribbons were awarded—there was no money for premiums—and the 25-cent ($4) admission ticket paid for lunch. The boys' show was a reminder that Kern County had not had a fair in four years.[363]

Business was still recovering from the post-war decline, and because of that, no county fair was held in 1922, but with assistance of the Farm Bureau, Civic Commercial Association and private sponsors, the Boys' Agricultural Club held a three-day show at the fairgrounds. A Californian reporter called it a district fair, but its agricultural part was only a modest showing of dairy cattle, horses, poultry and hogs. Still, rancher Albert S. Goode brought 10 of his finest Jerseys, and H.A. Jastro showed some yearling Hereford steers acclaimed the finest of baby beef. The club's show also had informational booths, one addressing the eradication of weeds, animal pests, and harmful insects.

The Californian reporter could have said the show was a mini district fair because it had a junior-cowboy rodeo—(staged by club members Earl Burgess and Cecil and Darrell Tracy of Buttonwillow),—a football game, the high school's band, and singing competitions among eight grammar schools. Rides included a roller coaster, merry-go-round, and something called the Whip, all of which helped pay for ribbons and trophies.[364]

The Californian observed, "The refreshment concessions operated by a number of sweet lassies of two Camp Fire groups drew crowds, as hot dog, ice cream, candy and similar edibles were vended." [365] Among the business owners showing agricultural lines were Fred Gunther and Arthur H. Karpe. Karpe,

126

known as a hard-nosed businessman, supported the show financially and had a history of helping hardworking young men establish in farming.[366]

Part of the show was held on the roof of the Stock Exchange Building downtown. There, the Chamber of Commerce displayed minerals and historical photographs, Arvin Farm Center displayed fresh produce, and the Bakersfield Garden Club provided a showing of flowers under a canopy of wire-netting that was covered with alfalfa.

Publisher Alfred Harrell wrote of the Boys' Club, "They are the ranchers of the future. They are the potential candidates for positions as leaders in a great industry. The experience they will thus gain in the conducting of a livestock exposition will doubtless do much toward whetting their ambitions and identifying them permanently with a well-chosen life work."[367]

To Harrell, county fairs were investments in the community: "It may safely be said that it is always a profitable investment, if not in direct financial results, at any rate in the stimulus it gives to the business and industrial life of the community in which it is held. There appears no good reason why a county fair on an ambitious scale should not be held annually in this city, which is the center of one of the most important counties of the state. The grounds of the Kern County Fair association are admirable for their purposes. They are lacking, however, in the necessary structures. The county fair here should be a permanent institution and the buildings should reflect the fact."[368]

# Fairs and Rodeos 1923

The Fifteenth District did not hold a fair in 1923, but five local farm districts did. Weed Patch, Mountain View, Edison-Fairfax, and Arvin held a fair at Vineland School, and it rivaled past county fairs in diversity: a furnished model home with a small garden, farm produce, floral exhibits, fine arts, sewing, fancywork, and canned and jarred preserves.

Tickets were drawn every hour for prizes, and at noon 3000 people enjoyed a free lunch under the direction of "barbecue artist" C.E. Castro who served 1200 pounds of beef, 150 pounds of red beans, 600 loaves of bread, 300 gallons of coffee, and pounds and pounds of potato salad prepared by families of the districts.[369]

Dozens of mothers brought dozens of babies to the well-baby clinic, and county physician Joe Smith commented he did not have to give the mothers much advice because "the babies of the district seem to be pretty husky specimens." [370] Afternoon activities included horse racing, a bucking-horse contest, and a mammoth tug-of-war.

A month later, Bakersfield Elks Club sponsored a three-day Wild West Rodeo at the fairgrounds, and 2500 visitors came out to see the acclaimed humorist, newspaper columnist, and Hollywood actor Will Rogers. Rogers told Bakersfield that the county's lackluster business conditions were simply a natural transition from wartime profitability to peacetime business.[371] Department store owner Joseph Redlick agreed. ""This depression we hear about isn't so much 'post-war depression', as the disability or unwillingness for merchants to adjust themselves to the old scale of profits they knew before the war. Oilmen got accustomed to selling their oil at $1.20 a barrel, and forgot that they had formerly made money on 60-cent oil.""[372]

Because of man-power shortfalls during the war, Uncle Sam eased visa requirements for Mexican field hands. With the peace the rules were re-tightened, and the guest workers went home, but fewer U.S. citizens returned to farm work. Farming problems worsened when Hoof and Mouth Disease appeared in the northern San Joaquin Valley, and agricultural income fell by $1,000,000 ($16,000,000). By spring 1924 the virus had not shown up in Kern County, but if that happened, all agricultural products would be quarantined—none could be shipped out of the county. Kern County Farm Bureau urged supervisors to take all precautions regardless of expense, and one of those was cancellation of the 1924 Kern County Fair.[373]

### Deadly No. 99

The for-profit fairgrounds association had become an ailing investment. In fall of 1924 Paul Derkum spoke before its investors and explained how he could make the Motordrome a destination for modern, high-speed auto racing. Improvements would be costly, but the board gave Derkum a lease on the Motordrome with broad management and decision-making power over the proposed changes.[374]

Contractor Clyde Hartman brought in two dozen men with Fresno scrapers. They banked the curves for higher speeds, leveled the track, added gravel and sand from Four Falls quarry on Kern Island Canal, and after repeated oiling and tamping, the speedway became a hard, dense surface. To guard the grandstand from fire, 1000 feet of four-inch water pipe was installed.[375]

Early in 1925, while work was underway, Derkum spoke before the Exchange Club, outlined the history of automobile racing in America, and displayed his photographs from 1913 when he advised on construction of the Motordrome. His vision for profitability included Cotton Is King Week, auto-racing on national holidays, and agricultural fairs. In fact, Derkum already had issued a sub-lease to the non-profit fair association, and that group was making plans for a 1925 fair.

In April, Derkum hosted a junior Olympiad which attracted 1000 pupils and their families from 13 city and 65 county schools. The show gave Derkum free publicity and it gave the public an opportunity to see what had been done to the Motordrome.[376]

Derkum's first show on the new track was Prosperity Sweepstakes that opened in the first week of May 1925. One-dollar ($16) tickets for the grandstand and bleachers sold fast, as did the special two-dollar tickets that allowed bearers to park inside the big oval and watch the races from there.

Prosperity Sweepstakes started when two somber, uniformed men appeared on the empty field, one bearing the Stars and Stripes and the other the flag of Frank S. Reynolds Post, American Foreign Legion. Following them came the Eagles Drum Corps and Woodmen of the World Band. The colors were posted, and the grand overture played.[377]

Race cars were pushed to the track. Most of them were powered by Ford Model-T engines that had displacements of 177 cu. in. (2.9 L) and compression ratios of 3.98:1, but otherwise the engines were highly modified. Jack Kemp of Bell, California entered Hooker Special No. 99, which had a Ford Model T chassis powered by a Model T block with a Miller dual-overhead camshaft. Kemp raced No. 99 in the 25-mile feature race and pushed it to a national dirt-track record of 85 mph.

Some people on the grandstand were aware that No. 99 was a death car. Two months before Prosperity Sweepstakes, driver Billy Reed was killed in it. Two weeks after Prosperity Sweepstakes, 27 year-old Kemp himself died in the car, and five months later, driver Gene Bingham lost his life in old 99.[378]

## 1925 Fair

Seventy-seven-year-old Henry A. Jastro who led the fair of 1908 was expected to do the same in 1925, but his heart condition worsened, and Professor Howard K. Dickson took up the job. A new dining hall was built, trees planted, and walkways and loud speakers installed. The non-profit fair association rented tents from Los Angeles for $12,000 ($185,000), which put five acres under shade. Dickson invited several San Joaquin Valley chambers of commerce to show at the fair, giving special attention to Corcoran, whose cotton float had won first prize at the San Francisco Diamond Jubilee. Dickson met with Bakersfield City Council about the flow of traffic between East Bakersfield and the fairgrounds, and the city subsequently paved Twenty-Fourth Street between M and Union. Dickson conferred with the Southern Pacific, and it installed a 250-foot railway spur onto the fairgrounds. That allowed Bakersfield's name to be added to the short list of Californian fairgrounds that had on-site, direct-rail shipping.[379]

The fair was the first since 1917, and the non-profit went to lengths to show it was for the people. Cash premiums were generous, and the premium books were mailed to 7000 county addresses. The non-profit broadened the livestock and horse shows, hired a midway and fireworks company, and installed electrical scoreboards and radios because the World Series would be underway at fair time.[380]

First-day attendance was 25,000, and day-by-day ticket sales were positive. King Oliver and the Dixie Syncopators was a popular attraction, but an unexpected hit was Kern County Union High School's automobile mechanics show. At the sound of the starting gun, student teams raced to jalopies at the opposite end of the Motordrome, where they drained the radiators, started the engines, and drove back to the grandstand. There they removed the cylinder heads, replaced the valves, started the engines, and made one loop of the track. The team crossing the finish line first got $10 ($160).[381]

Despite the encouraging attendance, the books disappointed. Days later when the association met for review, Secretary P.G. Clarke entered the meeting carrying two folders: his resignation and the financial statement showing that the association was $27,000 ($421,000) in the red. [382] Clarke's parting words surprised no one: "Your next task is in bringing about the purchase of the fairgrounds by the county to eliminate the prohibitive rental [of tents] which more than any other one thing caused the deficit this year. Working under the same handicap which was faced this year, it is a physical and financial impossibility for any group of men to carry on a fiscally-successful fair. Mistakes have been made, but none of them were costly, and were to be expected in the working of a board of men who, previous to this year, scarcely knew each other."[383]

## Armistice Day Remembrance

Armistice Day 1925 started with a subdued downtown parade. Business closed, and that afternoon there was a modest fireworks show at Griffith Field followed by a football game between the Drillers and Occidental College freshmen of Los Angeles. Frank Reynolds Post, American Foreign Legion rented the Motordrome, and at sunset free bus service started between the Motordrome and the closest streetcar stop.[384]

The show was a two-hour memorial reenactment of the Battle of the Argonne Forest honoring the brothers Frank and Claude Reynolds.[385] Californian columnist Scholer Bangs was there. "How one company of American Soldiers fought in the campaign of the Meuse-Argonne offensive, slowly but steadily gaining ground in the face of a crashing rain of death from the enemy and paying with blood for the victory of the last battle of the World War was seen by 10,000 people at the fairgrounds last night. With the devil-may-care mien of a group of gladiators saluting in the Coliseum with "Hail, Caesar! Those who are about to die salute thee" a company of Legionnaires with Major C.K. Badger at its head marched into view, wheeled in front of the judges' stand, and saluted. The colors carried by Sergeant Albert G. Barksdale were posted in front of the judges' stand while the thousands who looked on saluted. The High School band played "America." Ten minutes later, every light in the grandstand went out as a rocket with a train of red sparks climbed into the air and burst with a roar that shook the grandstands. From the enemy trenches hurled a mortar bomb which released a calcium flare, making the field as light as day and showing the first wave of Americans coming over the top with spitting rifles."[386]

No seat was unfilled, and the show was probably a money maker for the for-profit association, but 1923 and 1924 had been generally bad for business, and a month after the show the for-profit had to dip into reserves to pay stockholder dividends. The board decided it was time to sell the fairgrounds.

# Chapter 7, 1925

## County Buys the Fairgrounds
## Historical Collections
## Chamber of Commerce Building
## 1928 Fair

The county's new hospital on Flower Street was in use for a year when county supervisor James J. Wagy moved that the county sell the old hospital grounds on West Nineteenth Street and buy land for a fairgrounds. The motion did not get a second, but at the next meeting, the for-profit association brought petitions urging supervisors to buy its fairgrounds. A.H. Swain of the non-profit association was also there, and he too urged supervisors to buy it.[387] F.W. Browster representing the for-profit association said, "We, the directors, are between the devil and the deep blue sea. Creditors were after us for more money today—you people, of course, are the deep sea." [388] Following up on that, realtor J.H. Thornber remarked, "Unless the county owns grounds for another fair, it will be a fiscal impossibility, I believe, to get directors to manage another fair." [389] Supervisor Wagy responded, "We haven't the finances to buy, so we must do a great deal of casting about to find a way to make such a purchase. We've got to find the money first." [390] The next day the Bakersfield Californian wrote, "Taxpayers were aware that such a purchase would cause a slight increase in their tax rates, but that they were willing to assume it."[391]

The for-profit association wanted $105,247 ($1,609,000) for its fairgrounds, but the figure did not include Paul Derkum's lease. Derkum had been quiet about everything but now he announced he was out-of-pocket $18,846 ($301,000), and that amount did not include his monthly lease of $500 ($7800). [392] Said Derkum, "Continuous discussions have contained so much misinformation that I am impelled to give the facts regarding my own interests and activities. First, if the fairgrounds are sold, I must be reimbursed for my investment, which is as follows... *[expenses listed]*. The above figures represent only the actual outlay of cash and contract price. They do not include any amount for engineering ability, knowledge, and experience or of miscellaneous expenses of traveling and compiling the work. Neither do they include the extra expense of living in Bakersfield or salary for the eight months during construction."[393]

Kern County Land Company owned three parcels with potential as fairgrounds, but all needed expensive development. Kern County Farm Bureau, Commercial Association, and Edison-Fairfax Farm Center wanted the county to buy the for-profit fairgrounds, but Delano Businessmen's Association were opposed owing to its restricted access and soggy, sticky conditions when wet. [394] Supervisor John Hart wanted to send the question to a referendum, while others preferred to hear directly from the public. In the end, supervisors invited citizens to "advise this board as to whether or not they could arrange to make other and further use of said grounds by promoting automobile shows, stock exhibitions, cotton exhibits, harvest festival, midwinter fairs or other and further activities in such a manner as would enable the county to derive revenue from rents or lease such as would in part cause the said fairgrounds to be self-sustaining financially..."[395]

Supervisor Stanley Abel insisted the fairgrounds was worth no more than $70,000 ($1,078,400), others disagreed, and the back-and-forth went on for weeks, but in the final show of hands, it was four to one to offer the association $100,000 ($1,540,000), which included the matter of Derkum's lease. In March, April, and May of 1926, Notice of Intention to Purchase appeared in the Bakersfield Californian and public comment invited.[396]

Paul Derkum scheduled another Junior Olympiad in May, and the Californian wrote, "Every parent and patron of the schools will give heartiest co-operation in the effort to give every boy and girl in Kern county a change for clean, wholesome and a well-balanced program of activities to develop healthful living, good sportsmanship and citizenship." [397] Two thousand people watched a morning of sport and an afternoon of fun, and a Californian writer joined the silliness: "1:30 o'clock, Jingling Brothers and their sister's mammoth circus, featuring the ring-necked hyperunkus, the googleosaur, acrobats and other bats. Biological wonders never before seen in Kern county. Oodles of beautiful dancing girls and features from the Colosseum of old Rome. Clownamaniacs, from the one- and two-teacher schools of the central section of Kern county, in Ring No.1."[398]

Supervisors were deliberate and up front with the public about the prospect of buying the for-profit's fairgrounds, and Supervisor J.I. Wagy was surer than

137

ever it was going happen. A. J. Crites, then president of the for-profit fair association, may have thought he was helping things along when he warned the public that there would be no fair unless the county bought the fairgrounds. In fact, Crites already had ordered 600 chicken coops, 152,000 square feet of tenting and was in negotiations with a carnival company.[399]

On Friday July 3, 1926, county supervisors convened as a Board of Equalization, received public input, and at noon adjourned for the weekend. The Californian was optimistic: "The large fairgrounds site, scene of scores of automobile races, horse races, motorcycle races and county fairs, owned by a private group of stockholders, will probably become the property of Kern County tomorrow for a consideration of $100,000. When the board convenes Monday it will be in the nature of a public hearing to learn whether or not there are any protests against the purchase of the fairground. They will sit as arbiters in settling any protests arising in connection with assessments levied by the county assessor against property. When ratified by the Board, purchase will include the fastest one-mile track in the world that has a dirt surface as well as the stables and grandstand." [400] At the Monday meeting of supervisors, the question was called, and the fairgrounds' purchase squeaked through on a vote of three to two.

A day later Kern County Treasurer Jerry Shields and C.A. Barlow, secretary of the for-profit fair association, sat down at what must have been a very long table, and Shields deliberately counted out 1000 $100 dollar bills ($1,700,000). [401] The Californian wrote, "Purchase of the Kern County fairgrounds by the county supervisors assures the permanence of the county fair as an institution. It also places upon the shoulders of every resident of the county a share of responsibility. The fairgrounds is an asset, but it is one that must be used. It is an investment, and it must pay a profit. The grounds will pay profit upon one condition, and that is a general realization of its common ownership."[402]

Days later the Fifteenth District board met with county supervisors at the old hospital grounds, inspected the two-story lab building and decided it was solid enough to move to the fairgrounds for a business office. That meeting, and many more to come, preceded the fairgrounds' grand opening just two months later.[403]

During that time, the state reorganized its agricultural districts, and California Governor Friend Richardson appointed a new board for the Fifteenth District Agricultural Association. Named were R.C. Annin (Wasco), F.W. Brewster (Arvin), Angus J. Crites (Bakersfield), H.K. Dickson (Bakersfield), G.W. McClintick (Delano), C.A. Melcher (McFarland), and A.H. Swain and J.H. Thornber of Bakersfield. A.J. Crites became president. It was estimated that $39,000 ($650,000) was enough for a fair, and getting the money was not a problem. The Fifteenth District had $37,500 ($628,000) in reserve and expected $41,000 ($688,000) from ticket sales, which meant, barring bad weather, that a respectable nest egg would be left over for the next fair. The county rented its fairgrounds to the fair association for $12 ($192).[404]

Past fair associations had bought rain insurance, which in 1925 cost $500 ($7900). A.J. Crites examined his weather records going back to 1904 and confirmed what was already common knowledge: Rain always fell at least once at fair time. Crites noticed that in the same 21-year period, rain had fallen only twice between September 14 and September 18. He took that information to his board, and the Fifteenth District fair was scheduled for the third week of September 1926. Rain insurance was skipped.[405]

The south fence was moved 150 feet nearer the railroad spur, more parking spaces created, and 100 benches and four rest rooms built with "adequate sanitary toilet facility even for record-breaking fair crowds".[406] The old hospital lab building was in place.

The association rented 150,000 square feet of tenting from Los Angeles for $5000 ($77,000) and awarded contracts to Morris Mosquito Abatement, John Ramage Concert Band, A.B.C. Attractions (a carnival company), and contracted with Central California Ice Company at Union and Kentucky for the storage of fruit and produce. Bakersfield police officer W.E. Snell would take over traffic control, and Boy Scouts of America would wave-in cars and the five-minute buses from town.[407]

Schools were closed on Monday September 13, 1926, and at mid-morning gates opened at the largest county-owned fairgrounds in California. Families streamed into the carnival, some stopped at concession stands, others headed to six enormous tent pavilions: the 146 by 368-foot Machinery Hall; Hall of Varied Industries (100 by 300); Community Exhibits (100 by 300); Pure Foods and Home Industries (75 by 225); Kern County Schools (80 by 160); and Kern County Manufactured Goods and Agricultural Products (50 by 200), the last sheltering an 80-foot cotton exhibit.[408] To the west near a grove of trees, stood an open-air dance floor, stock barn, pens, corrals, and the railroad spur, sometimes called the fairgrounds' "private railroad track."[409]

Crowds were large every day. Premiums of $6800 ($104,900) and ticket sales and entry fees of $19,100 ($329,300) pointed to profitability. Also, the association expected to receive $37,500 ($646,000) from the state, but that didn't happen. In the lead-up to the fair someone slipped a digit, and the actual rebate was only $9000 ($150,000), but the county made up the shortfall, and as the Californian predicted, the loss was insignificant to 90,000 taxpayers.[410]

Clerical error was not the reason for the loss. During the fair the Sells-Floto Circus and 101 Wild West Show were open in another part of town and directed $15,000 ($259,000) away from the fair. Weeks later, Bakersfield City Council banned itinerant circuses and carnivals during fair time and the month before the fair.[411]

Over the next several months, supervisors spent $14,000 ($241,000) for ground leveling, irrigation lines, fences, stock sheds, rest rooms, a dance floor, business office, and electrical work in preparation for the 1927 fair.[412] The Farm Bureau, Chamber of Commerce, Civic Commercial Association, and Fifteenth Agricultural District Fair Association raised the premiums to $16,000 ($237,000).[413] Even though economic times were better, the Californian wrote prudently, "It may properly be regarded as not only a desirable privilege but a special duty of every citizen of Kern county to attend as many times as possible during the next five days and nights. The fair is designed to be helpful to all residents of the district, and it will be more than that if the people respond whole-heartedly and enthusiastically to the opportunities which it represents."[414]

## Historical Collections

Kern County Sports Club planned a winter sports complex for Breckenridge Mountain, and it would include a history center. The club rented space at 1802 Chester Avenue, brought in historical items, and encouraged the public to donate more. Their plan for a history center did not materialize, but the idea did. Bakersfield Lions Club, which had its own historical collection, felt it was time for Kern County to have an official museum. Lions' President Whit C. Barber met with Kern County Chamber of Commerce Secretary Lawrence Nourse and offered him the Lions' collection. Nourse accepted, and the two agreed that a fitting setting for all the historical material would be the new county library then waiting voter approval. Meanwhile the Lions' donation went into storage at the fairgrounds.[415]

The 1927 fair had domestic exhibits, school displays, arts and crafts, and the bounty from Kern's 12 farming districts. Day One was called Children's Day, and 9000 youngsters were admitted free. On Bakersfield Day, downtown stores closed at noon so employees and their families could attend the fair. Bench shows displayed handiwork, sewing samples, and home-made dresses, and following that, J.C. Penney Company held a fashion review and popularity contest.[416]

A huge 100 by 340-foot tent sheltered new automobiles, and nearby it was a 60 by 250-footer that shaded trucks and farming equipment. Across from the fast-food booths and buffet line, space had been made under the grandstand for a first-aid station. To the west, in the direction of the railway spur, were rabbit and poultry shows. In the first few days of fair week, a football game was played at the Motordrome, followed by horse racing—saddle, harness, trotters, and pacers. On Thursday and Friday, $1000 ($16,500) in prize money awaited the auto races. Building on the excitement, a performer named Sandow laid down on the racetrack and allowed a speeding car to pass over his body.[417]

On Elks Day, lodge members from across California were conspicuous in their regalia. The night entertainment included Otto Taglieber swan-diving from an 85-foot ladder and making hardly a ripple in the diminutive tank of water below.[418]

Gate and grandstand receipts ran neck and neck, and manager R.E. Cady reported positive cash flows, but when the fair ended, it was again in the red. The Farm Bureau suggested that the county handle the finances next time and let the Chamber of Commerce do the rest.[419] The Californian also made suggestions, but the Bakersfield Morning Echo merely blamed the state for its tight-fistedness: "The fair for the past three years has been conducted by the directors of the Fifteenth District Agricultural Fair Association, named by the governor. The district comprises Kern county, but it is said that the fair has not been adequately supported, leaving the directors of the association with a carry-over of indebtedness each season."[420]

## Chamber of Commerce Building

The long-desired permanent pavilion talked about since the 1890s was about to become a reality. In 1927 the county treasury was flush, and in the fall Kern County supervisors approved construction of an 83 by 300-foot pavilion. But that was not all. At the next board meeting, Charles H. Biggar, AIA, showed his plans for a two-story, 40 by 145-foot Spanish-style Chamber of Commerce Building with an estimated cost of $25,000 to $35,000 ($418,000-$545,000). [421] Downtown business grumbled about putting it on the fairgrounds, but most agreed that its best placement was on the main traffic artery through town. Ground levelling started in November. Not long after the foundation was poured, it was discovered that the footings were below the river's high-water mark. Diversion ditches had to be dug, and construction costs rose 40 percent. As work neared completion, the chamber of commerce which was then in the north wing of city hall, began packing its collection of minerals, promotional photographs, and historical items.[422] In March 1928 the new Chamber of Commerce Building opened to the public.[423]

## 1928 Fair

In September 1928 a crate of carrier pigeons arrived at City Hall, and the next morning they were released from atop the fairgrounds grandstand. A day later the mayors of Los Angeles and San Francisco called Bakersfield Mayor L.K. Stoner to announce that his "pigeongrams" had arrived heralding the Kern County Fair.[424]

Downtown business closed early on the first day, and as the mid-morning crowd streamed onto the grounds, newly poured sidewalks kept down the dust. Some paused to watch selections from H.M.S. Pinafore that were underway on the outdoor stage. Under a tent and showing for the first time at the fair was the Artist Club, which in a few short years would become the Kern County Art Association.[425] Forty youngsters from the Children's Shelter spent "several happy hours in the exhibit buildings and along the Midway, where they were passed into all the shows and the riding devices by courtesy of Messrs. Foley and Burk [the carnival company]." A Californian reporter who saw the poultry show wrote, "A covey of baby valley quail, just learning to fly, still take refuge under their bantam foster mother when disturbed, and the whirring of their tiny wings as they fly up has a novel suggestion of the out-of-doors."[426]

First-day ticket sales exceeded the 1927 count by 1000, and General Secretary R.E. Cady attributed it to the cooperative relationships among the Board of Supervisors, Farm Bureau, and Fifteenth Agricultural District. Attendance remained steady through the last day, but when the numbers were crunched, the fair spent more than it took in. Any mention of that was a digression: The county picked up the tab.[427]

In the spring of 1929, two huge concrete pads were created just south of the main gate, and as fair time drew near, two massive tents arose over their smooth surfaces, the Californian likening them to giant mushrooms making their annual appearance. Also new to the fairgrounds were oiled driveways, additional fencing, and a care-taker's cabin, designed by Symmes & Cullimore.[428]

145

June Dooley Rodriguez who lived there as a child recalled, "In 1929 my father *[Walter L. Dooley, then 57]* was appointed caretaker of the Kern County Fairgrounds by Roy Woollomes, Supervisor of District One. I was 2-1/2 years old when we moved to the fairgrounds. I remember living in our first house while the county built a new house for the caretaker. We were the first family to live in the house that is still on the grounds of what is now Pioneer Village. Our old *[first]* house was farther west from where it *[the present house]* is now. The house faced east toward the Chamber of Commerce building, which now serves as the Kern County Museum. To the west of our house were the barns. The old grandstand was north and continued toward the east. There was a baseball diamond to the south."[429]

Once again, each day of the fair was given a name: Bakersfield Day, Kern County Day, All-States Day, Children's Day, and Home Coming Day. The attractions closely mirrored the fair of 1928, with the exception of bicycle racing, equestrian gymkhana, and a Junior Olympiad, the last featuring a troop of girl tumblers from Standard School.[430]

Everything was interesting and exciting in its own way, but again the fair lost money. Nevertheless, president A.J. Crites and director Howard K. Dickson were gratified by how far the fair had come in so few years. Crites: "From an initial start of five years ago that proved to be a dismal failure, Kern county this year has proven itself capable of producing a fair that places it among high ranking fairs of the state's counties... The 1929 Kern County Fair, after five years of slow but certain progress, has finally reached a degree of success that cannot be denied. Its value as a factor in community life is assured."[431] The Californian remarked, "The co-operation afforded committeemen and fair workers by the hundreds of exhibitors was nothing short of perfected community spirit, and of such a nature as to ensure the success of next year's event."[432]

# Chapter 8, 1929

Great Depression—Work Camp
Rodeo—Work Camp in 1933
Pari-Mutuel Betting
Frontier Days—Basement Museum
New Grandstand

The Crash of Wall Street in September 1929 did not affect the county's economy right away, although supervisors shrank the fairgrounds budget. Money became tight, and in the spring of 1930 Paul Derkum asked the public to help fixing the track. Associated Oil donated clay from an abandoned oil pit, county trucks made 500 trips to deliver it, and Derkum was grateful. "All of this would have been impossible were it not for the magnificent support that is pouring in from every side for the Kern motorcycle officers in the effort to raise money for their widows' and orphans' fund."[433]

O.A. Kommers who was president of the Chamber of Commerce and director of the 1930 Fifteenth District fair signed a contract with Warren Brothers of San Francisco to ornament the fairgrounds with bunting and create a grand, colorful passageway from 19th and Chester to the fairgrounds.

The permanent pavilion saved the county the cost of tent rental, but some were still needed. The ones delivered in the fall of 1930 had fire-resistant

149

wire rope instead of hemp rope, and the installation was new to workers, and Kommers had to closely supervise.[434]

The first day had the expected hustle and bustle, but the afternoon was more sobering. Six hundred spectators filled the pavilion to see Kern County Superintendent of Public Works B.B. Meek and nominee for state governor James Rolph, Jr. discuss Kern's agricultural water problems. Framing the podium and softening the proceedings were masses of blooms from the Garden Club.[435]

The fair had five days of horse racing but no auto racing—which came a month later—but there were displays of new cars, and on one day the fair had a baseball game and miniature airplane exhibition. The pay events included a parachute-jumping show, notable because the jumpers landed directly in front of the grandstand.[436] One of them was a female, Miss Billie Brown, who a beguiled Californian reporter characterized as a "heroic little figure whose blue eyes and golden bob makes a person think she belongs in Bryn Mawr instead of in the air at altitudes varying from 18,000 feet down ... The only accident of the day was that in which pretty little Billie Brown, holder of the world's altitude record for parachute jumping, figured when a dangerous updraft of air caught her and swept her over the top of the grandstand, over the midway zone and into the parked automobiles south of the fairgrounds. There the 98 pounds of tricky parachute jumper cracked up on the side of an automobile and came out with a lot of thrills and a sprained ankle."[437] The evening show was Sunshine Idea featuring Fanchon & Marco's lavishly-costumed "Sunkist beauties" performing musical potpourris in perfect unison.

In the first year of the Great Depression, California's taxable income fell seven percent. Most agricultural districts in California had less than $700 ($12,000) in reserves, but the Fifteenth Agricultural Fair District had an astonishing $6251 ($109,000), and that allowed Paul Derkum to continue his racing shows. In October 1930, in preparation for Western Circuit Sweepstakes, Derkum and helpers worked late at the pit stops and fought rising dust in preparation for 55 prominent speed kings and their powerful machines. The show was a hit and focused state-wide attention on Bakersfield.[438]

Kern's economy softened through 1930, business struggled, and at the end of the year Kern County Chamber of Commerce's reports showed shrinking inventories and depressed oil production.[439] Tight budgets were the rule, and the state ordered its agricultural districts to streamline management and consolidate responsibilities. In January 1931 the Chamber of Commerce assumed the duties of the Fifteenth District Agricultural Fair Association, by then commonly known as the Kern County Fair.[440]

## Work Camp 1931

The growing numbers of unemployed men roaming the county was stark evidence that the bad times were here to stay. In 1931, Kern County Supervisor J. Perry Brite introduced the "Brite Plan" that made the pavilion a "work stockade"—the first of many to come in the state. [441] Fellow supervisor Richard Ashe advised the public, "When approached with a request for assistance, citizens should direct the supposedly needy one to the work camp. Professional beggars will give this county and its woodpile a wide berth, yet not one hungry person will go unfed. Our object is to make certain that no person actually willing to work will starve in Kern County."[442] Signs posted under bridges and along the river showed how to find the work camp. It sold no meals, and none were given away for free; an hour's work on the woodpile equaled one meal ticket.

By this time county supervisors had cut the fairgrounds budget by $17,000 ($305,000), and no fair was planned. Tulare County did not tamper with its, and in September 1931, Tulare had an agricultural fair. The Bakersfield Californian noted, "Since Kern county is not having a fair this year, the management of the Tulare County Fair particularly invites the people of Kern county to join in the Twelfth Annual Tulare County Fair at Tulare, September 22 to 26 inclusive."[443] The fair at Tulare had Children's Day, Governor's & Pioneer Day, Kern & Kings County Day, Farm Day, and Fiesta Day. When Kern County Chamber of Commerce was asked about holding an agricultural fair in 1932, its answer was "maybe". Should it be limited to Kern County exhibitors only? Would it attract visitors from the Los Angeles Summer Olympics? The topic lost steam, and nothing more happened.

Congress sent a $375M ($2.4B) bill to President Hoover to provide food and shelter for destitute Americans, but Hoover vetoed it, explaining that public funding discouraged philanthropy and undermined self-determination. Among the few relief bills Hoover did sign was the Federal Emergency Relief Act, but it did little for Kern's mounting poverty.

The fairgrounds work camp sheltered, fed and provided jobs, but it could not save all who were out of luck. In the spring of 1932, a body was discovered at a private campground north of the river. A man had hanged himself. In his pocket were two work-camp meal tickets.[444]

## Rodeo

Kern County provided clothing and food for destitute families, and the Lions Club delivered milk to hundreds of undernourished school children, but in 1932 Kern's economy worsened and donations to the Lions project dwindled. In response, the club rented the Motordrome for a Labor Day fundraiser. I.L. Wofford of Kernville and Edna L. Shaw of Miller Brothers' 101 Ranch Wildwest Show brought the Milk Fund Rodeo & Wild West Show to the Motordrome.[445] The Californian wrote, "I.L. Wofford, manager-director, has left nothing undone to give Bakersfield the greatest rodeo in its history. Hundreds of visitors are expected from towns of this San Joaquin valley, from Los Angeles, Hollywood and other towns across the ridge."[446]

On Saturday morning November 12, 1932, Rammages's Band and a dozen mounted riders formed a modest parade at Niles and Baker Street, headed south on Baker to East Nineteenth, turned west to Chester Avenue, and from there rode on to the fairgrounds. Fox Movietone News and Universal Studios filmed the rodeo, and for the next several weeks it screened in movie houses across the county. The fundraiser helped the Lions' project for a while, but philanthropy alone was not enough to meet the rising poverty.[447]

Desperate people took desperate measures to survive. Dance marathons and flag-pole-sitting are remembered today, but less well-known is B. Ward

Beam's "notorious ash-can derby" at Kern County Fairgrounds in early 1933. Drivers did not pay entrance fees, but the winners could sell their cars to Beam. He rarely paid more than $50 ($1000). His grand finale mirrored the desperation of the times: He always found two individuals so desperate for cash that they agreed to crash their cars head-on at 40 mph.[448]

## Work Camp in 1933

In January all beds at the work camp were full. A Californian reporter who visited there wrote,

"Men of all ages, from 16 to 70 are at the camp, many of the youths garbed in better clothes would grace a ballroom. Some of the older men, with sartorial & tonsorial service, would make splendid motion picture characters as bankers, lawyers, or physicians or members of some other profession. However, there are others, marred by the battles of life, who would offer frightening characterizations of screen gangsters or in similar bad-man roles.

"There are no social or color lines at the Kern County Work Camp where 300 men are being fed and sheltered in exchange for a few hours of labor. With enough work to keep their minds off troubles and to offer them enough exercise to keep them physically fit, and a warm place to rest at night, the men consider themselves lucky under the existing circumstances.

"White, yellow, black and red, the men of various colors and nationalities mix easily, for the prejudices of normal existence are forgotten when life settles to the basic principles of food and shelter. Consider the attractive blond chap whose muscles of steel and curly locks would put Bill Boyd of flicker fame to shame. Another youth with a black patch over

154

an empty eye socket has the gift of expression which would make him more than a mediocre writer of feature stories. There is a Jewish youngster, with snapping black eyes and handsome profile, who wears an Alpine hat and carries an air of joviality cockier than his headgear. Another chap, husky and good-looking carries a shiny steel hook where his right arm once swang a mighty fist.

"Then there is a slender youngster who lacked clothing enough to keep him warm in summer here. A traffic officer, owner of a discarded uniform, rigged him up in fine style. The lucky boy now sports the uniform—cap, coat, breeches, and puttees, and is the proudest fellow in camp. All he lacks is a shave and a haircut and the motorcycle and he would look good on Lieutenant Bob Powers' squadron of traffic officers.

"Bakersfield residents with jaded appetites should watch the motley crew attack their two meals daily. Each one eats more than a half loaf of bread every meal. They get steaming hot prunes, potatoes, coffee, mush, meat, and other types of substantial, wholesome and clean food from the Kern General Hospital Kitchen. More than 30 gallons of stew goes down their throats at each evening meal — a lot of stew in any way you look at it.

"The men work six hours each day and receive tickets enough for three meals. Yesterday, according to superintendent Hal Griffis, the men did $1,100 worth of cleaning-up work. The work is of such nature it is not competitive and does not keep local unemployed from an opportunity to labor. It is work which the city or county could not afford to do now but still it is worth a lot of money to the community.

"During the leisure hours the men read books and magazines donated by kind-hearted Bakersfield citizens. They "boil out" their clothing, cut one another's hair, shave, tell stories, or listen to the radio given them by Witham & Booth. A phonograph also adds to the entertainment.

"Kern County, one of the first districts to devise the work camp method of caring for the transient unemployed, is doing more than its share of charity work in that sphere. Then, too, petty crime, which generally follows an influx of strangers who are broke and hungry, is decreased. The more vicious crimes generally chronicled when hundreds of idle and destitute men gather in a small community are missing here, and there is little doubt but that the work camp is worth the trouble and expense to which society is burdened by its establishment, authorities declare."[449]

Early in 1933 the state took control of the camp and with Federal help created more work for citizens. The Californian: "With the close of the local relief camp, fortunately there is the opportunity for employment in government camps, and a number of young men will be benefited thereby, arrangement having been made for the establishment of four of such camps here in Kern County."[450]


Rodeo returned to the fairgrounds in 1933. "The spring round-up is on. High-heeled boots and spurs rattling on hotel lobby floors; horses' hoofs clattering on pavement; 10-gallon hats up and down the street; Indian tepees glistening under the sun all lead to the tense excitement gripping the community as Bakersfield awaits its second annual and greatest rodeo. Kern county will be living again the old days that made it the most colorful cow-town in the west."[451]

The parade was much the same as 1932, but this time there were trick riders and ropers, and personalities from radio and screen. Rodeo star and promoter Cuff Burrell brought his cowboys, bucking horses, and wild steers, and I.L. Wofford of Kernville, who had Hollywood connections, brought a First Nation show to the Motordrome. The Californian wrote, "Importation of an entire tribe of American Indians, with its tribal dancers, medicine men, fancy riders and warriors, and the establishment of an Indian village at Kern county fairgrounds for the second annual Bakersfield rodeo Saturday and Sunday was assured today upon return of Manager I.L. Wofford from Hollywood where the Indians are being used in motion picture work."[452] Hollywood moviemakers were accustomed to hiring California tribes. In fact a street in San Juan Capistrano was called Little Hollywood because the Juaneño Band of Mission Indians was often hired as extras for movies.[453]

In the winter of 1933 the camp was home to 60 men, and the number overwhelmed the sewer system. Workers hired by California State Relief Administration (SRA) solved the problem by digging an eight-inch sewer line between the pavilion and the city's branch line on K Street.[454]

June Dooley Rodriguez recalled the work camp in those days. "Our house was close to the railroad tracks and sometimes the "hobos" would stop and ask if there was some work they could do for something to eat. My mother always gave something. It was during the Depression and we children did not understand the severity of the times. In 1935 the county opened a

157

mess hall (we called it the soup kitchen) for unemployed men. They had entertainment for the men. I was eight-and-a-half years old and my brother was almost seven. We put on a boxing match for the men's entertainment. I was always a tomboy and enjoyed outdoor activities."[455]

Franklin Delano Roosevelt was elected November 8, 1932, and in the 43 days before his inauguration Federal relief funds flowed into California. Kern County Fairgrounds was awarded 19 make-work grants that paid for a rodeo arena, barns, and exhibit and storage buildings. Monday through Saturday, SRA and Kern County Relief sent men to Kern General Hospital, Kern County Airport, county mosquito abatement, and Bakersfield street maintenance.[456] Their paychecks fed and clothed their families.

## Pari-Mutuel Betting

California legislators always rejected legalized track gambling, and in the balloting of 1924 and 1932 the public also rejected it. In May 1933, California Governor James Rolph vetoed a pari-mutuel gambling bill, but this time the racing interests were ready, circulated petitions in a ballot initiative, and pari-mutuel betting was legalized by a margin of 13 percent. Under the new system, the winning bettors shared all the money wagered by the losers, minus a percentage of state tax.

Some taxation imposed on track gambling was earmarked for the state's agricultural fair districts, and the new law saved them. In 1933, eight agricultural fair districts were in operation. In 1946, there were 76.[457]

Ag shows put on by the Boys' Club substituted for county fairs, and in October 1933 it happened again when 200 students showed hogs, sheep, beef, and prize dairy stock. [458] The Californian observed, "Since discontinuance of the county fair, the agriculture students' show has been the only undertaking of this nature held here."[459]

The fairgrounds became a community recreation complex with priority given to baseball. Federal and state make-work programs put up two 200-seat bleachers, 600 night-baseball seats, 200 seats for junior baseball, as well as horseshoe courts, more parking spaces, a children's playground, and a grandstand that sat 1800. The massive concrete pads poured in 1920 for the big tents became lighted tennis courts.[460]

## Frontier Days

During the 1933-1934 academic year, salaries at Kern County High were cut 15 percent, and night-time classes in Americanism were eliminated. [461] The depressed economy affected everyone, some more, some less. At the fairgrounds, the cost of a ticket to horse racing was the same as the average hourly wage, 40 cents ($8). Notable was the three-jockey race in which each jockey had three horses. Riders broke from the gate, made one-and-one-half turns of the track and traded to the next horse.[462]

There was no fair in 1934. Instead, a new organization—Frontier Days Association—rented the county fairgrounds and put on a new kind of festival. The word "whiskerino" is from that period, and the following from the Bakersfield Californian explains what it means: "Bakersfield newspaper men today joined the scores of city and county employees, police offices and firemen engaged in the exclusively masculine art of whisker cultivation in preparation for the first annual Frontier Days celebration October 6, 7. Also today, City Manager Fred Nighbert, chairman of the Whiskerino contest, speaking from the lush depths of a President Madison beard, announced that virtually every business man in the city is asking his male employees to enter into the spirit of the celebration and let his chin foliage sprout. Chief of Police Robert Powers has offered a gold badge to the officer growing the homeliest beard."[463]

Frontier Days' first parade started mid-morning on October 6, 1934, and true to its theme, the spectators and western-garbed marchers sported cowboy hats, neckerchiefs, and loaded six-shooters. Californian columnist Larry Kimble observed, "The glamorous, red-blooded spirit of the old west in the day of '49 and the pioneer years that followed, when Kernville was Whiskey Flat and Bakersfield was a woolly frontier town with a smile for a gentleman and a rope for a hoss thief, was reborn this morning."

"No person could stand and watch the four-mile-long procession of prancing horses, plodding burros, hard-bitten cowboys and fair cowgirls, surreys, buckboards, Democrats, covered wagons, hayracks, perambulators, and bicycles which this morning wound through the streets of Bakersfield for hours to open the first annual Frontier day rodeo without feeling a thrill rarely equaled in this busy age of automobiles and airplanes. If there was a horse, mule or burro in Kern not in the parade it must have been hidden in the darkest and farthermost corner of the county."[464]

160

Kimble did not mention the Kern County Union High School and Junior College Band that led the high school's float showing its original building. It was a fond good-bye; days later the old structure was demolished.

Cowboys with families streamed onto the fairgrounds to see maverick calf-roping, girls' steer roping, wild-steer bulldogging, wild-cow milking, and bronco and Brahma bull riding. Grandstand and bleachers overflowed, and by the end of the week, Frontier Days 1934 attracted an all-time fairgrounds attendance record of 20,000.[465]

## Basement Museum

In 1934 the Chamber of Commerce Building was home to many county departments and several state and federal relief agencies. The crowding got so bad that county supervisors considered making basement space under the six-year-old Chamber of Commerce Building. County Engineer H. G. Pope advised against it, but money was available from Federal Civil Works Administration (CWA), and in December, county supervisors gave the go-ahead.

While digging was underway, State Emergency Relief Administration (SERA) took over CWA, and checks for the basement job stopped coming. In the summer of 1935, Kern County Grand Jury toured the unfinished basement and recommended that it be "cemented and completed to allow for storage and adequate protection of Chamber of Commerce and fair association property which, for the lack of space, is not being properly taken care of."[466] Kern County paid to finish the job.

# New Grandstand

For two decades the wooden grandstand had been repaired and painted, but SERA money was now available to replace it. County supervisors declared it unsafe, and in the spring 1935 it was razed. June Dooley Rodriguez saw it happen. "The old wooden grandstand was torn down, and a new one built of dirt was constructed while we lived there. The dirt was obtained by tearing down the racetracks."[467] The dirt was moved and compacted, steel posts were set and redwood seating bolted on. Salvaged lumber from the old grandstand was used in construction of the Sawtooth Building, its name deriving from the row of windows along its roof line. Today, Stramler Park occupies the site.

Kern County gave Frontier Days Association a five-year lease on the fairgrounds. One day before the start of Frontier Days 1935, elderly citizens dressed in western regalia met on Jackson Street in East Bakersfield for the "Grand March of a Thousand Pioneers". They ambled two blocks west, doubled back, and sat down to watch a two-orchestra dance at Jackson and Baker.[468]

The following day the Frontier Days Parade assembled at Baker and Niles Street, but this year the parade was less historically correct than before. The city had banned the open-carry of firearms, and Chief of Police Robert Powers said he would strictly enforce the rule, but the parade of horses, floats, bands, and marchers, was still wonderfully historic as it proceeded south on Baker Street, east on Nineteenth to Chester, and north to the disband point at 26th. From there the walkers and riders made their way to the fairgrounds.

The Californian reported, "The brilliant trick riding and roping of Montie Montana and his pretty wife, the trick riding of beautiful Alice Van, screen and rodeo star, the break-neck daring of two former world's champion cowboys, Clay Carr and Leonard Ward, the beautiful silver-mounted outfits of the General Petroleum Corporation, the Los Angeles Sheriff's Mounted Posse and the Gilmore outfit—all these and a hundred other spectacular events made it difficult to label any one as outstanding. Out-of-town rodeo notables declared that in two years Bakersfield's show has leaped into a place of prominence second to none of its kind in the nation." [469] Nevertheless, Frontier Days and Rodeo of 1935 was less profitable than 1934.

Kern's economy was on the mend. New-car sales were up 32 percent, and if used-car sales were figured in, the improvement was 80 percent. State and federal make-work programs, however, remained essential lifelines for many. In 1935, fairgrounds workers leveled and fenced pastures, installed irrigation systems, baseball backstops, concrete curbs, and they made thousands of adobe bricks for stables, corrals, and barns. A water-tank house was built.[470]

In 1936 Californian columnist Jim Day wrote, "The supervisors purchased the fairgrounds as a recreational center for the county, and so far the baseball diamonds at the site have supplied more "recreation facilities" than the rest of the park lumped together." Two months later Day wrote, "As many as 8000 persons have assembled on a single week night to watch softball games at the fairgrounds. From 1000 to 6000 persons assemble nightly to see softball games here during every day of the playing season. The playing season lasts all summer and into the fall. With the exception of baseball facilities and the use for one week end by the Frontier Days Association with its colorful pageant, the big fairgrounds plant is dormant and unused most of the year."[471]

Frontier Days/Western Roundup 1936 was another nostalgic return to the Old West. Cowboys from Oregon and Texas showed up on downtown sidewalks in every cut of sartorial garb and every feature of facial foliage. On the first morning of Frontier Days, 20 cattlemen from Walker Basin stoked their campfires at the fairgrounds and started their morning coffee. Hours later, at the parade, bands, marching associations, horse-drawn carriages, and beautifully caparisoned steeds made their way through downtown, and this time the parade included three-dozen riders from the Los Angeles Sheriff's Silver-Mounted Posse. Frontier Days/Western Roundup Rodeo 1936 broke all records for attendance.[472]

# Chapter 9, 1936

## Recovery—Agricultural Fair
## Sam Lynn Park—Museum Approved

Kern's recovery from the Great Depression matched that of the nation. In 1936-1937, Kern manufacturing was up nine percent, public utilities up 11, and employment and payrolls up 18, but Kern County's treasury was depleted, and supervisors did not have money to help destitute families. In March 1937, supervisors wired President Roosevelt for help.[473]

Fairgrounds director Mort A. Weatherwax was looking for another source of funds. Supervisors recently had granted use of the fairgrounds to a skeet club, and Weatherwax expected them to approve polo games, too, but the prospect of mixing horses and shotguns was an issue, and after examining historical records, supervisors concluded that the two together strayed too far from reasonable use.[474]

Weatherwax then rented the fairgrounds to the Elks Club, and it brought in Captain Bob Ward and his Hollywood Dare Devils. Their stunts were entertaining, but three were stunning: A speeding car smashed into a six-foot brick wall, an airplane crashed through a barn, and a performer strapped to the top of a car slammed through a flaming wall.[475]

## Frontier Days

Parade marshal for Frontier Days 1937 was radio and motion picture star Leo Carrillo, and the parade lived up to his fame with its 2500 mounted riders, 16 Belgian draft horses, scores of bands and floats, and hundreds and hundreds of marchers. Sidewalk standing room was non-existent.

This time, Frontier Days had a junior live-stock show, and it offered $3000 ($57,000) in premiums. Attendance was huge on the first day, but it was not a problem because Federal make-work programs had added an additional 7000 parking spaces. Highway Patrol Captain Leroy Galyen managed traffic control, Bakersfield police officers covered the ticket office, and mounted sheriff's deputies patrolled the fairgrounds perimeter.[476]

The rodeo sold 21,000 tickets. Boss Hugh Strickland's six-shooter started the steer and bronco-riding, which was followed by an amateur rodeo that had "real cowgirls and cowboys, the kind that ride herd, string fence poles and now and then do a little milking."[477] The youngster-and-old-timer steer-roping contest brought smiles—one partner was under 15 and the other over 50.

The pavilion was named "Happy Gulch". Half of it had tables and 600 chairs for the Cowgirls' Banquet, and the other half was ready for Fanchon & Marco shows, dance bands, Happy Gulch Bar, and a miniature version of Olvera Street Mexican Market.[478]

On the last day, buyers from local restaurants, cafes, and clubs, as well as meat packers from Sacramento and Los Angeles awaited the livestock auction. Frontier Days was a money maker, the association reporting $3000 ($57,000) in tickets, and when the space rent was added in, and premiums subtracted, $7500 ($142,000) was left for Frontier Days 1938.[479]


## Track Gambling

Late in 1937 county supervisor George Parish moved that the county disk the speedway for the safety of horses. Horses had not run there for several years. Was the sport of kings returning to the track?

Several weeks later, the Rochester Tigers and Salinas Packers played football on the field, and a month after that, Californian columnist Jim Day reported what many had expected: "Over a brand-new mile track the bangtails *[horses]* will run Sunday afternoon starting at 1 o'clock sharp, fairgrounds. Reversing the usual process of progress, the mile automobile track has given way to a mile running track. Over the old mile automobile track, I saw the ill-fated young Frank Lockhart send his roaring car to a new world's record. Now the automobile track is gone, supplanted by a horse-racing oval."[480]

The new course had all the appurtenances of a first-class horseracing track: a solidly-built 10,000-seat grandstand, betting machines, judging stands, paddocks, 200 stables, and the Clay Puett Starting Gate, which was the electrically-operated release mechanism then gaining popularity at tracks across the country. On the first day of races, 200 thoroughbreds ran eight quarter-milers, several intermediates, and a one-and-an-eighth-mile classic. Track manager Charlie Coit paid-out $4500 ($85,500) in pari-mutuel winnings, and for the next 10 weeks he held seven-more meets.[481] Then, everything fell apart.

Jim Day wrote in February 1938, "Horse racing folded up here this month because the public was not interested—stayed away from the track in droves despite the fact that some good races and more than modest purses were offered. As a matter of fact, the fairgrounds is a modern racing plant—with no races. The supervisors have not intimated what they intend to do with the fairgrounds."[482]

It is possible that Jim Day did not get the whole story. Complaints had been registered against Coit, and county supervisors ordered him to enforce the Santa Anita racing rules, which meant the rules of the California Horse Racing Board, which controlled doping and other corrupt turf practices. If Coit continued at the track, he would face three independent racing stewards, each of whom had authority over owners, trainers, jockeys, grooms, and even Coit himself. He conferred with his attorney and quit.[483]

## Agricultural Fairs

In June 1938, receipts at the U.S. Post Office on 18th Street were up 16 percent, and that figure and other encouraging news caused the Kern County Chamber of Commerce to call a conference on community needs, and among the points agreed upon was resumption of agricultural fairs. A vocal proponent was Professor Howard K. Dickson who had been responsible for the high-school livestock shows more than 10 years earlier. At the time of the conference on community needs, Dickson was President of the Fifteenth District Agricultural Fair Association, and he recently had urged Californian

Governor Frank Merriam to boost the racing-tax benefit for agricultural fairs.[484]

In August, Frontier Days gave the Fifteenth District space for a modest exhibit, and that made it eligible for the racing-tax benefit, but Frontier Days had no claim on those funds. Weeks before opening day, Frontier Days found itself in immediate need of $3000 ($57,000), and it tapped businesses along the parade route. Owners promised help, but when the route was changed, the bypassed merchants refused to pony-up. Kern County supervisors stepped in and rescued the association.[485]

Downtown was busy with activity. Frontier Days tickets at Nineteenth and Chester were $0.55 to $2.20 ($11 to $45), and people with extra cash could rent western get-ups at the Woman's Club booth in Motor Center Showroom. Days passed, and downtown blossomed with colorfully-dressed, city-slicker cowpokes.

One day before Frontier Days, East Bakersfield Progressive Club and the association sponsored a night-time dance at Jackson and Baker Street, and the cash prizes and seven-piece band attracted droves of dancers and spectators. The oldest couple in costume got $100 ($2150), the most comically-dressed dancer got $5 ($110), and the most comically-dressed couple got $2.50.[486]

Fifty-five-thousand people lined the sidewalks to watch Hollywood actor Mickey Eissa on his silver mount lead the six-mile-long, three-hour parade from Baker Street to Bernard to Chester, and thence to the breakup point at the Traffic Circle.[487] Comments heard along the way: "Pooh, I didn't know any pioneer women that would let their men get away with ragged beards like that guy has."—"Golly, this is some crowd, huh, Bill?"—"Mama, can I stand on the fender of that car?" "No!" "Why, Mama?"[488]

The fairgrounds filled with visitors. Some stopped and marveled as they entered, some headed directly to the pavilion, some to the Foley and Burke Carnival, and others to the Junior Livestock Show. Veterans' associations and Rising Concessions Company sold soft drinks and beer, but Rising had to work harder because it had to buy its supplies from local merchants.

Twenty thousand filled the grandstand to see the amateur cowboy show, and some spotted California Governor Frank Merriam in the Governor's Box. Later that day he was honored guest at the Cowgirls' Banquet.[489]

Frontier Days 1938 was a boon for business, and Department-store owner Malcolm Brock remarked, "Bakersfield vitally needs the Frontier Days activity each year."[490] Some citizens, though, were weary of Frontier Days, as shown in this letter to the Californian. "The very life and success of the Frontier Days' celebration is built upon the publicity that precedes that event. ... We have had, along with every celebrating California city, such rubber-stamp and well-worn hocus pocus as whiskerinos, cages, kangaroo courts, etc. ... By the shades of the mighty Barnum, renowned worshiper at the shrine of the myriad-tongued goddess of publicity, I pray for something new."[491] Rio Bravo 4-H did not wait for something new. While Frontier Days was going on, Rio

Bravo held a mini agricultural fair with livestock and domestic arts.[492]

Kern's economy grew four percent in the first half of 1939, and county supervisors directed the Chamber of Commerce to call a fact-finding meeting to find out how much interest there was in an agricultural fair. Panama Grange, Kern County Farm Bureau, Fifteenth District Agricultural Fair Association, Frontier Days Association, and independent businesses favored it, and they laid out the following division of duties: livestock show to the Fifteenth District; parades and rodeos to Frontier Days Association; commercial exhibits and the midway to the Chamber of Commerce.

The plan was taken to the Conference on Community Needs at Hotel El Tejon, and there it met resistance. Professor H.K. Dickson preferred that the responsibilities stay the same, while others presented other ideas. Each of them was delivered to county supervisors.

Kern County was in better financial health than ever. In previous months it had spent as much on fairgrounds improvement as the Federal government did, but county money was still an issue, and the supervisors' main question had nothing to do with who did what. Rather, could an agricultural fair pay its own way?[493] Their initial reluctance eased when they were told that the Fifteenth District would qualify for $17,900 ($349,000) from the pari-mutuel racing tax. After that, they agreed that "a livestock show, staged by the agricultural association, with the aid of state funds, could be enlarged to include somewhat more extensive exhibits."[494]

Europe was no longer at peace. On September 1, 1939, Nazi Germany invaded Poland, Britain and France declared war on Germany, and on September 3 German submarine U-30 sunk British liner Athena carrying more than 1000 passengers. Twenty-eight of the dead were United States citizens. Congress condemned the attack but did nothing more, and news of the European war filled the Bakersfield Californian. Activity at the fairgrounds continued unchanged.

Kern County supervisors transferred control of the fairgrounds to the Chamber of Commerce, and that summer, Bakersfield Recreation Commission had a summer youth-bicycle show on the track and supervised dozens of baseball leagues.[495]

In 1939, Frontier Days Secretary Emory Gay Hoffman announced that the Fifteenth District Fair would join in the sixth annual Frontier Days celebration. Frontier Days was still unsupported by dedicated funding, and it was then on shaky financial ground. Hoffman needed money for a free show, and county supervisors advanced him $2000 ($39,000).[496]

On opening day, a band played for the visitors as passed through the gates. Some paused to see Captain Lower and Bozo his Mind-Reading Dog before branching out to the carnival, rodeo, and livestock arena where young exhibitors showed their prize animals. Day-by- day crowds were large, and by the end of the week 55,000 people had come to the fair.[497]

The supervisors' cautious approach for "somewhat more extensive exhibits" was successful, and although the economy had improved, money was still a priority.[498] At a meeting of the Fifteenth District board, it was moved to do away with carnival, entertainment and concessions, but that motion had no second, and for good reason. All increased attendance, it attracted commercial exhibitors, and the space rent paid for improvements.[499]

To assess interest in a more comprehensive fair, the Chamber of Commerce mailed questionnaires and succinctly reported the response: "County fairs are becoming too humdrum and commonplace".[500] That answer was puzzling because the last Kern County agricultural fair was held 11 years earlier. Had the public equated Frontier Days with agricultural fairs? But some knew the difference, as reflected in this disdainful letter to the Californian: "They recently leased our fairgrounds for five more years from our Kern county dictators, and it seems the lease money does not take care of our fairgrounds. As I noticed recently in your paper they showed $8000 [$156,000] budgeted for the upkeep of the fairgrounds but no fair. - Taxpayer"[501]

In the week before Frontier Days 1940, shoppers in cowboy shirts, colorful neckerchiefs, riding pants and tight boots paraded on the sidewalks. W.C. "Billy" Willis and his Wandering Minstrels played at Nineteenth and Chester, Bakersfield Progressive Club performed sidewalk scenes from "Aaron Slick, From Punkin Crick", and those actors not needed at the moment scouted around for clean-shaven innocents to escort to whiskerino court, where the get-out-of-jail fine went to a good cause.[502]

A kids' parade formed in front of Washington School, at Niles and Baker Street, tramped south to East Nineteenth, and reversed back to the school. At Druid Hall on Sumner Street, also in East Bakersfield, Lackawanna Council, Degree of Pocahontas prepared a dance, and the young crowd headed over to Jackson and Baker Street for a chance to win cash prizes at a street dance. Workers at Hotel El Tejon, Stockdale County Club, and Union Avenue Plunge bandstand prepared their own dances, while employees from Motel Inn (Bakersfield Inn) were at the fairgrounds setting up for the Cowgirls' Banquet.[503]

On the morning of September 18, 1940, Bakersfield High Big B lettermen were setting up sidewalk bleachers, and Radio KPMC was preparing a live broadcast of the Seventh-Annual Frontier Days Parade. The Californian wrote it was the most-colorful parade ever seen in Bakersfield, but the novelty may have worn off because the newspaper gave it much less ink than before.[504]

All commercial spots at the fairgrounds were rented, and for the first time ever, both commercial and agricultural exhibitors received equal space. Agriculture used all its with 20 major exhibit divisions and hundreds of subdivisions. One new barn was so filled with visitors that the exhibits had to be moved to an older barn.

Awards and premiums were generous, particularly in the dairy competition where the top exhibitors "split a tasty melon" of $3971 ($77,000). That was also true in the Guernsey, Holstein, Jersey, and Dairy Shorthorn butter-fat competitions where the premiums totaled $2415 ($47,100). Four-H had its own competitions, but if those premiums were added to the rest, the total was $17,860 ($348,300).[505]

Presidential candidate Wendell L. Willkie's campaign train arrived in East Bakersfield on the last day of the show, and he and his supporters, many of whom had boarded at Caliente, stepped off and glad-handed well-wishers. Willkie's green limousine was unloaded, he was driven to the fairgrounds, and there

174

he spoke 15 minutes before 15,000 cheering Republicans. Hours later he was in Tulare.[506] Frontier Days 1940 ended, and in spite of the cheek-to-jowl humanity, none of the 75,000 visitors voiced a single complaint against "rollicking" Frontier Days.[507]

America was at peace in 1940, but news of the war filled the Bakersfield Californian. In October, Selective Service mailed 17,000 draft notices to Kern County men, and war anxiety grew. Twelve months later, America was still at peace when Washington exempted married men 28 years and older from military service, although single males were still subject to the draft. In September 1941, President Franklin D. Roosevelt signed the $3.6M ($66.8M) War Revenue Act, which raised taxes on personal and business income and levied excise tax on gum, soda, cigarettes, alcohol, gasoline, insurance premiums, gambling winnings, and much more. Kern citizens now paid more for movie tickets and rides on the little train at Kern County Park (Hart Park).[508]

In the summer of 1941, 100 cadet pilots arrived at Bakersfield and Taft airports while the Army was breaking ground for Army Air Corp training camps at Taft and Lerdo. By then so many military and defense workers were in Kern County that Frontier Days General Manager Eugene B. McCoy predicted a fall attendance of 100,000.[509]

County leaders scrambled to establish a wartime footing. In mid-September, Kern Defense Council launched 100 aircraft-spotting stations, and Mrs. J. E. Ketchem of the Women's Temporary Defense Committee advertised for female volunteers to staff them. At Sam Lynn Park, Kern County Sheriff John E. Loustalot swore-in 85 California State Guard volunteers.[510] Said Loustalot, "We know that in case of emergency we can fall back upon you, and we wish to thank you for giving up your time for the protection of the county."[511]

Manager McCoy was right about the increased attendance. A week before opening day, Ben Harrison and his Roaming Cowboys played downtown sidewalks, and whiskerino court collected fines at Nineteenth and Chester. On the morning of the big parade, Queen Corinne Cattani lead 13 bands, floats, mounted riders, and hundreds of marchers. Missing from the parade was the Southern Pacific Band, which then was at Kern General Hospital playing for patients, retirement-home-folks, and children from Stonybrook Tuberculosis Sanatorium. Also missing from the parade were workers at Kern County Park setting up for the Cowgirls' Banquet.

The wafting odor of hot dogs and hamburgers and the familiar sound of the merry-go-round and Ferris Wheel greeted fairgoers. Lines were long at the Rocket, the Whip, Jitter Buggy, Thimble Theater, Giggle Inn, Cuteland Cabaret, Ro-Lo Fun House, Odd-But-True, and Dedrik's Circus. From the grandstand, fairgoers saw equestrian drills and trick riding, and they gasped as rodeo-clown Pinky Gist dodged danger. Three hundred twenty exhibitors in the Junior Live Stock Show showed 1000 animals, and the premiums were $18,000 ($334,000). [512] Overheard was the comment "I think we should expand into a county fair."[513]

## Sam Lynn Park

Nineteen forty was the last year that the fairgrounds got a make-work grant. That $3000 ($58,500) leveled the north end of the racetrack and built a lighted baseball field, dressing rooms and bleachers. The Californian wrote, "The baseball plant will be known as Sam Lynn Park in honor of the late Sam Lynn, most active supporter of baseball in Bakersfield and the original backer of the city's Class C ball club."[514] Bakersfield Badgers were the first to use the field, but in the summer the park was modified for a night-time horse show. Wood chips covered the infield, white canvas back-drops surrounded the base lines, and as darkness fell, Hollywood trick-rider-and-roper Montie Montana and his silver-mounted posse played under brilliant lights.[515]

## Museum Approved

America was at peace in the fall of 1941, and Kern County supervisors focused on boosting Kern's image. When the Emery Whilton Wildlife Collection came up for sale, Kern supervisors outbid nearby counties and signed a lease-to-buy agreement with the Whilton family.

About that same time, the county bought the San Joaquin Exhibition Building that had been built for the 1939-1940 San Francisco Golden Gate International Exposition. The metal and glass structure was trucked to Gorman on Highway 99, and county prisoners reassembled it by the Lebec Hotel. In early 1942 the rehabilitated exhibition building opened as the Florafaunium to exhibit the Wilton collection.[516] The Bakersfield Californian wrote, "In the future it will become a county museum."[517]

Kern County Historical society donated its collection of books and historical artifacts to the county in 1940 [518] California Public Resources Code, Section 5120-5132, made it possible for historical societies to become agencies of local government, and later in the year society president Ardis Walker asked supervisors for that designation. It was an ambitious request for such a small organization and probably motivated by the same zeal that fellow member Alfred Harrell expressed six years earlier: "Kern county has a rich treasure house of history. On such a background its citizens have a right to be proud of its place in the state. The influence of the past is part of the cultural training of each new generation and makes for higher standards of citizenship." [519]

Ardis Walker urged supervisors to create a tax-supported museum, pointing out that Kern's growing population of newcomers made it "increasingly important that traditions of the county be instilled in its citizens." [520] He added that the museum would need a curator, historian, and advisors for best use of the historical materials. County supervisors tabled the matter, and days later Alfred Harrell wrote, "We have much of historic worth in the county, and it is timely now to begin to assemble it." [521]

At the next supervisors' meeting vice-president of the historical society Bernard C. Ely reiterated Walker's request, and supervisors agreed to store the county's historical collection at the Chamber of Commerce Building "until such time as other facilities are available." [522]

Weeks later Ely took signed petitions to the supervisors requesting them to authorize a county museum and hire a curator. Ely explained that the society was no longer interested in being a part of county government; rather, it preferred to advise it on best use of the county's historical materials. In May 1941, supervisors appointed a museum advisory board of society members, and ordered county counsel to draft paperwork establishing the Kern County Museum as a division of county government.[523] A board was named, and it began producing "much-needed" historical information for the Chamber of Commerce, Kern County Library system, county schools, newspapers, community groups, and Kern's "rapidly growing and diverse population." On December 7, 1941, the Empire of Japan attacked Hawaii, and the United States declared war. Progress on the Kern County museum ended, but during the war the historical society met at schools, members' homes, and in the Chamber of Commerce Building.[524]

# Chapter 10, 1941

War—Victory Foods Fair

Museum Grows—Fair of 1945

Four months before the attack on Pearl Harbor, U.S. Navy destroyer escorts were accompanying British supply convoys to mid-Atlantic, and from there the Royal Navy escorted on to Great Britain. On October 17, 1941, 1800 miles south of Iceland, U.S.S. Kearny (DD-432) was cruising in Convoy SC-48 when German submarine U-568 torpedoed the Kearny. Eleven U.S. sailors were killed and 22 injured. Days later, in the same general area, U-552 torpedoed and sunk the U.S.S Reuben James (DD-245) that was escorting Convoy HX-156. Ninety-nine U.S. sailors were killed, and the United States filed a formal protest. Seven weeks later, on the morning of Sunday December 7, 1941, Japan attacked Hawaii, and the next day the U.S. declared war on Imperial Japan, Germany, and the Kingdom of Italy.

In February 1942, President Franklin D. Roosevelt signed Executive Order 9066 that stripped U.S. citizens of Japanese descent of their civil rights. Two months later, in California, the U.S. Army removed families from their homes and moved them to Tulare, Turlock, and Salinas fairgrounds. All were sent on to remote internment camps. Kern County assisted in the enforcement of Executive Order 9066, but Kern County fairgrounds was not used for the deportations; rather, it was the location of three Victory Food Fairs.[525]

In March 1942, Kern County Fair President Albert S. Goode was asked about holding a Kern County Livestock Show, but he had no answer. Wartime rules cut the horse-racing tax, Lt. General J.L. DeWitt of Army Western Defense Command canceled the Sacramento State Fair, and Army caravans had bivouacked at Kern County Fairgrounds.[526]

Life in Bakersfield was changing but in some ways it stayed the same. At Maricopa on a Sunday in April 1942, horse races attracted nearly as many people as Sunday baseball did at Sam Lynn Baseball Park. In that month, too, the Mighty American Circus, called the "Biggest Show on Earth for the Price", played at Kern County Fairgrounds, and a month later, at Sam Lynn Baseball Park, 2500 fans filled the 3000-seat grandstand to watch the double hitter between the Santa Barbara Saints and the Bakersfield Badgers, the Badgers managed by Louis "Jack" Colbern of Brooklyn Dodgers fame.[527]

Days before the game, 21 year-old Badger outfielder Elmer "Oley" Olson found out his draft number was coming up, and he enlisted in the U.S. Coast Guard. Game two was Olson Day, the Badgers won 3-1, and two days later Elmer Olson left for boot camp. A few days later, night baseball came to an end when Western Defense Command imposed dusk-to-dawn dim-outs across California.[528]

Sears, Roebuck, & Co. still was selling rugs and furniture in 1942, but inventories everywhere were shrinking. Fifteen percent of railroad traffic was reserved for military use, a 35 mph wartime speed limit slowed deliveries, and business lost employees to the draft. In September 1943, Kern County Defense Council—mostly unknown before Pearl Harbor—was managing clerks, messengers, air-raid wardens, rescue workers, nurses, ambulance drivers, auxiliary police, and 7000 volunteer fire watchers—all hailing from the "wooded vastness of mile-high mountains to the vast expanses of the Mojave desert—in cities and at the crossroads—transcending anything in the history of the county."[529]

## Victory Food Fairs

Western Defense Command restricted public gatherings to 5000, and that caused the cancellation of Salinas Rodeo, Santa Barbara Fiesta, and the Kern County Livestock Show. County supervisors offered the Government full use of the fairgrounds, and in early 1942 the Office of Price Administration and Civilian Supply moved in to reign-in rent gouging and price fixing and administer the war-time ration-book program.[530]

In the summer, the Chamber of Commerce and Fifteenth District Agricultural Fair Association asked Lt. General DeWitt for permission to hold a livestock show. He spoke to California Governor Culbert Olson, and they agreed that the show was vital for the war effort. Approval, however, came with one caveat: The fairgrounds had to go dark in case of air raid. That requirement was quite doable, and Chamber of Commerce Director E.G. Hoffman began planning for the show.[531]

Food for Victory, held four days in September of 1942, offered "a maximum of good stock and top exhibitions of the animals but without the frills"—which meant no entertainment, carnival, or concessions.[532]

Horses from Arvin and Shafter were awarded premiums, and Mykrontz-Scarbert stables of Monolith swept the Palomino class, while in the Registered Belgians it was Sanger ranches that took the honors. One thousand five hundred youth representing the Kern County High Farm School, 4H, and Shafter and Wasco Future Farmers showed their sheep, hogs, beef, and dairy cattle. Ten thousand dollars ($168,000) was awarded, but many winners did not keep their money: A gaily-decorated table by the premium booth beckoned them to buy war stamps and war bonds.[533]

Awaiting the livestock auction were buyers from Rotary, Kiwanis, Kern Valley Packing, Clark Auction, Valley Cold Storage, Bidart Brothers, El Tejon Hotel, El Adobe Motel, Minter Field Cadet Mess, Shafter Central Market, and Los Angeles Union Stockyards. Private parties also bid, and when the hammer came down on theirs, most doubled the bid and gave half to the young owner and half to the Red Cross. Ten thousand came to Food for Victory, and when the ticket sales and expenses were reconciled, $20,000 ($335,000) was left for Victory Foods Fair 1943.[534]

Black-out restrictions that left Bakersfield nights in muffled half-darkness were still in effect in September 1943, Which meant that Victory Foods Fair again was held in daylight hours. For five days, civilians rubbed shoulders with civilian-defense workers, Red Cross, and soldiers from Gardner, Minter, and Muroc Army air fields. The Bakersfield Californian was delighted by the sheer number of sheep, hogs, rabbits, poultry, beef, dairy cattle, and the bounty from civilian victory gardens, and it extolled Kern's "continuity in the arts of peace."[535] One example of that was a mini fair held at Jefferson School in East Bakersfield. It had a pet show, an old-fashioned box social, and a display of canned tomatoes and dehydrated potatoes prepared for the school cafeteria by the Parent Teacher Association.[536]

## Museum Grows

In the spring of 1944 Kern County supervisors directed county counsel Norbert Baumgarten to start the paper work designating the basement of the Chamber of Commerce as the Kern County museum. An advisory board was appointed, and those named from Bakersfield were Clarence Cullimore, Angus J. Crites, E.L. Harmon, Hugh Jewett, O.R. Kamprath, C.D. Lavin, Roy W. Louden, Ethel Bacon McManus, Mrs. Ralph Sanders, and Miss Eleanor Wilson. From other areas were William H. Hitchcock (Shafter), Paul Hubbard (Randsburg), George Smith (Taft), and Ardis Walker (Kernville). Frank F. Latta was appointed part-time curator, and he set up a desk on the second floor of the Chamber of Commerce Building. [537] The Californian wrote, "The new directors are responsible for establishing and maintaining a museum for the artifacts and relics of early Kern county and historical papers and documents." [538]

The dim-out restrictions were lifted in late 1943, and in the fall of 1944 Hanford, Tulare, and Kings County held a "streamlined" three-day fair with a carnival.[539] Kern County Victory Foods Fair 1944 did not have a carnival, but Corporal Roy Larsen and his Minter Field Skyliners played at the pavilion next to shelves of fresh vegetables, home-canned goods, and school woodshop projects. The fair had dairy and beef cattle, sheep, goats, swine, rabbits, poultry, and pigeons but no premiums. When that news got out, fairgoers took up a collection.[540]

The equestrian side of Victory Foods Fair 1944 had trail and stock horses, Clydesdales, Arabians, Palominos, Percherons, Belgians, Morgans, Shetland ponies, three- and five-gaited saddle horses, jumpers, roadsters, and harnessed Standardbreds. Six thousand people saw it, and most agreed that it was a shoe-in for next fair. Attendance was 20,000, and Californian columnist Mae Saunders wrote, "With the end of the war, an even greater showing is believed possible."[541]

## Fair of 1945

The war continued for seven months. Nazi Germany surrendered on May 7, Imperial Japan on August 14, and somewhere between those dates the Fifteenth District ordered tents, ribbons and trophies for the 1945 fair, which opened for a five-day run on September 19, 1945 to the theme "Kern County, Horn of Plenty". Californian columnist Kappy Girton was there to take it in. "The old lure of the fair gripped Kern county today as residents thronged to the opening of the five-day Kern County Fair, the first regular one since Pearl Harbor. Five barns were full of well-bred horses, pens of fat sheep and swine, carefully groomed dairy and beef cattle and pink-nosed rabbits and proud chickens along with shelves of colorfully-preserved fruit and colorful, fresh garden products, farm machinery, educational exhibits and hot dogs."[542]

It had no midway, but there was entertainment: Little Theater Guild, East Bakersfield High Brass Quartet, Taft Youth Center Glee Club, and Our Lady of

Guadalupe Church Choir under the direction of Reverend Father Silvana Baquedano. Frank Noriega supervised the livestock show, and Walter Stiern supervised the agricultural show. Premiums for all exhibits—fruits and vegetables, food preservation, beef and dairy cattle, swine, sheep, rabbits, and poultry—totaled $20,000 ($340,000).[543]

Tri-County Racing Association supervised two days of harness and running races, and because the pari-mutuel betting machines could not be found, thousands of dollars in illegal betting passed between hands during the fair. The most thrilling and emotion-packed race was a harness dash between S.A. Camp's 26 year-old stallion who was running his final race and a two-year-old filly named Miss Beverly, who was running her maiden mile. The old fellow won, and Camp retired him to greener pastures.[544]

Residential housing was not built during the war, and after 12,000,000 men and women returned from war-time service, the country faced a challenge. Surplus military buildings at Minter Field were candidates for public use, but because of bureaucratic missteps, their sale was delayed for more than a year. In the spring of 1947, 100 Kern and Tulare County veterans vied for 57 frame buildings. Those unsuitable for housing, such as sheds, warehouses, and chapels, were offered to county government, and one of them wound up at Kern County Fairgrounds. In 2023 that 80 year-old structure was modernized as a cultural/historical center dedicated to First-Nation people who occupied this region for thousands of years. Kern County Historical Society meets there, and its members serve as guides and research associates.[545]

# Chapter 11, 1946

New Fairgrounds
Armories
Wayside School
Fair and National Horse Show
Miniature Cars
New Fairgrounds Development
Museum Grows
Earthquakes—1952, First Fair

In the spring of 1946, 101 Ranch Wild West Circus brought trick riding, fancy roping, and rodeo clowns to the fairgrounds. The Californian observed, "The clowns and their stunts kept the program from lagging."[546] In the fall, Frontier Days Association and the Fifteenth District held the Tenth Annual Fair— some calling it the Ninth Annual Harvest Festival. Whatever the name, General Manager Herb Vaughan promised the largest horse show yet.

The three-day affair opened on Tuesday September 26, 1946 with carnival, concessions, stock shows, agricultural exhibits, and manufactured goods. Visitors canvassing the exhibition building (no longer called the pavilion) were particularly attracted to two booths: the American Red Cross' motion picture exhibit and Arvin's display that had bales of cotton framing artful arrangements of fruits and vegetables. Free entertainment at the festival included La Altenitas Glee Club, the Gal Caballeros Trio from Our Lady of Guadalupe Youth Center, and a puppet show under the direction of Mrs. Ruth Reese—school counselor and member of the Bakersfield Recreation Commission.[547]

On the last day, auctioneer Charles Adams of Alhambra sold nine swine, 20 sheep, and 35 head of steers, all rated choice or champion under the Danish judging system. The turnstile count was expected to hit 75,000, but in the end it was 90,000. All exhibit space was carefully managed, and there was little room for much else. Street traffic was clogged and railroad crossings backed up. Professor H.K. Dickson shook his head, "Where it was a good site in 1924, it is very poor in 1946."[548]

### New Fairgrounds

Kern County Land Company had 179 mostly-undeveloped acres bounded by Union Avenue, Kern Island Canal, Belle Terrace, and Casa Loma Drive. The drainage was excellent and access to town unobstructed. Some months before the war ended, Kern County Land Company General Manager Hugh Allen offered that property to Kern County for $119,250 ($1,673,000). County supervisors had been expecting the state to distribute $500,000 ($7,400,000) to its agricultural districts, but there was

188

no way to know exactly when that would happen, so supervisors tabled Allen's offer. Shortly after the peace, Fifteenth District Vice President Howard Dickson alerted supervisors that the money was on the way, and in the summer of 1946 land company manager Hugh Allen and Kern County Supervisor C.W. Harty opened escrow on the acreage.[549]

The state paid for most of the buy, which meant it had first say over the development. Plans at the Division of the State Architect showed three pavilions, a 16,000-seat grandstand, racetrack, swimming pool, and National Guard armory. President of the Fifteenth District Albert Goode hoped the work would start soon, but post-war shortages slowed progress, and Kern County Planning said that opening day was at least two to three years in the future.


## Armories

What would happen to the old fairgrounds? Supervisor Charles P. Salzer said it had been good for community recreation and should stay that way. Others on the board, and the public too, had their own ideas, and eventually the matter was turned over to county planning.

While that was going on, Commander George S. Smith of the Eleventh Naval District was searching for a site for a new armory. The county offered him a slice of land south of the Chamber of Commerce Building, but Washington preferred property that faced Chester Avenue. After months of back-and-forth, the Navy accepted a 200 by 280-foot parcel at the northeast corner of the old fairgrounds. Twenty-Sixth Division,

U.S. Naval Reserve held an open house in the summer of 1948.[550]

Sacramento chose Bakersfield to receive a National Guard armory in 1947. The Office of the State Architect drew plans for a reinforced-concrete building on two-and-one-half acres at the southwest corner of the new fairgrounds, and Sacramento approved $199,000 ($2,213,000) for construction. Bidding opened in late 1952, and a year later the armory was occupied.[551]

## Wayside School

In the 1930s, President Franklin Delano Roosevelt signed the National Housing Bill, and it helped the construction of new homes immediately south of Bakersfield. One area was the 60-acre Wayside Rancho "1 mile south of the city limits *[Brundage Lane]* on Wayside Drive, 1/4 of a mile west of Highway 99 *[Union Avenue]*." [552] Homes were occupied in 1941, and a neighborhood school was needed, but the war halted construction.

The U.S. Army crossed the Rhine on March 7, 1945, Nazi Germany surrendered in May, and a month later Charles H. Biggar, AIA, showed his plans to county supervisors for a $199,000 ($2,900,000) school at P Street and Wayside Drive. Building materials were still in short supply, but U.S. War Production Board approved the construction. Planning started in 1946, and the school opened in spring of 1949. Today, the school shares a fence with the big fairgrounds parking lot on P Street.

While the school was being built, Wayside Drive was renamed West Casa Loma Drive, and the name stayed that way for the next 21 years. In 1969, West Casa Loma Drive between Union Avenue and South H Street became Ming Avenue—to match its western extension. The name Ming has historical significance. In 1895 a farmer Yen Ming, also known as Charles Ming, owned land around Casa Loma Drive and Panama Lane, and in 1922 there was a Ming Road just south of Brundage Lane.[553]

## Fair and National Horse Show

In 1947, Frontier Days Association and Kern County Fair Association held the Eleventh Annual Kern County Fair. Secretary-Manager George Wendt brought back the Great Western Livestock and National Horse Show, and he hired eight local experts and two specialists from out of state to judge 350 horses in the gaited, harness, saddle, and saddle-bred classes. That show was an extra-cost event, although general admission to the fair was free, the Fifteenth District being the last in California to offer no-cost admission. The horse show was well attended. Three of the more popular attractions on the fairgrounds were glass blowing, folk dancing, and a mineral and wildlife exhibit, the last held in the old Office of Price Administration Building.[554]

Livestock and poultry divisions were unchanged from 1946, with the exception of a rooster-crowing contest. One thousand four hundred exhibitors vied for $80,000 ($1.1M) in premiums, and Manager Wendt expected the six-day run and the generous premiums to attract 125,000 visitors. On the last day, 19,638 people entered the fairgrounds, which brought the grand total to 132,000—39,000 more than 1946.[555]

Frontier Days Parade 1948 began with a fly-over of 1st Fighter Group jets from March Field, and 30,000 spectators saw Grand Marshal and Hollywood actor Jackie Coogan lead the American Legion Rough Riders, six bands, nine additional mounted equestrian groups, seven divisions of floats, and several marching associations: Loyal Order of Moose, Royal Neighbors of America, Improved Order of Redmen, Lions Club, Missouri Club, Kern County Boat Club, Camp Fire Girls, and Daughters of Union Civil War Veterans.

The Californian wrote, "A float entered by the Business and Professional Women's Club, in which woman's place in business in 1848 and 1948 was compared, won first prize in the organization division. An entry by the Bakersfield Indians, in which a group of Indian maids marched single file behind their float, was awarded second prize." [556] Among individual entries was a boy riding his bicycle with a red hen perched on back. "The hen seemed to enjoy the ride but hopped off occasionally to investigate some attractive morsel on the street."[557]

Many hours earlier (at the old fairgrounds), young exhibitors awoke on beds of straw and fed and groomed their animals. Traffic picked up on Chester Avenue, reserved parking filled, and at 10 a.m. the north parking-lot gates were opened.

The day of free fairs had ended. Adult tickets were 50 cents ($6), 25 cents for children, and Boy

Scouts, Cub Scouts, Girl Scouts, Brownies, and Camp Fire Girls were ushered through without charge. A week earlier, 50,000 free tickets had been handed out at schools.[558]

Manager Lee Clark could now take a rest. The Great Western Livestock and National Horse had started, music was played in every corner of the fairgrounds, and Shafter, Wasco, McFarland, Kern Delta, and Magunden agricultural districts filled the exhibition hall. Live performances were underway on the outdoor stage, and each night, searchlights pointed the way to the fair. On the last night, fireworks filled the sky.

Gate receipts set a new record, but Bakersfield was not tired of excitement. Ten days later, a rodeo was held to benefit wounded veterans and their families, and the whiskerino police were again out rounding up the hapless smooth-shaven.[559]

## Miniature Cars

On weekends in the late 1930s a Eugene Myers directed miniature-car racing at Jefferson Park roller-skating rink—until neighbors complained of the noise. War stopped that kind of recreation, but when peace came, Kern County Recreation Commission had model-car racing at the old fairgrounds.

In the spring of 1947, Bakersfield Junior Chamber of Commerce hosted two days of a similar kind of model racing, but this time the little cars needed no racetrack. One car at a time was connected to a cable, which in turn was attached to a steel pole. When the engine was started and the little car released, it spun around and around picking up speed. The piercing shrieks of three-quarter-horsepower, alcohol-and-castor-oil-fueled engines was why they were called Little Whizzers. The Miniature Race Car Association was formed in 1948 and the steel-pole racetrack christened Myer's Memorial Speedway. In 1950 an Oakland whizzer hit 141 mph.[560]

## New Fairgrounds Development

Ernest L. McCoy, AIA, who was a member of the Fifteenth District board, assisted the state architect in planning the new fairgrounds. The fair of 1948 was underway at the old fairgrounds when a $300,000 ($3,400,000) water well was bought online at the new fairgrounds. At 107 feet it produced 2500 gallons a minute.

Three massive, prefabricated exhibition buildings with a price tag of $378,000 ($4,344,000) awaited state funding, the county to pay 24 percent and the state the rest. The pieces were delivered by train in the spring of 1949, but the assembly did not start until November 1950, which was when Norman I. Fadel Company of North Hollywood was awarded the contract. [561] The Californian explained: "Although $118,000 worth of material for the exhibit buildings had been on the ground for some time, officials feared that erection of the structures would be prohibited by a defense production order of October 31 [1949]. This order, which banned construction projects in 45 noncritical classifications, prevented awarding of the contract for the Kern job."[562]

Several miles east of Bakersfield on Breckenridge Mountain, a half-dozen modern-day Forty-Niners arose, saddled up, and headed down the hill to the 1949 Kern County Fair. They bedded down under the stars at night and arrived for opening day. While they were on their way, a National Guard F-80 jet fighter landed at Kern County Airport, and the next morning, early commuters saw it towed down Chester Avenue to the old fairgrounds.[563]

Aerial bombs signaled the start of the big parade. Grand Marshal and President of the Kern County Fair Association Albert S. Goode led it from 22nd and K to the break-up at Baker and Oregon Street. By then, KAFY, KERN, and KPMC Radio were at the fairgrounds broadcasting live.[564]

Frontier Days had an amateur horse show for the first time, but the Californian did not give it much coverage because the spotlight was on the National Horse Show, directed by Ken Lewis and Bakersfield Californian manager Walter Kane. Frontier Days, now 16 year old, had equestrian entries from Santa Monica, Santa Maria, Buellton, Snelling, Sacramento and Sonoma. The Miller Brewing Company sent its four-horse Clydesdale team, and those enormous, stately animals astonished little girls and boys, including this author.[565]

The horse show was impressive, but public turnout disappointed. Faultfinders said planning should have avoided fair time, while others insisted that richer cash prizes would have helped ticket sales, but that remark was uninformed.[566] Cash prizes in the

National Horse Show were $4000 ($49,000), comparing favorably with the Fifteenth District's premiums of $4600 ($57,000), and when both were combined, the Kern County Fair was among the top-paying fairs on the West Coast.[567]

Kern County Fairgrounds had very little room to spare, and no sheltered spaces were unused. The Californian wrote, "With fourteen communities entering exhibits and entry space practically taken in all divisions, the fair directors expressed regret at the limited space that will curtail the fair this year."[568] On the last day the Californian wrote, "The fireworks at 10 pm will emblazon the end of the historic fair which will undoubtedly be the last on the old grounds."[569]

Three years had passed since the county bought the new fairgrounds, and over that time it had spent $39,000 ($443,000) for basic infrastructure, which did not include the city's cost of extending P Street south to the fairgrounds. In 1949 there was still much work to do, but everyone anticipated a time when the Kern County Fair would have more space than it needed.

In late winter 1949, Disabled American Veterans sponsored a two-day circus at Sam Lynn Ball Park, and many visitors complained of the cold. On June 14, 1950, the Shrine Club brought back the same circus, the public was happy, and Californian columnist Jim Day wrote approvingly of the aerial acts, bare-back riders, clowns, trained bears, Dachshunds, and French Poodles.[570]

A few days later the Federal Government extended the Selective Service Act, and two days after that North Korea invaded South Korea. War news filled the Californian. During the 1950 fair, the 185th Regiment, California National Guard, was on the fairgrounds "to keep traffic moving and to prevent congestion", but there was no other mention of military.

The Bakersfield Californian thanked secretary-manager William H. "Bill" Leask for his organizational skill and wrote that the fair had "all the glitter and hustle and excitement that is expected of a county fair. Flags and pennants fluttered in the breeze, gray old buildings sported bright bunting and tinsel, and the smell of sizzling hamburgers wafted across the grounds. It was fair time, carnival time, and folks were arriving from all over the country to see what was going on."[571]

The 1600 livestock entries far exceeded 1949 and helped boost first-day ticket sales to an eye-popping 35,244. New to the fair was Joe Chitwood's Auto Destruction Derby, but the rest was mostly unchanged: livestock, home economics, crafts, minerals, floriculture, melodrama, bands, barber shop quartets, strolling troubadours, square-dancing, and a midway, and they made a huge turnout.[572]

The war in Korea changed the look of the 1951 parade. Leading it was a military color guard followed by an open convertible carrying former high school athletes and disabled veterans Robert Triplet and J.D. Sarver, both double amputees from the war in Korea. Behind them came a 75-piece Marine Corps band flown in from El Toro Marine Corp Air Station.[573]

The fair charged admission fees, and this time the public squawked.[574] The Californian wrote, "The fair manager and his assistants are paid by the state from money allotted to the agriculture district from the state's take at the horse racing tracks. Premium money comes from the same funds. All books are audited by the state. The Kern County Fair was one of the last in the state to charge admission. This was made necessary by the inclusion of many features which ran expenses up and were demanded by the public. One of the most important aspects of the Kern County Fair is its encouragement to young men and women who are interested in agricultural work."

It continued, "Here is their opportunity to win cash and honors for their year's project. This project, while it brings the cash and honor, does far more than just that. It provides an educational process which proves far more valuable in many ways than the cash which ends the year's work. It likewise provides an incentive for the development of self-reliance, discipline, development of proper work habits, and other benefits. The Fair likewise provides an opportunity for the various communities of the county to join in a common project and encourage neighborliness and to feel a mutual bond of accomplishment."[575]

Forty service clubs served light refreshments, and five served complete meals. There were 11 free vaudeville acts. The National Horse Show was gone— replaced by a junior horsemanship show and equestrian gymkhana. Both were extra-cost tickets.

One hundred twenty-two thousand visitors came to the 1951 fair, and it represented a 20 percent gain over 1950. Some of that success was due to innovative advertising, such as Placemat Treasure Hunt. Numbered place mats had been given out at local cafes, and customers who took theirs to the fair had a chance to win attractive prizes. The gimmick was popular and was repeated in 1952.[576]

Generations of farming families boosted fair attendance. In 1926, Dexter Garrett was a member of Future Farmers of America, and his dairy stock won ribbons. In 1951, Dexter's son Gary showed his Holstein and six Guernseys at the fair. [577] Said young Gary, "I'm learning from some of the same teachers who taught Dad—like Mr. Dickson, Mr. Knight, and Mr. Holmes."[578]

The Californian praised the fifteenth district for its commitment to youth, "Here is their opportunity to win cash and honors for their year's project. This project, while it brings the cash and honors, does far more than just that. It provides an educational process which proves far more valuable in many ways than the cash which ends the year's work. It likewise provides an incentive for the development of self-reliance, disciple, development proper work habits and other benefits. The fair likewise provides an opportunity for the various community of the county to join in a common project, to encourage neighborliness and to fell a mutual bond of accomplishment. This year's event offers ample proof of this, together with an outstanding tabulation in glittering array of the county's huge and varied natural resources." [579]

Agricultural instructor P.D. Spilsbury of Wasco High School thanked fairgoers for their support of 4-H, Junior Farmers and Future Farmers of America, and he recognized six leaders in the livestock industry: J.D. Camp, S.A Camp, E.J. Peters, Oscar Rudnick, Lester R. Smith and the late Lawson Lowe, all of whom routinely paid well-above market price for stock raised by youth. [580] Said Spilsbury, "The list of supporters of the young people in rural activities is a long one, but investment in the encouragement of the youth of the county is the soundest that can be made. Many of them will be the livestock leaders of tomorrow, and all will become excellent citizens of the communities in which they live."[581]

## The Museum Grows

The Florafaunium was shut down during the war, but with the peace, few visitors stopped to see it. Moreover, humidity and mountain weather had degraded the collection. In 1951, supervisors purchased the entire collection for $10,000 ($107,000) and moved it to the Chamber of Commerce Building in Bakersfield. The taxidermied birds went into an eight-foot glass case in the basement, the taxidermied deer, buffalo, bears, and lions were placed a ten-foot showcase on the main floor, and the 1800 mounted and labeled California wildflowers, leaves and grains went on display in the second-floor library.

In 1952 the Whilton collection attracted 50,000 visitors. Unfortunately, the collection was costly to protect from decay, and owing to the deterioration some said it would be worthless in five years. Today, more than 70 years later, all of the mounted specimens are gone, but the 1800 mounted flowers and seeds, collected by Inez Whilton, survive today. [582] Richard Bailey wrote in 1959, "The entire flower collection was made in triplicates *[copies]*. One set was retained by the Whiltons, another presented to the Department of Botany at the California Academy of Sciences, and the third given to Tulare High School." Today the Inez Whilton collection is a holding of the California Academy of Sciences in San Francisco.

In 1946 Frank Latta was named full-time curator and Yokuts tribal member John Garcia appointed his assistant. By then the two-decades-old Chamber of Commerce Building was home to Navy and Marine Corp recruiting, Farm Bureau, Kern County Recreation and Cultural Commission, Fifteenth District Agricultural Association, and the Chamber itself.

In the spring of 1949, supervisors discussed moving the office of the Chamber of Commerce to a larger building North of the River. Sensing an opportunity, the Californian wrote, "The county museum should have more space and adequate headquarters in which to display properly and attractively the many historical treasures in its possession. The museum performs a valuable and important educational service."[583]

In 1946, Frank Latta presented plans for a 13-acre village of historic buildings and also asked supervisors to buy the old county courthouse in Havilah. A detailed study was ordered, and months later the county approved the buy, but by then the deal with the owner had fallen through. Today a replica of the county's first courthouse stands at Pioneer Village. It had only a few buildings in 1951, but 50,000 visitors came out to see what had been done and tour the basement museum.

Frank Latta invited the public to contribute historical items to the new museum. Valuable and curious objects arrived: gun collections, cotton sacks, farm wagons, and Atwater Kent radios, to name but few. Latta's duties multiplied, and he moved his desk from the second floor to the basement to be nearer to his work.[584]

In the mind of the general public, the Chamber of Commerce Building was the Kern County Museum, and in the summer of 1952 supervisors made that a reality. To "eliminate many weaknesses" in the work of the Chamber of Commerce, they changed its name to Kern County Board of Trade and merged it with 11 other county boards then operating as the Associated Chambers of Commerce. Supervisor John Holt moved that the Kern County Museum be given use of the entire Chamber of Commerce Building, the motion passed, and Frank Latta was directed to compile an inventory of holdings, submit plans for operation, and establish guidelines for showing the county's collections. Chamber of Commerce employees began packing.[585]

## Earthquakes

On July 21, 1952, 10 miles south of Bakersfield, the White Wolf Fault registered a 7.2 quake, and four weeks later it registered a 5.8 quake. Between those dates, the fault registered 188 minor shocks. Chimneys were broken, buildings damaged, some were made unsafe, and some were ruined. Official county business continued, and the offices of Auditor, Assessor, Surveyor, Tax Collector, and Treasurer were moved to safer buildings. Some staff went to the old fairgrounds and some to the new fairgrounds.

The museum's new home sustained $40,000 ($413,000) in damage but was judged safe enough to remain open. [586] The basement was safe, but the outside stairway less so—halfway down the stairs a sign warned visitors to watch for low-hanging steam pipes, but they had been there long before the quakes. Frank Latta submitted plans for a fix, the pipes were removed, the floor lowered twelve inches, an interior stairwell built, and the outside stairway was filled in.[587]

## 1952, First Fair

The most up-to-date fairgrounds in California opened on Monday September 22, 1952 to the theme Mechanized America. All exhibit space was taken, and all was reserved for the next year. Ticket booths opposite the 40-acre parking lot on P Street had 50-cent ($5) for adults and 25-centers for kids. Just inside the gate were two landscaped, spotlighted model homes and next to them "tram trains" staffed by Junior Chamber of Commerce guides waiting to transport visitors to all corners of the fairgrounds. Along the way they marveled at their images on closed-circuit television and smiled as Bozo the Clown huffed and puffed his toy balloons into Disney-like characters.[588]

The midway was jammed and the exhibition buildings mobbed. "Community exhibits brought forth "oohs" and "ahs" from those who crowded around the colorful displays, each depicting the resources of the section represented." [589] No tickets were left at the 8000-seat open-air grandstand for the Junior Horse Gymkhana and Hollywood-Vaudeville Review.

The diversity was enormous, impossible to see in one visit, and despite two days of showers the crowds kept coming. The ticket count was 10,000 paid admissions and 55,000 free ones, which doubled the attendance of 1951. The state allotment came in at a whopping $65,000 ($730,000), but not many fairgoers knew or cared about that. All that mattered was the new county fairgrounds was a resounding success.[590]

# Epilogue

In the spring of 1962 Kern County Health Department used the fairgrounds in the administration of Type III polio vaccine, and its massive parking lot and Albert S. Goode Auditorium were helpful in that effort. Assisting were nurses, doctors, police, Boy Scouts, Girl Scouts, teachers, and PTA, and owing to their efforts, more than 182,000 citizens were made immune to the paralytic virus.

Year-around use of the fairgrounds grew, and off-season income soon rivaled the annual fairs. The auditorium's claim for size was eclipsed in 1962 with completion of Bakersfield Civic Auditorium—today Mechanics Bank Arena, Theater, and Convention Center.

Periodic national recessions crippled county fairs, and the Great Depression of the 1930s set it back 10 years. Many years later when the federal government declared the recession of 2007-2009 over, many locations were far from recovered. California had stopped funding its agricultural districts, and El Dorado County's agricultural district, to name but one, struggled to survive. As late as 2014, 15 agricultural districts were on the verge of shutting down permanently, but Kern's Fifteenth District weathered the storm. In 2018 the state resumed funding, and that year more than 460,000 people attended the Kern County Fair.

Coronavirus arrived in 2020, and fair attendance fell to 39,000. The next fair was cancelled, but the livestock show took place, and buildings at the fairgrounds were used for COVID inoculations. The fair came back in 2022, although visitors were urged to wear masks and get the COVID shot. Two of the days were set aside for cleaning and disinfecting. In 2023, 340,000 visitors attended the fair, which was still well below the 460,000 count of five years earlier.[591]

Why do we have fairs? In 1951 the Californian wrote, "The Fair likewise provides an opportunity for the various communities of the county to join in a common project, to encourage neighborliness and to feel a mutual bond of accomplishment."[592] Music, junk-food, midway, rodeo, giant pumpkins, newborn calves, fancy chickens, and lop-eared rabbits lend spice to community life, and unlike schools and libraries the fairs' benefits are immediate: They create jobs, pay taxes, and boost businesses. Some of the benefits are less tangible. People meet and fall in love at fairs, but the more common benefits are the memories and dreams of past fairs—the experiences that strengthen our racial, cultural, and religious fabric. After 150 years, the Kern County Fair is embedded in the psyche of the people.

# Questioning the Author

## Why write about old fairs?

Some years ago I found a pamphlet that said the story of the early fairs was waiting to be written. I remembered 1948 when my grandpa took me to the old fairgrounds to see a three-ring circus. The ringmaster cracked a long whip, the brass band hurt my ears, eight clowns jumped out of a midget car, and acrobats traded hands in midair. That was all I knew about the old fairs. Sometime later I researched the fair of 1893 and posted the story to my website.

About eight years after that, a retired-teacher friend told me about living at the old fairgrounds in the 1930s with her parents. Her story was valuable, first-person history, and I thought why not add it to some of my other stories and make a book about the old fairs. I started when COVID hit, and right away I knew I had a lot of work to do, but I dove-in anyway. It was a slow but interesting grind.[593]

## Isn't your old fair story still online?

Short answer, yes. Some years back when Ken Hooper was President of the Kern County Historical Society he helped me get online access to historical newspapers. While enjoying that resource, I discovered I'd made a lot of mistakes in the fair story, and I took it off my website. But it'd been pirated, and it's still floating around out there in cyberspace. Not much I can do about it.

## Why so many endnotes?

Kern historians didn't leave us many breadcrumbs, so I put them in for the next generation. By the way, if you're reading about a 1936 carnival, and the endnote says 1940, that's because newspapers don't give all the facts in one story. Also, if you're reading about a bridge and the endnote says Farmers' Meeting, that's because the bridge info is somewhere in the Farmers' Meeting story.

## You mentioned microfilm readers.

Online research sure beats making trips to the library to read microfilm, but the web doesn't have everything, but microfilm lets you dig deeper. The copies I made from both of them were helpful in fixing mistakes, but sleuthing around for the information took time. Sometimes it was a tug-of-war between Life and Art. Both demanded my attention, progress dragged, and there were times when I wanted to quit. Then I reached the point where I had too much in it to quit.

Winston Churchill is credited with saying "Writing a book is an adventure. To begin with, it is a toy and an amusement. Then it becomes a mistress, then it becomes a master, then it becomes a tyrant. The last phase is that just as you are about to be reconciled to your servitude, you kill the monster and fling him to the public." That sums it up, but for me there was also the feeling of loss for something that had been in my life for a long time.

## *So you published on-demand.*

That came from my friend Lee Harold Edwards who wrote articles for True West Magazine. He'd read Joe Doctor's *Shotguns on Sunday,* about badman Jim McKinney, and decided to write a fact-filled book about that guy. In 1988 Harold mailed his manuscript to a printer and in due time got back boxes and boxes of books. Selling the Killing of Jim McKinney was hard, and I remember him saying "Eighty miles from here, nobody cares about our history."

Chris Brewer of Exeter bought the remainders, and the last time I was in Brewer's shop he still had the book for sale. If Harold were here today, it'd give me a lot of pleasure to tell him that signed copies of the book are going for $47. I'm sure he was right about the 80-mile rule. I won't be storing books and trying to sell them.

## *Will it sell?*

Who knows? Your question reminds me of Edwin Lincoln McLeod who clerked for Hochheimer's store more than a century ago. McLeod collected Kawaiisu baskets in his spare time, and today the collection is a holding of the Hearst Museum of Anthropology, University of California, Berkeley. In

1951 the Bakersfield Californian wrote that McLeod was "a modest man whose hobby enriched not only his own life, but provided a unique historical heritage for posterity."[594] Now that's an accolade to treasure.

# Appendix

## Leaders in Early Fairs

Elisha Miles Roberts (1887). Agriculturalist, Kern County Supervisor

Mrs. Dr. L.S. (Doris) Rogers (1888), organizer

Henry Alexander Jastro (1889), Kern County Supervisor, General Manager, Kern County Land Company

J.M. Reuck, (1892), newspaper owner

Solomon Jewett (1892), agriculturist

W.H. Scribner (1892), merchant

Charles Averill Barlow (1912), banker and oil executive

Angus Jewett Crites (1912), oil executive

Alfred Harrell (1912), newspaper owner

John C. "Paul" Derkum (1913), promoter

Howard K. Dickson (1921), teacher

# Presidents,
# Secretaries, and Managers

Solomon Jewett (1892)

Henry A. Jastro (1902)

William G. Lutz (1907)

E.B. Fussell (1908)

Angus J. Crites (1925-1929)

O.A. Kommers (1930)

Howard K. Dickson (1940)

C.J. Cheek (1941)

Ardis Walker (1942-1943)

Albert S. Goode (1944-1945)

George W. Wendt (1946-1947)

Lee Clark (1948)

Bill Leask (1949-1950)

Lloyd H. Goad (1951-1952)

# References

*Bailey, Richard C.*
—"Emery M. Whilton Florafaunium Collection". "Beale Memorial Library List of Whilton Collection Materials Sent to Kern County Library, March 8, 1965. "Typewritten story on The Emery Whilton Florafaunium Collection by Richard C. Bailey" [Beale Memorial Library, McGuire Local History Room, Bakersfield, California]

—"Emery M. Whilton and his Wildlife Collection", Historic Kern, Quarterly Bulletin of the Kern County Historical Society, v. 9, no.4, May,1959

—"Collector's Choice: The McLeod Basket Collection." Thirteenth Annual publication of the Kern County Historical Society and the County of Kern through its museum, Bakersfield, California, (n.p), 1951

Bakersfield City Council, Minutes, City of Bakersfield, 1501 Truxtun Avenue, Bakersfield, California 93301

*Bates, Helen*
"15th District Agricultural Association, Kern County Fair, 1142 So. P. St 93307, Kern County Fair history, by Helen Bates" 15th District Agricultural Association, Kern County Fair 1142 So.P. St 93307. Helen Bates. Robert D. Dunlap, Secretary Manager. Pres. Lloyd Hokit, VP Julian Filoteo." (n.d.), (c. 1980) [Research Center, Kern County Museum, 3801 Chester Avenue, Bakersfield, California 93301]

*Boyd, William Harland*
—Chinese of Kern County, 1857-1960, *Kern County Historical Society*, Bakersfield, California, 2002, -"Homecoming Week Airplane Race", Kern County Historical Society, Quarterly Bulletin, March 1987

*Bremer, Jeff R.*, The Trial of the Century: Lux v. Haggin and the Conflict Over Water Rights in Late Nineteenth-Century California; Southern California Quarterly, July 1, 1999 (v 81, no. 2, p. 197-220) [https://dr.lib.iastate.edu/handle/20.500.12876/Rwyq AP3w]

*Karpe, Arthur H.*, Life with a Lusty Pioneer, Carlton Press, New York, N.Y. 1969

Carroll v. California Horse Racing Board, Civ. 6103, Supreme Court of California, Decided Aug 25, 1939 [www.caselaw.findlaw.com/ca-court-of-appeal/1785277.html]

*Cherny, Robert W.*, Gretchen Lemke-Santangelo and

*Richard Griswold de Castillo*, Competing Vision, a History of California, 2nd ed., updated August 26, 2022. San Francisco State University, Saint Mary's College of California, & San Diego State University, Self-published, 2022, [www.dropbox.com]

*Dane, Edith,* "Kernland Tales", Taft Daily Midway Driller (1949-1956) in Larry Peahl (ed.), Edith Dane, Kernland Tales, (2006).   [Manuscript, Kern County Library, McGuire Local History Room]

*Darling, Curtis*, Kern County Place Names, 2nd ed., (n.p.), Kings River Press, 2003

*Dick, Robert*, Auto Racing in the Shadow of the Great War, Streamlined Specials and a New Generation of Drivers on American Speedways, 1915-1922. McFarland & Company, Jefferson, North Carolina, 2019 [Fresno County Public Library, San Joaquin Valley Heritage & Genealogy Center. 2420 Mariposa Street, Fresno, California 93721-2285]

*Gates, Paul W.*, Land and Law in California: Essays on Land Policies, Purdue University Press, 2002

*Gia, Gilbert Peter*
—"Bakersfield Breweries, 1866-1920, v5"
[https://hcommons.org/deposits/item/hc:46601/]

—"Bashing Bakersfield, 1873-1922, a Look Back"
[https://hcommons.org/deposits/item/hc:49079/]

—"Dormitories_-bhs_1915_1955_v7_"
[https://hcommons.org/deposits/item/hc:15153/

—"Henry A. Jastro, Commodore of Kern County,
Biography, Kinships and Politics, 1848-1925, ver. 6",
[https://hcommons.org/deposits/item/hc:46623/]

—"Jails at Havilah and Bakersfield (California,
1866- 1963",
[https://hcommons.org/deposits/item/hc:15981/

—"Mme. Brignaudy in the Bakersfield Tenderloin,
1905-1933, v15"
[https://hcommons.org/deposits/item/hc:23495/]

—"One Hundred Years at Hart Park, 1890-1990"
[https://hcommons.org/deposits/item/hc:48749/]

—"Tarred & Feathered, Vigilantism in 1890, ver 2022"
[https://hcommons.org/deposits/item/hc:48639/]

—"What Happened To Bakersfield's Chinese
Cemetery?"
[https://hcommons.org/deposits/item/hc:48643/]

*"History of the Big Fresno Fair, the Road to Becoming
the State's 5th Largest Fair!"*
[https://cdn.saffire.com._History_of_The_Big_Fresno_
Fair]

*Hudnut, Herbert B., Jr.*, The Life of Richard Hudnut,
1828-1903, Supplement 2011. Self-published, Glens
Falls Printing, Glens Falls, New York, 2011 [McGuire
Local History Room, Beale Memorial Library,
Bakersfield, California]

*Igler, David.* Industrial Cowboys: Miller & Lux and the Transformation of the Far West, 1850-1920. Berkeley: University of California Press, 2001.

*Kern County Fire Department, 1927-1974,* Kern County Fire Department, (n.p.), Bakersfield, California, 1998

*Kern County Hall of Records*, 1655 Chester Ave, Bakersfield, California 93301*Kern County Tax Book*, January 1, 1870 [Genealogy Room, Beale Memorial Library, Bakersfield, California]

*Kern County Articles of Incorporation*, Kern County Land Company, September 2, 1890. Records of the California Secretary of State, California State Archives, Sacramento, California

*Littlefield, Douglas R.*
—"Late Nineteenth and Early Twentieth Century Private Land Ownership and Control of Rio Bravo Ranch" (Monograph, 1992), Littlefield Research Associates, Oakland, California
—Ruling the Waters, California's Kern River, the Environment, and the Making of Western Water Law, (2020), University of Oklahoma Press

*Morgan, Wallace Melvin*, History of Kern County, California: with biographical sketches of the leading men and women of the county who have been identified with its growth and development from the early days to the present. Historic Record Company, Los Angeles, California, 1914
[www.loc.gov/item/16006472/]

*Odell, Kerry and Marc D. Weidenmier*, "Real Shock, Monetary Aftershock: The 1906 San Francisco Earthquake and the Panic of 1907", Claremont Colleges Working Papers in Economics, n. 2001-2007 [http://hdl.handle.net/10419/94590]

*Parker, Donald L.,* Perilous Voyage of the Balloon American, Self-published. Castel Press, Pasadena, Californian, 1993

*Rogers, Will,* Letters of a Self-Made Diplomat to His President, Albert & Charles Boni, New York, 1926

*Rudy, Lynn Hay*
—Granddad: Hugh A. Blodget in Early Bakersfield. Self-published, Jenner, California, 1999
—Old Bakersfield Sites and Landmarks, 1875-1915. Self-published, Jenner, California, 2000

*State of California*
—Bulletin, Department of Agriculture, v. 13-15, 1924, Appendix to the Journals of the State and Assembly of the 32nd Session of the Legislature of the State of California, 1895, v II. [www.google.com/books]

—First Annual Report of the State Market Director of California, Appendix "F", Proposed State Market Commission Act. 1916.[www.google.com/books]

—Transactions of the California State Agricultural Society During the Years 1868 and 1869. D.W. Ordwicks, State Printer, Sacramento, 1870. [www.google.com/books]

—Transactions of the California State Agricultural Society During the Year 1894. Sacramento, California, State Office, State Printing, 1895 [https://www.google.com/books/edition/Report_of_the _California_State_Agricultu/ ajQPAQAAIAAJ?hl=en]

*Turner, John,* White Gold Comes to California. Book Publishers, Inc., Fresno, California, 1981

*United States Department of Commerce*, Bureau of the Census. Estimates of Population of the United States, 1910, 1911, 192, 1913, 1914, 1915, 1916, And 1917 Including Result of the State Enumerations made in 1915. Washington, Government Printing Office, 1918

*United States War Production Board*, War Production News for Northern California and Nevada. May 26, 1942, Vol. 1, n. 31, 1355 Market Street, San Francisco, California

*Wallace, Joseph Samuel*, Recollections of a High School District, 1893-1968: An Informal History of the Kern County Union High School and Junior College District, 1893-1968. (n.p.), (n.d.) (c. 1980

*Williams, Amy,* "First Newspapers, Brief history of Fresno County Pre-1891 News Journalism", Clovis Station Free Press, V. 17,n. 21, July 15, 2000, [www.clovisnews.com]

*Zonlight, Margaret Aseman Cooper*, Land, Water and Settlement in Kern County, California, 1850-1890, Arno Press, 1979

## Journals, Pamphlets, Maps, Letters

Activities of Kern County Union High School Department of Agriculture. "Cycles in our K.C.U.H.S. Agriculture Department Development" K.C.U.H.S. Boys' Agriculture Organization, Bakersfield Chapter Future Farmers of America, Bakersfield, California. May 1934, pp 41, 43. [www.google.com/books]

Atlas of Kern County, 1901. Randall & Denne, 1901 [McGuire Local History Room, Beale Memorial Library, Bakersfield, California]

Bender & Hewitt, Bakersfield Map, November 1898

Bensel and Maitland, Bakersfield & Kern County Directory 1891-1892 [McGuire Local History Room, Beale Memorial Library, Bakersfield, California]

Billboard
—March 7, 1942, "Sizing Up the Season"
October 11, 1947,
—March 28, 1952, "Bakersfield Sets Mark-132,000 Kern County Fair"

Breeder and Sportsman, San Francisco, California, Breeder and Sportsman Publishing Co., 1882-1919 [www.biodiversitylibrary.org/bibliography/58597]

California Farmer Combined with California Cultivator, v. 46, 1916 [https://www.google.com/books/edition/California Cultivator/YMBJAQAAMAAJ?hl=en&gbpv=1]

"Irrigation Age", Vol. vi, n. 1, Jan 1894, "Map of Rosedale Colony", [Google Books. The_Irrigation_Age/mp4VAQAAIAA/]

Kern County Land Company, Map of
Rosedale Colony, 1892
[https://exhibits.stanford.edu/ruderman]

Official Program, First Annual Celebration, July 4,
1911. [Pamphlet file, Sports, Museum Research
Center. Kern County Museum, 3801 Chester Avenue,
Bakersfield, California, 93301]

Pacific Reporter, v. 65, June 25 —July 30, 1917

"Southern Pacific Company v. State of Arizona, #152",
p. 303. West Publishing Company, St. Paul.
[www.google.com/books]

Southwest Contractor and Manufacturer,
Jul 24, 1909, p. 6   [www.google.com/books]

Quarterly of the Kern County Historical Society
v. 53, n. 2, Bakersfield, California, Summer, 2003

Randall & Denne, Index Atlas of Kern County,
California: Containing over Five Million Acres of Land,
Consisting of Agricultural, Grazing, Fruit and Mineral
Lands and Its Wonderful Oil Producing Lands, San
Jose, California, 1901

Rodriguez, June Dooley. Letter to Gilbert Peter Gia,
April 2019

Sunset Magazine, June 1911, v. 26, p 633

# Newspapers

Bakersfield Californian, Bakersfield, California

Bakersfield Morning Echo, Bakersfield, California

Blue and White, Bakersfield High School [Bakersfield High School Archive, 1241 G Street, Bakersfield, California, 93301; Museum Research Center, Kern County Museum, 3801 Chester Avenue, Bakersfield, California, 93301]

Capistrano Dispatch, Capistrano, California, [www.thecapistranodispatch.com/a-bit-of-hollywood-back-near-little-hollywood/]

Colusa Sun, Colusa, California

Daily Californian, Bakersfield, California

Daily Evening Gazette, Bakersfield, California

Dispatch Democrat, Ukiah, California

Fresno Expositor, Fresno, California

Fresno Republican, Fresno, California

Fresno Weekly Republican, Fresno, California

Hanford Journal, Hanford, California

Hanford Sentinel, Hanford, California

Hanford Weekly Journal, Hanford, California

Kern County Californian, Bakersfield, California

Kern County Democrat, Bakersfield, California

Kern County Gazette, Bakersfield, California

Kern County Weekly Courier, Bakersfield, California

Los Angeles Herald, Los Angeles, California

Los Angeles Times, Los Angeles, California

Morning San Louis Obispo Tribune,
San Louis Obispo, California

Pacific Rural Press, San Francisco, California

San Diego Union and Daily Bee, San Diego, California

San Francisco Call, San Francisco, California

San Francisco Chronicle, San Francisco, California

San Jose Daily Mercury, San Jose, California

Shafter Press, Shafter, California

Sumner Standard, Kern City, Bakersfield, California

Tulare Times, Visalia, California

Weekly Californian, Bakersfield, California

# Endnotes

[1] Sacramento Daily Union, Mar 26, 1866, "A New County South"; Daily Alta Californian, Apr 6, 1866, "New Counties"

[2] Kern County Weekly Courier, Jan 25, 1873, "Population And Health"

[3] Kern County Weekly Courier, Oct 29, 1870, "Census Of Kern County"

[4] Kern County Weekly Courier, Sep 6, 1870, "Kern County, Its Agricultural Grazing And Mineral Lands; Resources, Climate And Productions"; Shafter Press, Aug 16, 1951, "Courageous Pioneers, Creators Of State Fairs"; "Transactions Of The California State Agricultural Society During The Years 1868 And 1869"

[5] Kern County Weekly Courier, Sep 6, 1870, "Kern County Its Agricultural, Grazing And Mineral Lands Resources, Climate And Productions"

[6] Pacific Rural Press, Oct 7, 1871, "Southern District Agricultural Association"; Aug 24, 1872, "Pure-Blood Stock Sales"; Kern County Weekly Courier, Nov 18, 1871, "Fine Sheep"; Sep 14, 1872, "Jewett & Saxe Took Two Premiums..."

[7] Kern County Weekly Courier, Nov 26, 1870, "Bakersfield Races"; Dec 24, 1870, "The Races"; Mar 4, 1871, "One Of Our Race Days"; Southern Californian, Feb 18, 1875, "A Race-Track Is Being Graded..."

[8] Kern County Weekly Courier And Southern Californian, Feb 18, 1875, "A Race-Track Is Being Graded, One-Half Mile Length...."; June 26, 1875, "At the bull fight on Thursday we learn..."

[9] Kern County Weekly Courier And Southern Californian, June 26, 1875, "At the bull fight on Thursday we learn..."

[10] Kern County Californian, "Mar 3, 1883, "Horse-Racing"

[11] Feb 18, 1876, "D.S. Lightner Is Laying Out A Race Track..."; Kern County Weekly Courier, Feb 26, 1876, "The Great $30,000 Race Is A Thing Of The Past."; Kern County Weekly Courier, Apr 22, 1876, "The town has been well supplied...."; Jul 20, 1876, "The races at the Hot Spring on the 12th inst., came off with great..."; Kern County Californian, Feb 3, 1883, "Races! Races! Races! At The Fairground Track"; Morgan, p. 70

[12] Kern County Californian, Apr 7, 1883, "The Foot-Race Of The Season Comes Off At The Fair Ground Track Sunday"; Sep 4, 1884, "Base Ball Notes"; BC, May 18, 1950, "Circus Train Set To Unload"

[13] Southern Californian & Kern County Weekly Courier, Jun 6, 1878, "Gone From Our Gaze"

[14] Ibid.

[15] Bakersfield Daily Evening Gazette, Jul 16, 1884, "It Is A Satisfaction In The Older Residents Of This Valley To See Some Of The Old Foggy Ideas..."; Gia, "Bashing Bakersfield, 1873-1922, A Lookback"

[16] Gia, "Tarred & Feathered, Vigilantism In 1890"

[17] Kern County Weekly Courier, Sep 6, 1870, "Kern County, Its Agricultural Grazing And Mineral Lands; Resources, Climate And Productions"; Apr 22, 1871, "Kern Island"; Kern County Weekly Courier, Jan 25, 1873, "Population And Health"; Gia, "Mme. Brignaudy in the Bakersfield Tenderloin"

[18] Kern County Weekly Courier, Aug 23, 1873, "All persons indebted to the later firm...."; Kern County Democrat, Jun 29, 1877, "It Is Currently Reported, And The Report Is Probably True That Haggin Has Purchased..."; Morgan, p. 67

[19] State Of California, Transactions Of The California State Agricultural Society During The Years 1868 And 1869", p. 16; Kern County Californian, Oct 6, 1888, "The Sixth Annual Fair Of The Fifteenth District"; www.Fresnofair.Com/P/Education/Museums/Big-Fresno-Fair-Museum/History-Of-Horse-Racing; Igler

[20] San Francisco Chronicle, Oct 19, 1877, "The Duchy Of Kern"; San Jose Daily Mercury, Jan 12, 1878, "A Ring Organ's Defense"; Kern County Gazette, Oct 2, 1880, "Kern County Well Represented At State Fair"; Quarterly of the Kern County Historical Society, Vol 53, No. 2; California Supreme Court, Lux v. Haggin, p. 919, 923-24 (Cal. 1886); Los Angeles Daily Herald, Feb 13, 1886, "Cheap Homes For Settlers, In Parcels Of 160 Acres Or More In Kern And Tulare Counties"; Kern County Californian, Sep 30, 1889, "Arid Land Committee"; Kern County Californian, Feb 8, 1890, "If Persons Having The Names Of Personal Friends In Whom They Would Like To…."; Fresno Republican, Jan 1, 1891, "Kern County"; Atwood; Zonlight, p. 259

[21] Kern County Californian, Jul 23, 1887, "Kern County To The Front"

[22] Kern County Californian, Feb 11, 1888, "Mechanics' Institute"

[23] Kern County Californian, Sep 1, 1888, "Kern County Products, From The Examiner"; Breeder And Sportsman, Sep 1, 1888, "Kern County At The Fair"; Kern County Californian, Sep 1, 1888, "Kern County Products - From The "Examiner"; Sep 15, 1888, "The Mechanics' Fair At San Francisco Will Close…"; Pacific Rural Press, Sep 22, 1888, "Close Of The Mechanics' Fair – County Exhibits"

[24] Pacific Rural Press, Sep 22, 1888, "Close Of The Mechanics' Fair – County Exhibits";

[25] Kern County Californian, Feb 15, 1890, "Kern County. A Fine Description"

[26] Kern County Californian, Oct 12, 1889, "The Mechanics' Fair"

[27] Kern County Californian, Sep 7, 1889, "The Kern County Exhibit, From Mechanic's Fair Daily"; Oct 12, 1889, "The Mechanic's Fair"; Los Angeles Herald, May 7, 1890, "Bakersfield, May 6—For The World's Fair"

[28] Los Angeles Times, Jul 9, 1889, "The Burned Town"; Sacramento Daily Union, Jul 11, 1889, "Bakersfield Needs No Help"; Jul 14, 1889, "Plucky Bakersfield"

[29] Kern County Californian, Aug 30, 1889, "Plenty Of Money"

[30] Kern County Californian, Oct 12, 1889, "County Fairs"

[31] DC, Feb 22, 1890, "That Kern County Needs Fair Grounds And ..."; Sanborn-Perris Map Seal, "Bakersfield, Kern Co. Cal. Jan. 1890"

[32] DC, Jan 5, 1892, "Kern Fair Grounds Association"; Williams

[33] Kern County Californian, Apr 26, 1890, "Work upon the race track and fair grounds..."

[34] Kern County Californian, Sep 27, 1890, "Eighth Annual Fair" (Advertisement)

[35] DC, Jan 17, 1891, "Kern County Exhibit"

[36] DC, Sep 17, 1891, "The District Fair"

[37] DC, Oct 3, 1891, "On Monday The Fifteenth District Agricultural Fair Will ..."

[38] DC, Dec 14, 1892, "Kern County Fair Grounds Association Incorporated March 15th..."

[39] Kern County Californian, Mar 15, 1890, "The Agricultural Fair Association"; Aug 16, 1890, "The Valley Of The Kern" (Advertisement); Littlefield, "Kern County Articles Of Incorporation, Kern County Land Company, Sep 2, 1890"; DC, Feb 29, 1892, "For Fair Grounds" (Invitation For Bids); Jul 16, 1892 "The Fair Grounds"; Kern County Californian, Sep 19, 1892, "The Kern County Fair"; Sep 29, 1892, "The Coming District Fair"

[40] DC, Aug 5, 1892, "Know Thyself"

[41] Ibid.

[42] DC, Jan 21, 1892, "The Fair Grounds Proposition"; Bakersfield Weekly Californian Jan. 23, 1892

[43] DC, Feb 18, 1892, "The Kern Fair Ground Association Ready For Incorporation"; Weekly Californian, Feb 20, 1892, "A Good Race Course And Fair Ground Located Within Two Miles Of This City..."; Kern County Californian, Feb 22, 1890, "That Kern County needs fair grounds and a race track..."; Feb 25, 1892, "Meeting Of The Stockholders, Permanent Organization"; DC, Mar 2, 1892, "The Fair Grounds. Meeting Of The Stockholders This Afternoon"; Mar 4, 1892, "The Act Of The Stockholders Of The Kern..."; Mar 28, 1892, "The Ground Selected; May 24, 1892, "The Fair Grounds"; Cherny

[44] The Californian, Mar 2, 1892, "The Fair Grounds. Meeting Of The Stockholders This Afternoon"

[45] DC, Feb 18, 1892, "For Fair Grounds"

[46] DC, May 24, 1892, "The Fair Grounds"; Williams

[47] DC, Jan 5, 1892, "Kern Fair Grounds Association"

[48] DC, Jan 7, 1892, "Subscribe To It"; Feb 16, 1892, "Shall We Have A Fair?"

[49] DC, Mar 8, 1892, "Something Much Needed"

[50] DC, Mar 16, 1892, "The Driving Club"; The Californian, Mar 28, 1892, "The Ground Selected"; Kern County Hall Of Records, Lease 0002-0202, Jun 1, 1892

[51] DC, May 20, 1892, "The Fair Grounds"

[52] DC, May 26, 1892, "The Fair Grounds"

[53] Hanford Journal, Dec 15, 1891, "From Tulare Times--The lease of the racetrack and grounds..."

[54] DC, May 12, 1893, "How Kern Grows"

[55] Weekly Californian, Sep 24, 1892, "The Kern Fair Great Preparations Being Made"

[56] DC, Jul 16, 1892, "The Fair Grounds"; Oct 6, 1892, "The Coming Fair"; Fresno Expositor, Sep 19, 1892, "Kern County Fair, A Grand Pavilion Exhibit And Splendid Racing Programme"; DC, Sep 29, 1892, "The Coming District Fair";

[57] DC, Sep 7, 1892, "A Protest"

[58] Bakersfield Weekly Californian, Sep 10,1898, "District Fair Notes"

[59] DC, Sep 29, 1892, "The Coming District Fair"

[60] The Californian, Oct 6, 1892, "The Coming Fair. Reorganization Of The Board Of Directors."; Sumner Standard, Oct 13, 1892, "Never In The History Of Bakersfield Has There Been Such Bustle And ..."; DC, Oct 11, 1892, "The County Fair"

[61] DC, Sep 19, 1892, "The Kern County Fair"; Weekly Californian, Sep 24, 1892, "The Kern County Fair"; DC, Sep 29, 1892, "The Coming District Fair"

[62] The Californian, Oct 25, 1892, "Come To The Fair"

[63] Sumner Standard, Oct 27, 1892, "The Fair"

[64] The Californian, Oct 25, 1892, "At The Track"

[65] Sumner Standard, Oct 27, 1892, "The Fair"

[66] Sumner Standard, Oct 13, 1892, "Never In The History Of Bakersfield Has There Been Such Bustle And ..."

[67] The Californian, Oct 25, 1892, "The Pavilion"

[68] Bakersfield Weekly Californian, Sep 24, 1892, "The Kern Fair"; Oct 6, 1892, "The Coming Fair"; Oct 29, 1892, "Summing Up. The Fair And Its Influence On The People Of Kern"; Colusa [California] Sun, Nov 21, 1892, "A Palace Made Of Jelly -- New York Ledger"

[69] Sumner Standard, Oct 13, 1892, "Never In The History Of Bakersfield Has There Been Such Bustle And ..."

[70] Ibid.

[71] Sumner Standard, Oct 27, 1892, "The Fair"

[72] Ibid.

[73] Ibid.

[74] Sumner Standard, Oct 27, 1892, "The Fair"

[75] DC, Sep 6, 1892, "The Coming Fair. Reorganization Of The Board Of Directors"; Nov 2; Fresno Morning Republican, Nov 4, 1892, "Kern's Fine Exhibit"

[76] Sumner Standard, Oct 27, 1892, "The Fair"

[77] Ibid.

[78] DC, Oct 27, 1892, "Still She Booms"

[79] DC, Oct 29, 1892, "Summing Up. The Fair And Its Influence On The People Of Kern"

[80] Sumner Standard, Oct 27, 1892, "Chattering damsels and their attractive swains..."

[81] Ibid.

[82] Fresno Morning Republican, Nov 4, 1892, "Kern's Fine Exhibit"

[83] Daily Californian, Oct 26, 1892, "The District Fair"

[84] Weekly Californian, Oct 29, 1892, "The District Fair"; DC, Feb 8, 1893, "The Public Are Cordially Invited..."

[85] DC, May 12, 1893, "How Kern Grows"

[86] DC, Jun 6, 1893, "Fourth Of July. How It Will Be Celebrated In Bakersfield"

[87] DC, Oct 20, 1893, "The Chain Gang Is Doing Good Work On Chester Avenue..."

[88] DC, Mar 1, 1893, "Local News: The Kern Driving Club..."; July 19, 1893, "The County Fair"; Oct 12, 1893, "The Eleventh Annual Fair, 15th Agricultural District"; Oct 13, "Work Was Started This Morning Remodeling..."; Oct 16, 1893, "Eleventh Annual Fair" (Advertisement); Oct 17, 1893,"The Fair"; Oct 30, 1893, "City And Vicinity"

[89] San Diego Union And Daily Bee, Apr 22, 1894, "La Fiesta - Old Spanish Games Revived At Coronado"; DC, Aug 18, 1894, "Fiesta! Fiesta!" (Advertisement)

[90] State Of California. Transactions Of The California State Agricultural Society During The Year 1894

[91] DC, Mar 18, 1895, "British Club Races"; Aug 3, 1894, "Three Days' Races"

[92] DC, Apr 22, 1895, "Preparations Are Well Under Way..."; Apr 23, 1895, "The Floral Fair"; San Francisco Call, Jun 14, 1895, "Forty-Second Exhibition Of The State Agricultural Society"

[93] DC, Apr 8, 1895, "Business Men's Excursion"; Apr 13, 1895, "To Entertain The Half-Million Club"; Apr 15, 1895, "Floral Fair"; Apr 17,1895, "The Half-Million Club Excursion Did Not "Pan Out""; Apr 23, 1895, "The Half-Million Club"

[94] DC, Apr 15, 1895, "The Races"; Aug 1, 1895, "The County Club Of Kern County Have Received..."; Dec 23, 1895, "Bids For Race Track Privileges"

[95] DC, Apr 28, 1896, "Pony Race Meeting, May 2, 1896"; May 4, 1896, "County Club Races"

[96] DC, Dec 24, 1896, "Blue Rock Shoot"

[97] DC, Apr 27, 1896, "League Of Progress"

[98] DC, May 15, 1896, "Kern County's Exhibit"; April 27, 1897, "Bakersfield Spring Race Meeting"; Sep 6, 1897, "Counties Co-Operate"; Sep 24, 1897, "The Los Angeles Fair"; Fresno Republican, Oct 15, 1897, "Fair Building Needed In This City"; Pacific Rural Press, Feb 26, 1898, "Tulare Grange; Santa Cruz Evening Sentinel, Jul 7, 1898, "Can Not Santa Cruz Get Up A Fair This Fall?"; DC, Jul 14, 1898, "Fire"; DC, Nov 1, 1900, "The Population By Townships. Federal Census For Kern Co. In Detail"

[99] DC, Jun 7, 1899, "A County Fair For This Fall"

[100] DC, Jun 3, 1899, ""Governor Gage has appointed as directors..."

[101] DC, Jun 7, 1899, "A County Fair For This Fall"

[102] DC, Aug 4, 1899, "No Fair This Year"; Nov 2, 1900, "Bakersfield's Building Boom"

[103] DC, Aug 29, 1900, "Races, Races, Races";
Oct 24, 1900, "Kern County Fair And Race Meeting";
Nov 1, 1900, "The Population By Township";
Nov 22, 1900, "Fair Week!";
Nov 27, 1900, "Reduced Rates"

[104] DC, Jun 16, 1900, "District Fair In November";
Aug 11, 1900, "A Fair Will Be Held This Fall"

[105] DC, Oct 19, 1900, "A Call Comes For General Exhibit"

[106] DC, Oct 31, 1900, "In Preparations For The Fair"

[107] DC, Aug 11, 1900, "A Fair Will Be Held This Fall";
Sep 5, 1900, "The Coming Race Meeting"; Nov 1, 1900,
"First Day Of The Agricultural Fair"; Nov 2, 1900,
"Second Day Of The Fair"; Nov 3, 1900, "The Closing
Day Of The Fair"

[108] DC, Jan 4, 1901, "Agricultural Park"

[109] DC, Jan 3, 1901, "Agricultural Park, Event Of The
Season"; Jan 7, 1901, "Motor Tandem Beat Horses.

[110] DC, Mar 21, 1901, "Other counties in the state
are making..."

[111] Hanford Sentinel, Aug 1, 1901,
"Discussed Fair Exhibit"

[112] Hanford Sentinel, Oct 17, 1901, "E.E. Bush is making
preparations..."; Hanford Daily Journal, Oct 21, 1901,
"Annual Fair"; Oct 24, 1901, "Special Edition.
The Opening Of The Fair"

[113] San Francisco Call, May 3, 1902, "Bakersfield Citizens
Who Have Charge Of Arrangements For The Street Fair";
May 8, 1902, "Business San Francisco Goes Forth
To Greet The Opulent San Joaquin"

[114] Hanford Sentinel, Feb 6, 1902, "The 15th Agricultural
District, Comprising The County Of Kern...";Morning San
Louis Obispo Tribune, May 22, 1902, "Kern County Fair"

[115] DC, Jul 1, 1902, "Money Easy For The Fair"

[116] DC, Oct 8, 1902, "Opening Day Of County Fair"

[117] DC, May 13, 1902, "When Jastro Bossed Gage";
ME, Mar 27, 1909,
"Legislature Was Quite Expensive"

[118] DC Oct 19, 1902, "Out At The Race Track";
Los Angeles Herald, Oct 8, 1902, "Kern County's Fair"

[119] DC, Oct 9, 1902, "First Night At The Pavilion";
Oct 8, 1902, "Opening Day Of County Fair"

[120] DC, Oct 8, 1902, "Opening Day Of County Fair"

[121] Ibid.

[122] DC, Oct 11, 1902, "Premiums Awarded By The Committees"; Oct 8, 1902, "Notice To Exhibitors"; Oct 9, 1902, "First Night At The Pavilion"

[123] DC, Mar 22, 1902, "Funds For Our Exhibit"; Hanford Sentinel, Mar 27, 1902, "To Exhibit At St. Louis"; DC, Dec 31, 1902, "A Fourth Story And Roof Garden To Be Added To Southern Hotel"

[124] Hanford Sentinel, Sep 3, 1903, "Kern County Coming In Line"; Oct 1, 1903, "Judges Selected"; Sep 15, 1904, "After This Business Had Been Attended To ..."; San Francisco Call, Oct 10, 1905, "Central California Fair Has Auspicious Opening"; Hanford Weekly Journal, Oct 13, 1905, "Wednesday's Races"; DC, Aug 8, 1906, "Kings County Fair Oct 1 To 6"

[125] DC, Jul 14, 1905, "Race Meet At Fresno"

[126] DC, Sep 27, 1905, "A New Style Of A Horseless Carriage"

[127] DC, May 3, 1906, "How Local Fund For Relief Was Raised"; San Francisco Chronicle, Apr 25, 1906, "Vast Army Has Left The City; DC, Dec 31, 1906, "Stockholders' Annual Meeting"

[128] DC. Aug 8, 1906, "Kings County Fair Oct 1 To 6"

[129] BC, Jul 17, 1907, "Auto Stage Line From Mojave"; Aug 16, 1907, "Drummers Use Automobile"

[130] BC, Nov 16, 1907, "Broke Record To M'kittrick"

[131] Taft Midway Driller, February 4, 1950, "Kernland ales By Edith Dane"; Dane, Edith

[132] BC, Jan 30, 1911, "Auto Men To Meet Tonight"; Feb 22, 1911, "Cadillac Wins In Great Bakersfield-Fresno Race"; Nov 10, 1911, "Second Road Race To Fresno Being Planned For Washington's Birthday"

[133] BC, Apr 14, 1911, "Big Auto Show Opens Tonight At The Armory"; April 14, 1911, "Armory Hall Is Passing As A Public Meeting Place"

[134] BC, Jun 19, 1911, "Twenty Entries Assured For Races—George Adair Will Start—Money Comes In"; Jul 3, 1911, "Civic Parade This Evening"; Jul 3, 1911, "Official Program Of The Day's Celebration"; "Official Program, First Annual Celebration, Jul 4, 1911"; Gia, "Bakersfield Breweries, 1866-1920, v5"

[135] BC, Jul 5, 1911, "Buick Crew Had Narrow Escape"

[136] BC, Jun 23, 1911, "Tevis Cup Will Be Ready Tomorrow"

[137] BC, Jun 29, 1911, "Gus Schamblin Offers A Prize For The Automobile Races But The Conditions Differ From Those Governing Prizes Thus Far Offered"

[138] ME, Jan 17, 1912, "Along Automobile Row"; BC, Feb 17, 1912, Maricopa Trustees Object To Speed Of Automobile Racers"; Feb 19, 1912, "Entries Close Tomorrow Night For Washington's Birthday Road Race"; ME, Feb 20, 1912, "Thirteen Automobiles Entered In 212 Mile Race On Washington's Birthday"; Feb 22, 1954, "T.E. Klipstein, County Oilman, Dies In Hospital"; BC, Feb 24, 1912, "Here Are The Donators Who Made Big Road Race Possible"

[139] BC, Apr 30, 1912, "200 Autos At The Disposal Of The Supervisors"; May 1, 1912, "San Diego, Shasta And Santa Cruz Want Convention; Excursion This Afternoon"

[140] BC, Mar 12, 1913, "Buy Auto On Time And Pay Dealer Immediately"

[141] BC, Mar 12, 1913, "Klipstein Wins Wager On Trip To Los Angeles"; Mar 12, 1913, "Stage To Run Between Caliente And Kernville"; May 25, 1908, "Kissel Kar Wins Back The Record"

[142] DC, May 1, 1891, "The Town Of Kernville"; Kern County Tax Book, p. 23; DC, Jun 15, 1903, "The Passing Of Richard Hudnut"; ME, Jan 11, 1911, "Hudnut Driving Park Association"

[143] DC, Aug 18, 1892, "The Californian, Some Of Its History In The Early Days"; Mar 5, 1897, "In Connection With Matters Political..."; Jan 25, 1898, "There Will Be Another Daily"; Jun 2, 1898, "Entered The Standard Office"; Mar 3, 1898, "Thomas Jefferson Packard Has Moved And Says Check To The Enemy"; Lynn Hay Rudy, Old Bakersfield Sites & Landmarks, p. 28

[144] Kern County Californian, Apr 30, 1881, "Fresh Milk"; Jan 20, 1883, "Pasturage"; "Hudnut Addition To Bakersfield", Tract Map Book 1, Apr 1, 1888, Apr 7, 1888, Dec 15, 1888. County Maps, Kern County Hall Of Records; DC, Aug 11, 1895, "The Convention. A Representative And Harmonious Gathering"; Bender & Hewitt, Bakersfield Map, 1898; Bensel And Maitland, Bakersfield & Kern City Directory 1899; Los Angeles Herald, Feb 21, 1901, "Big Improvement In Bakersfield"; DC, Mar 26, 1901, "Block To Be Taken From Fire Limits"; BC, Sep 22, 1933, "Notice Of Sale Of County Real Property At Auction"; Hudnut, p. 53

[145] DC, Jun 23, 1906, "Driving Club To Be Organized"

[146] DC, Oct 20, 1906, "Hudnut Driving Association"

[147] Hudnut

[148] DC, Jun 23, 1906, "A Driving Club Will Be Organized"; Sep 28, 1906, "Hudnut Park Driving Ass'n Preparing To Incorporate"

[149] Hanford Journal, Oct 5, 1906, "The proposition presented to a number of our business people yesterday..."

[150] Hanford Sentinel, Jan 31, 1907, "Progress In Fair Circuit"; DC, Feb 14, 1907, "Appropriation For County Fairs"

[151] BC, Mar 23, 1907, "New Brick Building For Burned Cosmopolitan Block"

[152] DC, Dec 29, 1906, "First Meet To Be In February"; Jan 14, 1907, "Notice To Contractors"; Feb 20, 1907, "Contract Awarded For Driving Track"; Mar 20, 1907, "Grandstand For Race Track"; Mar 21, 1907, "Races At Hudnut Park Tomorrow";

[153] BC, Jul 12, 1907, "Richard B Will Go On Campaign"

[154] DC, Apr 6, 1907, "Good Entry Lists For Early Closing Events Of County Fair"; Mar 3, 1937, "Local Garage Man M.T. Debolt Recalls Racing Days Of Old Bakersfield 1907"

[155] BC, Jul 2, 1907, "Final Arrangements    For Fourth Complete"

[156] BC, Jul 15, 1907, "The Hudnut Club"

[157] BC, Jul 17, 1907, "Board Of Trade And Hudnut Club"

[158] BC, Sep 12, 1907, "Money For County Fair"

[159] Ibid.

[160] BC, Sep 18, 1907, "Abandon Fair And Race Meet"

[161] Sacramento Union, Sep 10, 1907, "Kern County To
The Front"; Hanford Journal, Sep 19, 1907, "The Hudnut
Driving Club Directors Yesterday..."; BC, Sep 17, 1907,
"No County Fair This Fall"; Sep 18, 1907, "Abandon Fair
And Race Meet"
[162] ME, Oct 2, 1907, Tulare County's Fair Has Opened"
[163] BC, Nov 14, 1907, "Stalls All Full At Hudnut Park";
Nov 28, 1907, "Program For The Races Today"
[164] BC, Jan 15, 1908, "Hudnut Club Plans Baseball
Grounds And Pavilion"; Feb 14, 1908, "Hudnut Club
Arranges Races"; Mar 21, 1908, "Racing At Hudnut Park
Tomorrow"; May 25, 1908, "Much Interest In Auto Race";
May 28, 1908, "Horses Fit For Sunday Races"; "May 30,
1908, "Excellent Program Of Races Offered For
Tomorrow"; Jul 6, 1908, "Record Crowd Sees Celebration"
[165] BC, Jul 6, 1908, "Record Crowd Sees Celebration"
[166] DC, Jul 13, 1891, "Charles Howard's balloon
ascension and drop..."
[167] Daily Californian, Apr 14, 1894, "Balloon Ascension";
Gia, "Bakersfield Breweries, 1866-1920, v5"
[168] DC, Jul 16, 1891, "Tehachipa [sic] Items";
Dec 1, 1900, "Agricultural Park, Bakersfield"
[169] DC, Sep 7, 1904, "Balloonist Will Jump From
5000 Feet From Mid-Air"
[170]DC, Jul 2, 1907, "Final Arrangements For Fourth
Complete"; Jul 5, 1907, "Aeronaut's Bill Is Not Paid";
Gia, "What Happened To Bakersfield's Chinese Cemetery?"
[171] BC, Jun 18, 1908, "Propose Annual County Fairs"
[172] BC, May 30, 1908. "The Merchants Association";
Jun 18, 1908, "Propose Annual County Fairs"
[173] BC, Jun 25, 1908, "Fair Association Will Sell Stock"
[174] BC, Aug 25, 1908, "More Than $2,000 Has Been
Secured For County Fair"
[175] BC, Sep 18, 1908, "40 New Stalls At The Track";
Sep 28, "H.A. Jastro To Open Fair"; Oct 1, "Democrats In
Convention. H.A. Jastro Speaks"
[176] BC, Jun 24, 1908, "Fair Association Has
Constitution"; Sep 16, 1908, "To Transfer The Hudnut
Park"; Sep 18, 1908, "Change Name Of Club";
Sep 18, 1908, "Driving Association To Become The Kern
County Agricultural Association"; ME, Oct 5, 1908,
"Order To Show Cause"

[177] ME, Jul 25, 1908; Randall & Denne, Index Atlas Of Kern County

[178] BC, Oct 7, 1908, "Exhibition And Admission Tickets To The County Fair"

[179] BC, Sep 18, 1908. "40 New Stalls At The Track";

[180] BC, Sep 2, 1908, "Official Program For Labor Day Celebration"

[181] BC, Sep 19, 1908, "Special Rates For Fair Week"; Oct 7, 1908, "Exhibition And Admission Tickets To The County Fair"

[182] BC, Jun 18, 1908, "Propose Annual County Fairs"; Sep 18, 1908, "40 New Stalls At The Track"; Sep 23, 1908, "Automobile Day At The Track"; Oct 13, 1908, "The Kern County Fair Is Formally Opened"

[183] BC, Oct 12, 1908, "List Of Exhibitors Growing Hourly"

[184] BC, Aug 11, 1909, "Hustle Work For Big Fair"; Oct 7, 1908, "Exhibition And Admission Tickets To The County Fair"

[185] BC, Oct 9, 1908, "Greatest Exhibition In History Of County"; Sunset Magazine, Jun 1911, v. 26, p. 633

[186] BC, Sep 28, 1908, "H.A. Jastro To Open Fair"; ME, Oct 13, 1908, "The Kern County Fair Is Formally Opened"

[187] BC, Oct 12, 1908, "List Of Exhibitors Growing Hourly"

[188] BC, Oct 9, 1908, "Greatest Exhibition In History Of County"

[189] ME, Oct 13, 1908, "W.C.T.U. Rest Tent At Fair Grounds"

[190] BC, Sep 28, 1908, "H.A. Jastro To Open Fair"; Morgan, "Kern County Land Company hired W.A. Eardley in 1905 as superintendent of Kern River Mills.

[191] BC, Sep 15, 1908, "All Ready For Labor Day"; Sep 28, "H.A. Jastro To Open Fair"; Oct 7, "A Big Midway And Many Attractions For The Fair"; Oct 9, "Greatest Exhibition In History Of County"; Oct 9, "Two Ostriches At The Coming Fair"; Oct 13, "The Kern County Fair Is Formally Opened"

[192] BC, Oct 1, 1908, "A Big Midway And Many Attractions For The Fair"; Oct 12, 1908, "List Of Exhibitors Growing Hourly"

[193] BC, Oct 19, 1908, "Fair Was A Great Success"

[194] BC, Oct 9, 1908, "Greatest Exhibition In History Of County"; Jul 7, 1909, "Richards' Captive Balloon For Fair On September 6"

[195] BC, Sep 23, 1908, "Automobile Day At The Track"; Oct 9, 1908, "Greatest Exhibition In History Of County"

[196] BC, Sep 23, "Automobile Day At The Track"; BC, May 25, 1908, "Much Interest In Auto Race"

[197] BC, Sep 25, 1908, "Announcement Of Fair Features"; Sep 29, 1908, "Bert Dingley May Come To Fair"; Oct 1, 1908, "A Big Midway And Many Attractions For The Fair"; ME, Oct 3, 1908, "The Kern County Fair Is Formally Opened" newspapers spelled the location both Famosa and Famoso.

[198] ME, Oct 3, 1908, "The Kern County Fair Is Formally Opened"

[199] Ibid.

[200] BC, Oct 19, 1908, "Fair Was A Great Success"

[201] BC, Nov 27, 1908, "Frank Free On Way Here"

[202] Daily Californian, Sep 19, 1899, "To Wipe Out The Malaria Belt"; Daily Californian, Feb 18, 1900, "Adios To The Panama Slough"; Feb 19, 1901, "Ordinance Against Tearing Up Streets"; Mar 26, 1901, "Block To Be Taken From Fire Limits"; ME, Jun 21, 1910, "More About City Refuse"; Gia, "Where Bakersfield Threw Its Garbage, 1872-1992"

[203] BC, Mar 17, 1909, "A Statement Of Finances"

[204] San Francisco Call, Dec 25, 1908, "Auto Track For Bakersfield"

[205] Ibid.

[206] BC, Jul 5, 1909, "A Big Crowd Enjoys Day At Picnic Grounds On Oak St."; Jun 9, 1909, "Eagles' Independence Day Celebration To Be Public"

[207] BC, Jun 19, 1909, "Fair Directors Discuss Plans"; Jul 5, "Racing By Electric Lights"

[208] Kern County Californian, Mar 9, 1889, "By Order Of J.B. Haggin"; Sanborn Fire Map, Bakersfield, July 1892; Hanford Journal, Oct 22, 1901, "Bakersfield, Oct. 21"; DC, July 31, 1902, "Power Transit And Light Company"; Los Angeles Herald, Mar 22, 1909, "Aeronautic Notes"; BC, Mar 22, 1909, "Fox And Hayden Buy A Printing Plant"; May 15, 1909, "Kites Fail, Will Use Balloon Now"; May 17, "One Picture Taken, Balloon Breaks Away"; May 24, "Oil Man And Their Talk"; May 24, "Ted Richards, The Aeronaut..."; Jan 31, 1910, "Aviator Reaches Altitude Of 1,019 Feet In Flight In Curtiss Biplane"' Parker, p. 33, 36; ME, Nov 30, 1910, "Bakersfield Will Get Natural Gas Soon"

[209] BC, Jun 14, 1909, "New Grounds Selected For Eagles' July Celebration"; Jul 5, 1909, "A Big Crowd Enjoys Day At Picnic Grounds On Oak St."

[210] BC, May 10, 1909, "Benefit Game For Aeronaut"

[211] BC, May 11, 1909, "Benefit Game On Saturday"; Jul 5, 1909, "Big Crowd At The Eagles Picnic (Continued From Page 1)"

[212] ME, Jul 4, 1909, "Want To Know About The Fair"

[213] ME, Mar 27, 1909, "Legislature Was Quite Expensive"; BC, Jul 22, 1909, "Eager To Buy Fair Shares"; Aug 13, "Are Boosting County Fair"; ME, Sep 1, 1909, "Amusements Unusually Good (Continued From Page 1)"

[214] BC, Apr 29, 1909, "Fair Directors Will Meet Soon"; May 2, "Agricultural Fair Association Formed"; BC, July 21, 1909; Southwest Contractor And Manufacturer, Jul 24, 1909, "Bakersfield: The Kern County Fair..."; ME, Sep 1, 1909, "Improvements At The County Fair"; ME, Jun 20, 1922, "William J. Doherty" (Obituary)

[215] ME, Sep 1, 1909, "Liberal Premium List Offers"; Sep 1, 1909, "Second Annual County Fair Promises To Be Great Success"

[216] ME, Sep 1, 1909, "Will Be A Success"; "Amusements Unusually Good"; "Second Annual Fair Bakersfield, September 6th To 11th Inclusive" ( Advertisement); "The County Fair– Big Addition To Last Year's Facilities For Exhibitors"

[217] ME, Sep 1, 1909, "Fast Horses For Fair Races"

[218] ME, Sep 1, 1909, "Liberal Premium List Offers"

[219] Ibid.

[220] ME, Sep 1, 1909, "Improvements At The County Fair";
Sep 1, "Many Entries Are Expected";
Sep 1, "September 6th To 11th Inclusive"
(Advertisement)

[221] ME, Sep 1, 1909, "Amusements Unusually Good
(Continued From Page 1)"

[222] Ibid.

[223] BC, Aug 20, 1909, "Fast Horses For Fair Races;
Newspapers spelled the name as both Famosa and Famoso.

[224] ME, Sep 1, 1909, "Arrange Two Auto Road Races
For Fair Week"

[225] BC, Aug 20, 1909, "Fast Horses For Fair Races";
ME, Sep 1, 1909, "Amusements Unusually
Good Continue From Page 1)"

[226] Ibid.

[227] BC, Jul 7, 1909, "Richards. Captive Balloon For
Fair On September 6";

[228] ME, Sep 1, 1909, "Amusements Unusually Good";
Sep 1, 1909, "Plenty Of Fun Is Promised On
The Midway"; Sep 1, 1909, "September 6th To 11th
Inclusive" (Full Page Advertisement); Parker

[229] BC, Sep 13, 1909, "The County Fair"; Sep 27, 1909,
"Fair Figures Show $32 Gain"

[230] ME, Dec 23, 1909, "Barney Oldfield Will Race Here
Next Wednesday"; ME, Dec 30, 1909, "Oldfield Breaks
The Record At Hudnut Park"

[231] ME, Dec 4, 1909, "Fair Directors Hold Meeting";
BC, Dec 4, 1909, "Earlier Date Is Planned For Fair"; BC,
Dec 17, "May Mortgage Hudnut Park"

[232] ME, May 9, 1909, "Bakersfield Has ..."

[233] ME, Sep 1, 1909, "Progress On Road Is Satisfactory";
Los Angeles Times, Dec 18, 1911, "State Highway
Commission"; Jan 28, 1912, "Our Neighbors. Why KC Is
The Land Of Opportunities."

[234] ME, Jan 30, 1910, "Hamilton Flies In Curtiss Biplane
At Hudnut Park Today"; BC, Jan 26, 1910, "Merchants
Back Aviation Meet"

[235] BC, Jan 26, 1910, "Merchants Back Aviation Meet";
ME, Feb 1, 1920, "The Biplane At Close Range (Continued
From Page 1.)"

[236] BC, Jan 26, 1910, "Merchants Back Aviation Meet"; ME, Feb 1, 1910, "Thousands See Aviator Fly At Hudnut Park"

[237] BC, Jan 31, 1910, "8,000 Persons Wildly Cheer Hamilton In Airship Flight"; Jan 31, 1910, "Hamilton Sports In The Air (Continued From Page 1)"

[238] Ibid.

[239] BC, Jan 31, 1910, "8,000 Persons Wildly Cheer Hamilton In Airship Flight"

[240] BC, Jan 31, 1910, "Parachute Leap Is Made Following C.K. Hamilton's Flights In Curtiss Biplane"

[241] Ibid.

[242] BC, Feb 22, 1910, "Wireless Fails To Reach Park"

[243] BC, Feb 14, 1910, "Wireless Phone In Parachute Leap"; Feb 21, 1900, "Ted Richards Ready For Balloon Flight With Wireless Telephone"; Feb 23, 1910, "Good Events At Hudnut Park"

[244] BC, Apr 8, 1910, "Track Teams On Edge For Meet"; ME, Apr 9, 1910, "Plan To Bring 2 Aeroplanes And Dirigible Balloon Here April 30"; Apr 17, 1910, "Kruse Tract No More For Circus"

[245] ME, Aug 14, 1910, "Back To The Farm"; DC, Sep 17, 1910, "Kern's Oil Exhibit In Great Demand"; ME, Sep 18, 1910, "Oil Exhibit Is In Big Demand"

[246] BC, Jun 19, 1909, "Fair Directors Discuss Plans"; Jul 23, 1909, "Car Line Loop Will Not Be Ready For Fair"; Mar 29, 1910, "Bailey Opposes Gift Franchise To Corporation"

[247] BC, May 9, 1910, "Commencement's Chief Feature"; Jun 7, 1910, "Model Farm School Plan Presented To Supervisors"; Wallace, p. 56

[248] BC, Jun 8, 1910, "Hudnut Park Bought For Agricultural Farm", Jun 10, 1910, "Farm School Is Much Commended"; Aug 2, 1910, "Begin Work On The Farm School"

[249] ME, Sep 28, 1910, "Changing Hudnut Park Into High School Farm"; Sep 30, 1910, "Agriculture For Freshman"; Oct 1, 1910, "Transform Park Into A Model Ranch"

[250] BC, Nov 21, 1924, "Motion Pictures Taken At High School, Feature Agricultural Development Work"; "Activities Of Kern County Union High School Department Of Agriculture", May 1931, p. 47-51; Gia, "Dormitories_Bhs_-1915_1955_V7_"

[251] BC, Sep 29, 1933, "County Plan To Trade Property Rights Opposed"; Oct 25, 1934, "Statement Of Minutes Of The Meeting Of The Board Of Supervisors"; Gia, "The Jails At Havilah And Bakersfield (California), 1866-1963"

[252] BC, Oct 14, 1933, "Three Lanes Of Traffic, Larger Subway Slated"; Kern County Fire Department

[253] BC, Jul 5, 1911, "Great Auto Races That Will Lead To Greater Still"

[254] ME, Apr 26, 1913, "New Race Track Fills Popular Demand"

[255] BC, Apr 5, 1912, "Bakersfield's Motordrome Is Assured"; ME, Feb 8, 1913, "Project Given Impetus And Assured Of Wide Support"; ME, Apr 26, 1913, "Jastro Has Aided Fair Association In Their Many Toils"; April 26, 1913, "Be A Real Booster-Buy Kern Co. Fair Ass'n Stock"

[256] BC, Apr 5, 1912, "Bakersfield's Motordome [sic] Is Assured; The Race Association Purchases The Old Race Track"; ME, Apr 6, 1912, "Old Fair Grounds Purchased For A Motordrome"

[257] BC, Jan 14, 1914, "Title Is Now With Kern County Fair Association"; Feb 7, 1913, "Annual Fairs Again"; ME, Feb 8, 1913, "Project Given Impetus And Assured Of Wide Support"; April 26, 1913, "Be A Real Booster-Buy Kern Co. Fair Ass'n Stock"

[258] ME, Apr 26, 1913, "New Race Track Fills Popular Demand"

[259] April 26, 1913, "Be A Real Booster-Buy Kern Co. Fair Ass'n Stock"

[260] BC, Apr 5, 1912, "Bakersfield's Motordome [Sic] Is Assured; The Race Association Purchases The Old Race Track"; ME, Feb 8, 1913, "Project Given Impetus And Assured Of Wide Support"

[261] ME, Apr 6, 1912, "Old Fairgrounds Purchased For Motordrome"; Apr 26, 1913, "New Race Track Fills Popular Demand"; Apr 27, 1913,"Drainage Of Fairgrounds"

[262] ME, Feb 23, 1913, "Bakersfield Will Soon Have Finest Racetrack In State"; BC, Jan 6, 1925, "Review Of Automobile Racing In Nation Given By Derkum At Club Luncheon Here"

[263] ME, May 1, 1913, "Fair Association To Offer City Site For Park. To Hold Celebration On July Fourth"

[264] ME, Apr 26, 1913, "New Race Track Fills Popular Demand"; Apr 27, 1913, "7000 See Opening Races On New Speedway"

[265] Los Angeles Herald, Apr 19, 1913, "Big Speed Card, Bakersfield's Auto Lure"; Apr 25, 1913, "Barney Meets Teddy In Fiat"

[266] BC, Jan 10, 1913, "Will Hold Motor Races At New Park"; Los Angeles Herald, Apr 19, 1913, "Big Speed Card, Bakersfield's Auto Lure"; ME, Apr 27, 1913, "7000 See Opening Races On New Speedway"; ME, May 14, 1913, "Association Calls Off Negotiations For Valley Race"

[267] Los Angeles Herald, Apr 19, 1913, "Big Speed Card, Bakersfield's Auto Lure"; ME, Apr 27, 1913, "7000 See Opening Races On New Speedway"; BC, Apr 28, 1913, "Oldfield Breaks A World's Record On New Track"

[268] ME, Apr 27, 1913, "7000 See Opening Races On New Speedway"

[269] ME, Apr 27, 1913, "Oldfield Goes Mile In 49 Seconds"; Apr 27, 1913, "Fifty Mile Race Today For $5,000..."

[270] Los Angeles Herald, Apr 19, 1913, "Big Speed Card, Bakersfield's Auto Lure"; ME, Apr 27, 1913, "7000 See Opening Races On New Speedway"; BC, Apr 28, 1913, "Oldfield Breaks A World's Record On New Track"

[271] ME, Mar 12, 1913, "Great Road Race Via Valley July Fourth"; "May 14, 1913, "Association Calls Off Negotiations For Valley Race"

[272] Los Angeles Times, Jun 1, 1913, "Twenty-Five Thousand Purse Lures Fast Cars"; Jun 30, 1913, "Race Course Patrol Ready"

[273] Los Angeles Times, Jun 13, 1913, "The Times
Pathfinder Blazing Race Trail"
[274] BC, Jul 4, 1913, "Table Showing Time Of The First
Thirty-Five Cars To Arrive Here"
[275] BC, Mar 12, 1913, "Cars Due To Reach Here
At 9 A.M., July 4, 1913, Going To San Francisco"; Los
Angeles Herald, Apr 19, 1913, "Big Speed Card,
Bakersfield's Auto Lure";
Los Angeles Times, Apr 25, 1913, "Barney Meets
Teddy In Fiat"
[276] ME, May 14, 1913, "Association Calls Off
Negotiations For Valley Race"; Jul 5, 1913, "Overland,
Studebaker And National Bring Home Honors In
The Local Speed Contests"
[277] ME, Jul 5, 1913, "Overland, Studebaker And National
Bring Home Honors In The Local Speed Contests"
[278] Los Angeles Herald, Jul 5, 1913, "$50 Car,
Second, Wins College For Driver"; ME, Jul 5, 1913,
"20 Cars Reach Sacramento By Sunset; Buick Sets New
Mark Los Angeles To Bakersfield";
"Overland, Studebaker, And National Bring Home
Honors In The Local Speed Contests"; "Crowd Turns Out
Early To See Racers Check In At Speedway"
[279] BC, Sep 29, 1913, "5000 People See Races At Track On
Sunday"
[280] BC, Aug 5, 1913, "Oldfield May Be Here For
Land-Air Meet"
[281] BC, Oct 2, 1913, A Week Of Festivities And
Nation-Wide Advertising Of The City And County
Projected By The Citizens"
[282] ME, Oct 9, 1913, "Old-Home Week Started On Way
(Continued From Page One.)"
[283] Ibid.
[284] Ibid.
[285] BC, Jan 14, 1914, "County Advertising Home Coming
Week"; ME, Jan 23, 1914, "Old Home Week Boost Labels
Bring Publicity To County"; BC, Apr 3, 1914, "Work On
Bleachers Started This Morning"; Apr 8, 1914, "Home
Coming Week Revives Horse Racing"; Apr 27, 1914,
"Citizens Unanimous In Praise Of Home Coming, Voice
Expressions As To Benefits To The Community"

[286] BC, Apr 20, 1914, "First Day Program For Home Coming Festivities"; Apr 20, "Steam Whistles Will Usher In Celebration"; Apr 21, "Official Home Coming Program"; Apr 21, "Bakersfield Extends Hearty Greeting To Home Coming Guests"; Apr 22, "Christofferson Is First To Arrive Here In Air Race"; Apr 22, 1914, "Hundreds Of Gorgeous Floats In Parade Start The Week Of Festival"; ME, Apr 22, 1914, "The Serious Question"

[287] BC, Apr 23, 1914, "Rodeo Started Off With Flourish By Cowboys On Parade"

[288] BC, Apr 11, 1914, "East Bakersfield And The General Committees Work In Harmony For Carnival Features For East Side"; Apr 21, 1914, "Official Home Coming Program; ME, Apr 21, 1914, "Bakersfield Extends Hearty Greeting To Home Coming Guests"; Boyd, "Homecoming Week Airplane Race"

[289] ME, Apr 24, 1914, "Best Riding In West Seen At Bakersfield Rodeo"

[290] Kern County Weekly Californian, Aug 14, 1875, "A General Rodeo Has Been Going On..."

[291] ME, Apr 24, 1914, "Stolen Ford Car Was Recovered At Kingsburg"

[292] ME, Apr 28, 1912, "Don't Forget To Visit Kellogg Orange Acres" (Advertisement); Apr 9, 1914, "Trustees Will Grant Permission To Hold The Street Carnival"; BC, Apr 20, 1914, "First Day Program For Home Coming Festivities"; Apr 20, "Steam Whistles Will Usher In Celebration"; ME, Apr 20, 1914, "Carnival Tents Go Up Today", "Two Carnival Companies Are On The Ground And Erecting Their Tents"; BC, Apr 21. 1914, "Official Home Coming Program"; Pacific Reporter, v.65. "Southern Pacific Company v. State Of Arizona", (152), p. 303

[293] BC, Apr 21, 1914, "Official Home Coming Program"; Apr 22, "Christofferson Is First To Arrive Here In Air Race"

[294] BC, Apr 23, 1914, "Rybitski May Ask Second Place On Protest In Big Air Race"; ME, Jul 5, 1914, "Aviator Rybitsky Who Made Valley Flight, Is Killed"

[295] BC, Dec 3, 1913, "Half-Mile Track Among The Many Improvements At The Fair Grounds"; Jan 14, 1914, "Title Is Now With Kern County Fair Association"

[296] BC, Apr 11, 1914, "Bakersfield Snubbed Oldfield, Barney Is Mad And Shows It"; ME, Apr 16, 1914, "Plan To Have All Ford Race"; BC, Apr 22, 1914, "Oldfield In Cyclone Fiat Beats Aeroplane; Makes Record In 5-Mile Trial"

[297] BC, Apr 22, 1914, "Oldfield In Cyclone Fiat Beats Aeroplane

[298] BC, April 25, 1914, "Los Angeles Visitors, 150 Strong, Storm Bakersfield And Boost For City, San Diego Represented, Too"

[299] BC, Apr 27, 1914, "Citizens Unanimous In Praise Of Home Coming, Voice Expressions As To Benefits To The Community"

[300] BC, Jan 12, 1914, "Will Transfer Title To Race Track Grounds"; Jan 14, 1914, "Title Is Now With Kern County Fair Association"; May 16, 1914, "Kern County Will Have First Place In Exhibits At The Fair"; Jul 1, 1914, "Legal Notices"; Jul 17, 1914, "Agricultural And Horticultural County Fair This Fall"; Aug 3, 1914, "Farmers Agree To Plans For Big Kern County Fair Next October"; Oct 7, 1914, "It Might Have Been"

[301] BC, Oct 17, 1914, "Annual Pure Food Show As Well As Exhibition Of County Products To Take Place Of Proposed Fair."

[302] Ibid.

[303] BC, Oct 17, 1914, "Annual Pure Food Show As Well As Exhibition Of County Products To Take Place Of Proposed Fair."; ME, Oct 29, 1914, "Pure Food Show Is Open Evenings"

[304] Dispatch Democrat, Aug 28, 1914, "The World's First Indoor Aeroplane Flight, Panama-Pacific International Exposition, 1915"

[305] ME, Oct 24, 1914, "Horse Races At Race Track Today"; Nov 1, 1914, "Lincoln Beachey And Barney Oldfield Will Contest In The Great..."; BC, Nov 16, 1914, "Lincoln Beachey To Fly At The Race Track On Next Sunday Afternoon"

[306] BC, Nov 23, 1914, "Lincoln Beachey Proves Himself Master Of The Air"

[307] BC, Jan 6, 1915, "Notice Of Assessment"; ME, Feb 11, 1915, "San Joaquin Valley Briefs"; BC, Feb 16, 1915, "Kern County Day At The Fair"; Mar 22, 1915, "Kern Wild Flower Day Was Delano Woman's Idea"; Aug 13, 1915, "Many Visitors To Kern County Exhibit"; Aug 23, 1915, "Mineral Exhibit Of Kern County At Exposition"; Sep 7, 1915, "Good Crowd Takes In Motorcycle Events"

[308] BC, Oct 17, 1914, "Annual Pure Food Show As Well As Exhibition Of County Products To Take Place Of Proposed Fair"; Mar 23, 1915, "Home Coming Celebration Last Of April"; ME, Apr 11, 1915, "Spring Festival" (Advertisement); BC, Apr 28, 1915, "Home Coming Ball"

[309] BC, Oct 3, 1915, "Big Event Planned For Washington's Birthday"

[310] Ibid.

[311] ME, Feb 9, 1915, "Elks Will Pull Off Auto Race, Ball Game On February 22"

[312] BC, Sep 25, 1915, "Fresno Fair Feature Innovation This Year"; ME, Sep 26, 1915, "District Fair-Fresno"; Oct 6, 1915, "Fresno Fair Receipts"; US Department Of Commerce, Bureau Of The Census

[313] BC, Jul 3, 1916, "Carnival Spirit To Rule City This Evening"

[314] BC, Jul 5, 1916, "Merry Throng Dances Out Best Fourth Celebration Ever Held In This City; Pleasing Exercises"

[315] BC, Mar 25, 1916, "Kern County Fair Is Topic At Meeting"; Mar 27, 1916, "Agricultural Fair Association Plan Is Approved By Farm Bureau"; Pacific Rural Press, Apr 1, 1916, "Kern County Fair Association"

[316] First Annual Report Of The State Market Director Of California, p. 106

[317] ME, Oct 25, 1916, "Farmers Lead In Fair Association"; BC, Dec 19, 1916, "$3184.65 Net Profit From First County Fair Shown In Reports"

[318] BC, Sep 12, 1916, "Grounds Plans For The County Fair Are Adopted"; ME, Sep 23, 1916, "Moose Lodge Reserves Space At County Fair"; Oct 17, 1916, "Thoroughbred Stock Arriving For Display"; BC, Oct 23, 1916, "First Annual Fair Ready To Swing Open Gates To Thousands"

[319] BC, Sep 24,1916, "Fair Directors Find Enthusiasm On Every Hand"

[320] Oxnard Daily Courier, Sep 12, 1916, "Ventura County Fair Assn. At Seaside Park"

[321] BC, Oct 19, 1916, "Burke Appeals To Fair Exhibitors To Act Now"

[322] ME, Oct 1, 1916, "The Farmers Show" (Advertisement); BC, Oct 23, 1916, "First Annual Fair Ready To Swing Open Gates To Thousands"; Oct 28, 1916, "Tonight Is Carnival Night At Fair. Big Exposition To Be Open All Day Tomorrow"

[323] BC, Sep 24,1916, "Fair Directors Find Enthusiasm On Every Hand"; ME, Oct 17, 1916, "Thoroughbred Stock Arriving For Display"; BC, Oct 19, 1916, "Burke Appeals To Fair Exhibitors To Act Now"; Oct 28, 1916, "Tonight Is Carnival Night At Fair"; Oct 28, 1916, "Big Exposition To Be Open All Day Tomorrow"

[324] BC, Oct 24, 1916, "Gates Of Great Agricultural Fair Swing Wide At Formal Opening Of Exposition Today"

[325] BC, Oct 19, 1916, "Burke Appeals To Fair Exhibitors To Act Now"

[326] BC, Oct 28, 1916, "Movies Of Great Parade Are Taken"

[327] BC, Sep 24, 1916, "Fair Directors Find Enthusiasm On Every Hand"; Oct 28, "Tonight Is Carnival Night At Fair; Big Exposition To Be Open All Day Tomorrow"

[328] ME, Sep 23, 1916, "Farm Tractors Will Be Demonstrated Here"; Oct 17, 1916, "Thoroughbred Stock Arriving For Display"; Oct 24, 1916, "Fair Program Today"; Oct 24, 1916, "Fair Directors Find Enthusiasm On Every Hand"

[329] BC, Sep 12, 1916, "Grounds Plans For The County Fair Are Adopted"; ME, Sep 23, 1916, "Farm Tractors Will Be Demonstrated Here"

[330] BC. Sep 28, 1908, "Good Exhibits For The Fair"

[331] ME, Oct 17, 1916, "Thoroughbred Stock Arriving For Display"; Oct 24, 1916, "Here's Program Of Attractions For This Week"

[332] ME, Oct 26, 1916, "Big Crowd Expected, Stores Will Be Closed'

[333] BC, Oct 19, 1916, "Entries Close At Midnight Next Monday";

334 ME, Oct 29, 1916, "World's Record For Bakersfield In Ten Mile Race, Is Claim"; Dick, Auto Racing In The Shadow Of The Great War; H.C.S. came from Harry Clayton Stutz' initials.

335 ME, Oct 24, 1916, "Fair Program Today"; Oct 24, "Farmers' Day To Be Opening Event"

336 BC, Oct 28, 1916, "Tonight Is Carnival Night At Fair; Big Exposition To Be Open All Day Tomorrow"

337 BC, Oct 24, 1916, "Gates Of Great Agricultural Fair Swing Wide At Formal Opening Of Exposition Today"; ME, Oct 24, 1916, "Here's Program Of Attractions For This Week"; Oct 26, 1916, "Big Crowd Expected, Stores Will Be Closed"

338 ME, Nov 5, 1916, "$10,140 Fair Bills Have Been Cleared"

339 BC, Dec 19, 1916, "$3184.65 Net Profit From First County Fair Shown In Reports"

340 BC, Oct 25, 1916, "Judge Frees Man Who Wants To See Fair"

341 BC, Sep 25, 1916, "In Appreciation"

342 BC, Sep 24, 1916, "Petition To Have County Own Property"

343 BC, Oct 13, 1917, "Fair Pavilion"; Oct 24, 1916, "Petitions To Have County Own Property"; ME, Oct 26, 1916, "County Fair Grounds"

344 ME, Oct 13, 1917, "A Good Fair"

345 ME, Oct 26, 1916, "County Fair Grounds"

346 Ibid.

347 BC, Apr 14, 1917, "Spirit Of Our Patriotism"

348 ME, Sep 28, 1917, "Three Bands Will Play Opening Day";

349 BC, Oct 6, 1917, "Horses Owned Here Figure In Race Meet Today"; Oct 11, 1922, "Avenue Of Fine Poplars Marked South Boundary Of Jewett Property"

350 BC, July 11, 1917, "Fair Premiums To Total $15,853"; ME, Sep 28, 1917, "Three Bands Will Play Opening Day"; ME, Sep 28, 1917, "County Fair Story"; Oct 13, 1917, "A Good Fair"; Oct 13 1917, "Fair Entertainment"; BC, Dec 8, 1916, "El Monte Has A Population Of Possibly..."

351 ME, Oct 14, 1917, "In Every Farm Center"

[352] BC, Oct 12, 1917, "Fair Pavilion Projected By Local Auto Dealers"

[353] BC, Aug 8, 1946, Pipefuls By Jim Day"

[354] BC, Oct 12, 1917, "Fair Pavilion Projected By Local Auto Dealers"; Apr 30, 1918, "To Build    Pavilion At Kern Fair Grounds"

[355] BC, Sep 1, 1918, "Airplane Races With Motorcycle At Track Today"; Sep 2, 1918, "Tice Captures All Honor In Motor Race Events"; Oct 22, 1918, "Bill Pickens, King of Racing Promoters, and Jack Prince..."; Oct 26, 1918, "Sports Chatter"; Apr 9, 1924, "Funeral Is Held For Edward Tice"

[356] BC, Oct 17, 1918, "23 Influenza Cases In City Reported, Says Dr. P.J. Cuneo"; ME, Oct 20, 1918, "Thousands See Aviators Land"; Oct 20, 1918, "Not Under Check Yet"

[357] BC, May 28, 1919, "May Recruit Cowboys Into U.S. Service"

[358] BC, Sep 23, 1920, "See The Great San Joaquin Classic"

[359] ME, Sep 14, 1919, "Boxing, Racing At Hanford Fair"; Dec 29, 1919, "County Fair Favored By Kern C. Of C."

[360] ME, Oct 15, 1920, "Cotton Day Program"; Oct 16, 1920, "Pageant Will Form In 5 Divisions Led By Municipal Band"; Turner, p. 41

[361] ME, Oct 15, 1920, "Bakersfield Will Open Hospitable Doors To Visitors"

[362] BC, Sep 26, 1921, "Boys' Club Will Stage Fair And Livestock Show"

[363] ME, Sep 11, 1921, " 'Ag' Department Denotes Growth Of High School"

[364] BC, Oct 5, 1922, "Program Of Events For Afternoon"

[365] Ibid.

[366] Karpe

[367] BC, Sep 15, 1922, "The Boys' Fair"

[368] BC, Aug 17, 1922,"The County Fair"

[369] BC, Aug 29, 1923, "All Ready For Weed Patch Fair"

[370] ME, Sep 2, 1923, "Weed Patch Fair Mecca For Three Thousand Persons"

[371] BC, Sep 11, 1923, "Elks To Banquet In New Building"; Oct 27, 1923, "Big Elks' Rodeo Opens With Best Talent In West"; BC, Oct 29, 1923, "Keen Competition On Final Day Of Annual Elk's Fiesta"; Will Rogers

[372] BC, Aug 24, 1923, "All Department Can't Flourish At Once, Merchant's Reminder"

[373] BC, Mar 29, 1924, "Kern County Farm Center Feels Alarm Over Spread"; Oct 5, 1924, "The Prod Of Adversity"

[374] BC, Oct 15, 1924, "Fairgrounds Are Leased To Paul Derkum; Plans Big Improvement"

[375] BC, Apr 14, 1916, "Moonlight Picnic"; May 9, 1925, "Barney Oldfield Is Official Starter"; May 9, 1925, "Speed Kings Ready For Flag"; Oct 23, 1924, "Money, Men And Mules Transform Old Race Track Into Speedway"; Nov 25, 1924, "Los Angeles Men Inspect Speedway, Success Assured"

[376] BC, Jan 6, 1925, "Review Of Automobile Racing In Nation Given By Derkum At Club Luncheon Here"; Mar 10, 1925, "Plans For County Fair Progressing"; ME, Apr 22, 1925, "Opening Of New Track Postponed"; BC, Apr 30, 1925, "Stage Set For Great Olympiad Tomorrow"

[377] BC, May 9, 1925, "Speed Kings Ready For Flag"

[378] BC, May 9, 1925, "Kemp Breaks Old Speedway Record"

[379] BC, Mar 21, 1925, "New Speedway May Be Completed Soon"; Sep 5, 1925, "S.P. Laying New Track For Fair"; Sep 22, 1925, "County Fair Directors In Session To Form Program"; Gia, "Henry A. Jastro, Commodore Of Kern County"

[380] ME, May 17, 1925, "Premium Books To Be Mailed Out In Very Short Time"; May 17, 1925, "Great Crowds Expected Here Next October"

[381] ME, May 17, 1925, "Many Features To Entertain During Kern County Fair"; BC, Sep 22, 1925, "County Fair Directors In Session To Form Program"; Blue And White, Oct 6, 1925

[382] BC, Sep 25, 1950, "Old Records Show Evolution Of County Fair During Nearly Half Century Since 1902"

[383] ME, Nov 10, 1925, "$27,203 Deficit For County Fair Shows In Report"

[384] BC, Nov 9, 1925, "Program For Armistice Day"

[385] ME, Nov 3, 1925, "Armistice Day Celebration Here Will Be One Of Biggest Events Ever Sponsored By Local Legion"

[386] BC, Nov 12, 1925, "Battle Of Argonne Brings Armistice Celebration To Dazzling Conclusion Here"

[387] ME, Nov 3, 1925, "Wagy Announces Plan As Feasible Manner Of Acquiring Ground"; 15th District Agricultural Association, Kern County Fair

[388] BC, Nov 9, 1925, "Fair Directors Petition For Purchase Of County Ground By Supervisors"

[389] Ibid.

[390] Ibid.

[391] Ibid.

[392] ME, Dec 28, 1925, "Kern May Acquire Fair Site At Approximately $123,000"; BC, Jan 5, 1926, "Derkum Issues Statement For Public On Fair Ground Problem"

[393] BC, Jan 5, 1926, "Derkum Issues Statement For Public On Fair Ground Problem"

[394] BC, Feb 9, 1926, "Final Decision On Purchase Of Fairgrounds Is Again Deferred"

[395] BC, Mar 2, 1926, "Delano Business Men Are Against Kern Purchasing Local Speedway"

[396] BC, Mar 23, 1926, "Speedway Of Paul Derkum Included In Total Price"

[397] BC, May 2, 1926, "Junior Olympiad Here Tomorrow"

[398] Ibid.

[399] BC, Jul 1, 1926, "Kern Fair Conducts Meet"

[400] BC, Jul 5, 1926, "Supervisors Of Kern County To Close Purchase Of Fairgrounds"

[401] BC, Jul 6, 1926, "Fairgrounds And Speedway Bought By Kern Supervisors"; Jul 19, 1926, "Board Supervisors Complete Purchase Of Fair Site Here"; Jul 20, 1926, "Kern Pays Fair Board For Site With Greenbacks"; ME, Jul 20, 1926, "County Invests $106,000 In Fair Site And Shafter Farm"

[402] BC, Jul 6, 1926, "Fairgrounds And Speedway Bought By Kern Supervisors"; Jul 7, 1926, "A Responsibility"

[403] BC, Jul 9, 1926, "Supervisors Of County May Use Old Structures At Fair Grounds"; Jul 10, 1926, "Improvement Of Grounds Delayed"

[404] BC, May 24, 1926, "May Let Bid For Fair Premium Book"

[405] BC, Sep 17, 1926, "Kern Fair Success; No Rain Insurance"

[406] BC, Aug 24, 1926, "Leveling Of Fairgrounds Now Nearing Completion"

[407] BC, Jul 27, 1926, "Fair Directors Give Contracts"; Jul 10, 1926, "Improvement Of Grounds Delayed"; Aug 13, 1926, "Far Exhibit Will Be Kept In Cold Storage To Insure Quality"

[408] BC, Jul 15, 1926, "Fair Directors Complete Plans For Housing Of Many Exhibits"; Jul 21, 1926, "Increase Space At Fairgrounds For Exhibits At September Show"

[409] BC, Aug 9, 1926, "C.W. Nelson Speaks At Boosters Club"; Aug 26, 1926, "Work Being Rushed To Make Park One Of Most Conveniently Laid Out Of Any In State Of California" Sep 13, 1926, "Kern County Fair Opens At 10 O'clock (Continued From Page One)"; Bates

[410] BC, Sep 28, 1926, "Kern County Fair Board Holds Meet"

[411] BC, Oct 12, 1926, "Financial Report Of 1926 Kern County Fair Shows $3967 Deficit"

[412] BC, Aug 18, 1927, "Estimate Kern Population At 90,000; Growth Shown By Poll"

[413] BC, July 11, 1927, "Fair Premiums To Total $15,853"

[414] BC, Sep 11, 1927, "The County Fair"

[415] BC, Mar 10, 1927, "Club To Exhibit County Fossils"; Aug 11, 1927, "Lions Club Makes Plans For Museum"; Sep 19, 1927, "Board Hears Plans For C. Of C. Home"; Sep 5, 1927, "The Proposed Library"; "Sep 19, 1927, "Check Receipts Of County Fair"; Oct 18 1927, "Approve Plans For C.C. Building"; Oct 20, 1927, "Splendid New Home For C. Of C. At Fairgrounds"; Dec 3, 1927, "Commerce Body Reviews Edict Of Fire Board"; Dec 10, 1927, "Lions Club May Mark Historical Sites In County With Monument"; Feb 23, 1928, "Kern Pioneers Will Assemble To Aid Museum Plans Of Club"; Mar 6, 1929, "County Park As Site Of Museum Urged By Hart"; Gia, One Hundred Years At Hart Park, 1890-1990

[416] BC, Sep 12, 1927, "Finest Display In History Of Kern Ready For Event"

[417] Ibid.

[418] BC, Sep 14, 1927, "Gate Check Shows 15,000 See Exhibits"; Sep 12, 1927, "Finest Display In History Of Kern Ready For Event"; ME, Sep 13, 1927, "Program For Today At Fair"; Sep 13, 1927, "Program For Today At Fair"; Sep 13, 1927, "Children Free Guests At The Fair"; Sep 15, 1927, "Expect Fair Attendance Records To Fall"

[419] BC, Sep 19, 1927, "Check Receipts Of County Fair"

[420] ME, Oct 2, 1927, "Offers Finance Plan For Fair"

[421] BC, Nov 29, 1926, "Fairgrounds Work Planned, Sanatorium Building Ordered"; ME, Jan 11, 1927, "State Will Start Work On Chester Avenue Footbridge"; BC, Oct 18, 1927, "Ask $50,000 Fund Used For New Kern Highway"; Oct 20, 1927, "Splendid New Home For C Of C. At Fairgrounds"

[422] BC, Sep 19, 1927, "Board Hears Plans For C. Of C. Home"; Oct 18 1927, "Approve Plans For C.C. Building"; Oct 20, 1927, "Splendid New Home For C. Of C. At Fairgrounds"

[423] BC, Nov 18, 1927, "Commerce Body Now In Office At Fairgrounds"; Mar 4, 1928, "Celebration To Mark Dedication Of C. Of C. Plant"; Mar 25, 1928, "Plan Dedication Celebration For C. Of C. Building"; Apr 23, 1928, "Funds Allotted For Completing Drainage Plan At Fairgrounds"

[424] BC, Sep 14, 1928, "Replies Are Received From "Pigeongrams"

[425] BC, Sep 12, 1928, "Fine Art Exhibit At Fair Praised"; Sep 13, 1928, "Capacity Crowds Throng Huge Exhibit Areas"

[426] BC, Sep 13, 1928, "Poultry Display Fair Sensation"

[427] BC, Sep 12, 1928, "Fair Attendance Records Broken"; ME, Sep 14, 1927, "Gate Check Shows 15,000 See Exhibits"; BC, Sep 29, 1928, "Fair Sets Record"

[428] BC, Aug 30, 1929, "Canvas Crew Starts Job At Fairgrounds"; Oct 25, 1929, "Notices To Contractors"

[429] June Dooley Rodriguez letter to Gilbert Peter Gia, Apr 2009

[430] BC, Sep 5, 1929, "Varied Program Of Events"

[431] BC, Sep 5, 1929, "Varied Program Of Events Scheduled (Continued)"; Sep 10, 1929, "Program Varied On First Day Of Great Exposition"

[432] BC, Sep 16, 1929, "Final Report To Be Made Public Following Meet Kern Executives"

[433] BC, May 20, 1930, "Kern Speedway To Be Perfect Avers Manager"

[434] BC, Sep 5, 1930, "Workmen Hang Exhibit Tents At Fairgrounds"; Sep 29, 1930, "Record-Breaking Throng Attends Exposition For Closing Events"

[435] BC, Sep 6, 1930, "City Decorated In Anticipation Of County Fair"; Sep 25, 1930, "Nominee For Governor Assures Kern County Interest In Problem"

[436] BC, Sep 6, 1930, "Garden Club's Big Flower Show To Be Held At Fair"; Sep 20, 1930, "Sunshine Featured In Novelty Program"; Sep 24, 1930, "All Of Bakersfield Will Be At The Fair Tomorrow"; Sep 25, 1930, "Dixie Pointer And Heroakel Take Big Events First Day"

[437] BC, Sep 25, 1930, "Nominee For Governor Assures Kern County Interest In Problem"

[438] BC, Nov 1 1930, "Drivers Testing Speedy Cars At Track; Greatest List In History"; Jan 1, 1931, "President O.A. Kommers Outlines Achievements During Season Of 1930"

[439] BC, Jan 1, 1931, "President O.A. Kommers Outlines Achievements During Season Of 1930"

[440] Ibid.

[441] BC, Oct 14, 1931, "County Work Camp Will Feed Hungry Transients (Continued From Page One)"

[442] BC, Oct 14, 1931, "Transients Will Be Fed After Hour On Woodpile"; Apr 18, 1932, "Find Body Of Unknown Man At Camp"

[443] BC, Sep 23, 1931, "Tulare Invites Kern People To Fair"

[444] BC, Apr 18, 1932, "Find Body Of Unknown Man At Camp"

[445] BC, Aug 4, 1932, "500 Barrels Of Flour Given To Jobless; Added Supply Ordered"

[446] BC, Oct 4, 1932, "Great Barbecue And Rodeo Will Be Held To Aid Lions' Milk Fund"

[447] BC, Aug 30, 1932, "Equipment For Kern Rodeo And Frontier Parade Is Being Sought"; Nov 11, 1932, "Colorful Western Days To Be Relived During Big Kern Rodeo"; Apr 13, 1933, "Wild Steers And Untamed Horses Will Show Here"

[448] BC, Jan 20, 1933, "Plan Junk-Heap Car Race; Motorized Wrecks To Compete"

[449] BC, Jan 19, 1933, "Men Of Many Colors And Creeds Gathered At Kern Labor Camp"

[450] Ibid.

[451] BC, Apr 21, 1933, "Community Takes On Air Of Old West For Big Round-Up"

[452] BC, Apr 18, 1933, "Tribe Of Indian To Locate At Fairgrounds For Rodeo"; Capistrano Dispatch, May 14, 2010, "A Bit Of Hollywood Back Near 'Little Hollywood", Https://Www.Thecapistranodispatch.Com/A-Bit-Of-Hollywood-Back-Near-Little-Hollywood/

[453] Los Angeles Times, Jun 2, 1991, "Hollywood Drama : A Historical Neighborhood In San Juan Capistrano"

[454] BC, Dec 27, 1933, "Drunkenness In Public Will Be Banned By City. Approve Sewer"

[455] June Dooley Rodriguez letter to Gilbert Peter Gia, Apr 2009

[456] BC, May 11, 1933. "Labor Camp Meals Served At Only Three Cents Each"; Sep 8, 1933, "Tentative Improvements For Kern County Planned"

[457] BC, Jun 29, 1933, "Technicality Only Basis For Action"

[458] BC, Sep 29, 1933, "Livestock Show Scheduled Soon"

[459] Ibid.

[460] BC, Oct 6, 1933, "Recreation Unit Is Formed Here"; Feb 23 1934, "Kern Property Being Prepared For Recreation". In Pari-Mutuel Betting Systems Winning Bettors Share All The Money Wagered By Losers, Minus A Percentage Deducted For Tax.3

[461] BC, May 10, 1933, "15 Per Cent Cut In Salaries For Local Teachers"

[462] BC, May 29, 1934, "Horses To Run Here Tomorrow"

[463] BC, Sep 6, 1934, "Newsmen Of City To Hide Under Shaggy Bush Piles"

[464] BC, Oct 6, 1934, "Huge Throng Sees Review Of 1894 Era"; "Miles Of Horsemen And Vehicles Of Long Ago March Before Throngs Along City Streets"

465 Minutes Of The Bakersfield City Council,
Sep 24, 1934, "Adoption Of Emergency Ordinance
No. 442"; BC, Oct 6, 1934, "Events Tomorrow To Be
Among Most Daring In History. Whiskerinos To Be
Judged Afternoon"
466 BC, May 29, 1935, "Last Report Of Grand Jury
Asks For Improved Library""
467 June Dooley Rodriguez letter to Gilbert Peter Gia, Apr
2009; BC, Apr 4, 1935, "Aged Structure Will Be Replaced
Soon By Earth And Steel Unit"
468 BC, Apr 8, 1935, "Frontier Group Given Contract On
Fairgrounds"; Oct 4, 1935, "Dinner, Parades, Dances And
Rodeo Events For Saturday And Sunday; Many Visitors
Coming"
469 BC, Aug 7, 1935, "Bakersfield Event Praised As One Of
Nation's Finest; Big Western Show Thriller";
Sep 23, 1935, "Guns Taboo During Frontier Day Fete"
470 BC, Jan 19, 1935, "Sale Of Motor Vehicles Shows Huge
Gain Here"; Apr 8, 1935, "Frontier Group Given Contract
On Fairgrounds"; Oct 4, 1935, "Dinner, Parades, Dances
And Rodeo Events For Saturday And Sunday; Many
Visitors Coming"; Fresno Public Library, San Joaquin
Valley Heritage & Genealogy Center,
[https://Livingnewdeal.Org/Projects/Old-Kern-County-
Fairgrounds-Bakersfield-Ca/]
471 BC, Mar 24, 1936, "Pipefuls By Jim Day";
May 6, 1936, "Pipefuls By Jim Day"
472 BC, Oct 2, 1936, "Saturday Parade Looms As One Of
Greatest In Western History"; Oct 7, 1936, "Rodeo Arena
Chief Expects World Records To Fall Here";
473 BC, Feb 27, 1937, Editorial Page, "Speaking of
employment ...";
Mar 9, 1937, "Supervisors Ask Federal Aid On Transient
Problem
474 BC, Feb 27, 1937, "A Widened Program"
475 BC, Mar 31, 1937, "Daredevil Stunt Program Slated";
Apr 3, 1937, "Death-Defying Crash To Be Presented
Here Sunday"

[476] BC, Sep 1, 1937, "Frontier Event Directors
Expect Record Crowds During Three Days
Of October 1, 2 And 3"; Sep 25, 1950, "Old Records Show
Evolution Of County Fair During Nearly Half Century
Since 1902"; Oct 2, 1937, "Frontier Rodeo To Be
Repeated Here On Sunday"

[477] BC, Sep 11, 1937, "Kern Cowboys, Cowgirls Will Enter
Contest"

[478] BC, Feb 27, 1937, "Speaking Of Employment ...";
Feb 27, 1937, "A Widened Program"; Mar 1, 1937,
"Action Delayed On Fairgrounds"; Mar 9, 1937,
"Supervisors Ask Federal Aid On Ancient Problem";
Sep 29, 1937, "Space For 7000 Automobiles To Be
Provided For Frontier Crowd"; Sep 30, 1937, "County
Pioneers Will Be Honored By Frontiersmen";
Sep 15, 1941, "Opens Tonight Then Daily 12 To Noon..."
(La Siesta Lounge Advertisement)

[479] BC, Sep 30, 1937, "Future Farmers Will Direct Show"

[480] BC, Nov 25, 1937, "Pro Teams Clash At Fairgrounds";
Dec 31, 1937, "Pipefuls By Jim Day". In 1928
Lockhart died in the crash of a Stutz Black Hawk Special.

[481] BC, Dec 11, 1937, "Horse Race Season Opens Sunday"

[482] BC, Feb 21, 1938, "Pipefuls By Jim Day"

[483] BC, Feb 17, 1938, "Court Rulings Affect Tracks";
Carroll v. California Horse Racing Board

[484] BC, Feb 24, 1938, "H.K. Dickson To Head Event For
Local Ranchers"; Aug 1, 1938, "Post Office Receipts Show
Increase For Quarter Here"

[485] BC, Aug 26, 1938, "Groups Chosen For Collecting
Parade Awards"; Aug 27, 1938, "Frontier Parade
Solicitors Plan Big Drive On Monday"; Sep 29, 1938,
"Governor Merriam To Take Part In Kern Celebration"

[486] BC, Sep 30, 1938, "Gay Street Dance Is
Slated Tonight"

[487] BC, Sep 23, 1938, "Costume Offices Open"

[488] BC, Oct 1, 1938, "55,000 View Big Parade";
BC, Oct 1, 1938, "Giant Ribbon Extends Six Miles, Has 35
Floats"; Sep 25, 1950, "Old Records Show Evolution Of
County Fair During Nearly Half Century Since 1902"

[489] BC, Sep 24, 1938, "Fun-Making Devices And Many Concessions Are Contracted By Heads Of Bakersfield Event"; Sep 29, 1938, "Governor Merriam To Take Part In Kern Celebration"; Oct 3, 1938, "Record Throng Attends Rodeo Show In Arena"

[490] BC, Aug 19, 1938, "Value Of Frontier Days Is Stressed At Local Session"

[491] BC, Jun 16, 1938, "Frontier Days Protest"

[492] BC, Aug 19, 1938, "Rio Bravo Fair Plan Drafted"

[493] BC, Jan 12, 1939, "County Fair To Be Meet Topic"; Jan 14, 1939, "County Fair Decision Left To Community Needs Meet"; Jul 20, 1939, "C. Of C. Survey Shows Upgrade In Business"

[494] BC, Jan 23, 1939, "County Fair Plan Deferred Until Next Year"

[495] BACA, Jun 7, 1940, "Schedule Released For Pair Of Loops"; Jul 20, 1940, "Kern Bike Champion To Be Crowned Here"

[496] BC, Apr 27, 1939, "Premium List Is Greater Than In 1938"; Aug 19, 1939, "Cattle Field Day Held For Kern Dairymen"; Oct 17, 1939, "Agricultural Directors Are Satisfied With Stock Show"

[497] BC, Oct 17, 1939, "Agricultural Directors Are Satisfied With Stock Show"

[498] BC, Apr 27, 1939, "Premium List Is Greater Than In 1938"; Sep 25, 1939, "Radio"; Oct 4, 1939, "Kern Livestock Show Slated Tomorrow At Fairgrounds"

[499] BC, Oct 17, 1939, "Agricultural Directors Are Satisfied With Stock Show"

[500] BC, Jan 1, 1940, "Kern Chamber Directors Report On Year's Program (Continued From Page Seventeen Preceding Section)"; Jun 7, 1940, "Schedule Released For Pair Of Loops"; Jul 20, 1940, "Kern Bike Champion To Be Crowned Here"; Sep 10, 1940, "Exhibit Divisions Claimed Filled To Capacity"

[501] BC, Sep 11, 1940, "Circus And Frontier Days"

[502] BC, Sep 16, 1940, "Western Frolic To Bring Week Of Festivity"

[503] Ibid.

[504] BC, Sep 16, 1940, "K.C.U.H.S. Athletes Will Take Part In Parade";
Sep 20, 1940, "Western Shows To Mark Peak Of Festivity"; Sep 20, 1940, "Complete Radio Programs (Continued From Page Fourteen)"

[505] BC, Jul 17, 1940, "Annual Frontier Day Show Set September 21"; Sep 10, 1940, "Exhibit Divisions Claimed Filled To Capacity; Sep 20, 1940, "Champions Are Crowded In Judging At Kern Livestock Show"; Sep 20, 1940, "Western Shows To Mark Peak Of Festivity"; Sep 20, 1940, "Complete Radio Programs (Continued From Page Fourteen)"

[506] BC, Sep 20, 1940, "Flays Arms Laxity, Urges Industry Spur"

[507] BC, Sep 16, 1940, "Western Frolic To Bring Week Of Festivity"

[508] BC, Oct 17, 1940, "Draft Registration May Surpass 17,000"; Sep 15, 1941, "Throngs Jam Annual Kern Stock Show On Opening; Sep 18, 1941, "Local Boards Reclassify Kern County Men Over 28"; Sep 20, 1941, "New Record Of 100,000 Predicted"; Gia, "One Hundred Years at Hart Park, 1890-1990"

[509] BC, Jun 5, 1941, "Lerdo, Taft Men Set Up Tent, Get Welcome";

[510] BC, Sep 15, 1941, " U.S. Navy Stripped For Fight Against U-Boats"; Sep 17, 1941, "Gardner Dedication Is Set November 11"; Sep 18, 1941,"85 Volunteers To Man 100-Center Kern Network"; Sep 20, 1942, "President Signs "Everybody's" Tax Bill"

[511] BC, Sep 17, 1941, "Volunteer Home Defense Corps Is Mustered"

[512] BC, Sep 15, 1941, "Frontier Days Calendar"; Sep 15, 1941, "Boys! Girls! Grown Folks, Too!"; Sep 18, 1941, "Many Floats, 13 Bands To Join Riders In Parade"; www.Legacy.Com/Us/Obituaries/Bakersfield/Name /Corinne-Lambert-Obituary?Id=33003189

[513] BC, Sep 20, 1941, "Officials And Exhibitors Praise County Stock Show"

[514] BC, Dec 4, 1940, "Work Begins On Ball Park At Fairgrounds"

[515] BC, Jun 5, 1940, "Frontier Days Horse Show To Be Held In Lynn Park"; Sep 16, 1940, "K.C.U.H.S. Athletes Will Take Part In Parade"; Sep 20, 1940, "Western Shows To Mark Peak Of Festivity"

[516] BC, Nov 26, 1940, "County Building At Lebec To House $200,000 Exhibit"; Bailey

[517] BC, Aug 20, 1941, "Kern Museum Slowed By Shortages"; Sep 13, 1949, "County Finds No Money For Florafaunium"

[518] BC, Jan 1, 1940, "Kern Chamber Directors Report On Year's Program (Continued From Page Seventeen Preceding Section)"

[519] BC, Jan 8, 1934, "Saving A Heritage"

[520] BC, Nov 13, 1940, "Historical Society Urges Creation Of Kern Museum"

[521] BC, Nov 13, 1940, "A County Museum"

[522] BC, Dec 16, 1940, "Supervisor Abel Reports Money All Allotted"

[523] BC, Feb 26, 1941, "County Museum Requested By Kern Historical Group", Mar 3, 1941., "Historical Society Seeks County-Sponsored Museum"; May 10, 1941, "T.J. Foley Is Appointed To Housing-Authority Post"

[524] BC, Feb 26, 1941, "County Museum Requested By Kern Historical Group"; Oct 27, 1947, "San Joaquin Indians Invented Barbarian "Root Of All Evil""; Jan 5, 1948, "Random Notes"

[525] BC, Apr 21, 1942, "New Large-Scale Ouster Speeded By Dewitt"

[526] BC, Mar 6, 1942, "Military Ruling May Hamper Kern Fair"

[527] BC, Apr 25, 1942, "Mighty American Circus" (Advertisement)

[528] BC, May 12, 1941, "Take First Steps On Establishing History Agency"; Apr 22, 1942, "California League Information At Glance"; Apr 25, 1942, "Maricopa Slates Bangtail Session"; Apr 25, 1942, "Sunday Is Olsen Day At Ball Park"; Apr 25, 1942, "2500 See Manager Colbern Lead Team To Win Over 1941 League Champions"; War Production News For Northern California And Nevada, War Production Board, May 26, 1942; Jul 25, 1942, "Ex-Badgers"; Aug 19, 1942, "Sears August Furniture And Rug Sale"; Aug 19, 1942, "Story Of The Patriotic Potatoes"; Aug 19, 1942, "Kern To Dim Out For War Tonight"; Jan 26, 1944, "Elect Frontier Group Leaders"

[529] BC, Sep 17, 1942, "7000 Volunteers In Kern Defense Setup"

[530] BC, BC, Sep 25, 1947, "Thousands See Many Exhibits"

[531] Billboard, Mar 28, 1942, "Sizing Up The Season"; BC, Jul 17, 1942, "1942 Fair Gets Final Okay"

[532] BC, Sep 2, 1942, "Final Plans Okayed For Livestock Show"

[533] BC, "Kern Fair Opens"; Sep 3, 1942, "Champion Parade Planned At Fair"

[534] BC, Sep 2, 1942, "Final Plans Okayed For Livestock Show"; Sep 7, 1942, "Record Sales Close Kern Livestock Fair"; Shafter Press, Sep 8, 1982, "Livestock Auction At Kern Fair Has Much History:

[535] BC, Jan 9, 1943, "Lower Allotment For County Fair"; Aug 12, 1943, "County Fair To Head Program"

[536] BC, Sep 3, 1943, "Random Notes"

[537] BC, Sep 15, 1944, "Kern Museum Board Of Directors Set"; Dec 29, 1951, "50,000 Visitors Tour Kern Museum Exhibits. By Frank Latta"

[538] BC, May 29, 1944, "Kern Museum To Be Opened"; Sep 15, 1944, "Kern Museum Board Of Directors Set"

[539] BC, Sep 25, 1944, "20,000 See Huge Food Fair"

[540] BC, Aug 23, 1944, "Elementary School Pupils Will Exhibit At Fair"

[541] BC, Aug 28, 1944, "Entries Pour In For Horse Division Of Foods Fair"; Sep 25, 1944, "20,000 See Huge Food Fair"; Sep 25, 1944, "4000 Pack Grounds For Annual Horse Show Finale, By Mae Saunders"

[542] BC, Sep 19, 1945, "Colorful 5-Day Festival Opens"

[543] BC, Aug 10, 1945, "$28,000 In Prizes Listed For Winner As Fair Officials Announce Premiums"

[544] BC, Sep 19, 1945, "Colorful 5-Day Festival Opens"; Sep 19, 1945, "Into The Stretch!"; Sep 19, 1945, "Events Slated For Kern Fair"; Sep 24, 1945, "Thousands See Kern Fair Close"

[545] BC, Apr 1, 1947, "Vets Promised Minter Homes In Agreement"; "Vets Promised 57 Barracks At Minter, Continued From Page Nine"; May 21, 2023, "Native American Education Center On Track For Opening In September"

[546] BC, Apr 5, 1946, "Wild West Show Re-Enacts Scenes Of Cowboy Life"

[547] BC, "Sep 21, 1946, "Event Will Draw 200 Purebreds"; Sep 30, 1946, "Steer Sale Sets Mark At Auction"

[548] BC, Mar 2, 1946, "Board Asks County To Buy Land"; Jul 9, 1946, "Board To Buy New Fair Site"; Sep 12, 1946, "New County Fairgrounds Will Be Californian's Best Show Site"; Sep 30, 1946, "90,000 Persons See 1946 Exhibits At County Fair, Continued From Page Nine"

[549] BC, Mar 2, 1946, "Board Asks County To Buy Land"; Aug 27, 1946, "Board Adopts Charity Law"; Sep 12, 1946, "New County Fairgrounds Will Be California's Best Show Site"; Sep 30, 1946, "150-Acre Purchase Is Proposed"; Sep 30, 1946, "90,000 Persons See 1946 Exhibits At County Fair, Continued From Page Nine"

[550] BC, Sep 12, 1946, "New County Fairgrounds Will Be California's Best Show Site"; Sep 12, 1946, "150-Acre Purchase Is Proposed"; Oct 28, 1946, "Salzer Motion For Dismissal Fails, 4 On Investigating Unit; Oct 29, 1946, "Fairgrounds Site Chosen For Armory"; Nov 1, 1946, "Supervisors Close Deal With Navy Over New Armory"; Mar 6, 1947, "Navy Calls Bids On $167,000 Armory"; Jun 14, 1948, "R.O.A. To Tour Naval Armory"

[551] BC, Feb 8, 1947, "City Gets Priority For Guard Armory"; Oct 16, 1950, "Fair Officials Work To Get Set For 1951"; Jan 11, 1951, "$127,000 Armory Asked For Delano Guardsmen"; Nov 3, 1952, "Bids For New National Guard Armory Advertised Today"

[552] BC, May 28, 1938, "Nine More Homes Boosting Total In 27 Days"

[553] BC, Apr 5, 1909, "A Revelry Of Wood Choppers Ends
In Murder"; May 23, 1914, "Board Of Trade Exhibit";
Oct 6, 1922, "Glorious Days Presage Winter Sleep By
Thelma Bernard"; Aug 10, 1945, "Plans-Made For
$199,000 New School"; Oct 12, 1945, "Grammar School
Site Change Studied At Meeting Of Board"; Jan 9, 1969,
"Rename Casa Loma Drive"; Feb 4, 1969, "Casa Loma
Drive Between Union Avenue And South H..."

[554] BC, May 3, 1947, "Money To Total Nearly $10,000";
Sep 25, 1947, "Thousands See Many Exhibits"; Sep 26,
"Horses Vie For Honors At Show"

[555] Billboard, Oct 11, 1947, "Bakersfield Sets Mark---
132,000"

[556] BC, Sep 28, 1948, "Colorful Kern County Fair Opens
Gate Today, Continued From Page 1"

[557] BC, Sep 21, 1948, "Jackie Coogan, Former Star, To
Head Parade"; Sep 27, 1948, "Gates To Swing Wide On
Big Show Tuesday"; Oct 12, 1948, "Community Theater
To Have Workshop, Rehearsal Room"

[558] BC, Sep 28, 1948, "Parade Opens Annual Fair"

[559] BC, Sep 27, 1948, "Gates To Swing Wide On Big Show
Tuesday"; Sep 29, 1947, "Successful Fair" (Editorial); Sep
27, 1948, "Kern County Fair"(Ad); Oct 4, 1948, "73,752
See County Fair Make Record"; Oct 7, 1948, "Whiskerino
Court Opens Here Monday"; Oct 7, 1948, "Clean Shaven
To Face Trial, Continued From Page 17"

[560] BC, Jan 8, 1947, "Tiny Racing Cars Open State-Wide
Meeting Saturday"; Jun 17, 1947, "Albert Wilbur Voted
$540 Boost In Salary"; Jan 24, 1948, "Miniature Race
Meet Set For Here Sunday"; Mar 25, 1948, "Miniatures
Open Racing Meet Sat."; Sep 25, 1950, "Oakland Man Set
Midget Car Record"; Jun 4, 1956, "Let's Review Salzer's
Record!"

[561] BC, Aug 13, 1948, "State Okays Fairgrounds Contour
Plans"; Mar 12, 1949, "State Agency To Pass Fund
Request"; Oct 16, 1950, "Fair Official Work To Get
Set For 1951"; Oct 27, 1949, "Rapid Action On
Fairground Plan Ordered"

[562] BC, Nov 18, 1950, "State Awards Contacts For
New Fair Buildings"

[563] BC, Sep 24, 1949, "Horsemen Set For Historic Ride To Fair"; Sep 26, 1949, "Jet Fighter Trundled To Fair Exhibit"

[564] BC, Sep 26, 1949, "Annual Agricultural Exhibit, Horse Show Set For Week's Run"

[565] BC, Jun 8, 1949, "Horse Show For Youths Suggested For Kern Fair"

[566] BC, Nov 11, 1949, Junior Horse Show Unit Plans 1950 Exhibition"

[567] BC, Sep 30, 1949, "Horse Show Ribbons Go To Equestriennes"; Oct 1, 1949, "Colorful, Thrill-Packed Week End To Climax Fair"

[568] BC, Sep 14, 1949, "Directors See 100,000 Gate At Kern Fair"

[569] BC, Sep 29,1949,"Many Events Fill Calendar Of Kern Fair For Friday"

[570] BC, Dec 16, 1949, "Vets Start Telephone Drive To Boom Circus"; Jun 14, 1950, "Pipefuls By Jim Day"

[571] BC, Jun 27, 1950, "Air, Sea, Fight Ordered On Invaders"; Jul 7, 1950, "Draft Ordered In Emergency"; Sep 26, 1950, "Fair's Bright Hurly-Burly Gets Under Way"

[572] BC, Sep 30, 1950, "County Fair Nears End Of Biggest Season Here"; Sep 30, 1950, "High Stakes Await Victors In Horse Show"; Sep 30, 1950, "Thrill Show Features Precision Auto Daredevils"; Oct 2, 1950, "Aristocrats Of Horse World Win Rich Prizes In Kern Show"

[573] Shafter Press, Sep 19, 1951, "Fair Parade Honors Two Local Veterans"

[574] BC, Jan 11, 1951, "Association To Abandon Annual Kern Horse Show"; Oct 1, 1951, "Cutting Horse Trials Wind Up County Fair"

[575] BC, Sep 26, 1951, "Kern Fair Opens To Throng"

[576] BC, Oct 2, 1950, "Random Notes"

[577] BC, Feb 22, 1951, "1951 County Fair Will Be Held At Old Grounds"; Shafter Press, Sep 19, 1951, "Wide Appeal Of Kern Fair Is Praised"; BC, Oct 28, 1951, "All-Time Record Attendance Seen At County Fair"

[578] BC, Sep 26, 1951, "Gary Garrett, 15, Follows In Dad's Footsteps At Fair"

[579] BC, Oct 26, 1951, "Kern Fair Opens To Throng"

[580] BC, Sep 26, 1951, "New Turnstile Mark Set At County Fair"

[581] BC, Oct 6, 1951, "The Reader's Viewpoint. Help Youth"

[582] BC, May 12, 1941, "Take First Steps On Establishing History Agency"; Aug 20, 1941, "Kern Museum Slowed By Shortages"; Oct 10, 1949, "Pioneer Village Plans Set; Work Starts Soon"; Feb 25, 1950, "Florafaunium Worthless In Five Years"; Apr 27, 1950, "County Will Move Lebec Florafaunium"; Jul 15, 1952, "Kern Associated Commerce Group Plans Completed"; https://Scvhistory.Com/Scvhistory/Lw3247.Htm

[583] BC, Mar 29, 1947, "County Chamber Previews New Building Plans"; Aug 22, 1949, "Museum Needs Space"; Sep 12, 1949, "Twenty Years Ago, Kern Chamber Opened Home"

[584] BC, Aug 22, 1948, "Board Approves Pioneer Village"; "Dec 29, 1951, "50,000 Visitors Tour Kern Museum Exhibits, By Frank Latta"; The Chamber Of Commerce balcony was added in 1958.

[585] BC, Jul 15, 1952, "Kern Associated Commerce Group Plans Completed"; Jul 15, 1952, "County Museum Takes Over Entire Chamber Building"; "Museum Gets More Space. Continued From Page 13"; Jul 16, 1952, "Random Notes"

[586] BC, Sep 5, 1952, 'Superior Court Moves To County Farm Building"; Mar 10, 1953, ""Courthouse" Now At Old Kern Fairgrounds"

[587] BC, Aug 27, 1952, "Board Will Reopen Budget Next Tuesday"; Dec 31, 1952, "Earthquakes Set Work In Museum Back, Says Latta"

[588] BC, Sep 19, 1952, "Kern County Fair" (Map); Sep 23, 1952, "Tonight's Fair Program"; Sep 29, 1952, "147,922 Attend Kern Fair"

[589] BC, Sep 22, 1952, "Bigger, Better Show Opens"

[590] Billboard, Nov 29, 1952, "Kern County Fair, Bakersfield"

[591] BC, Mar 28, 1962, "Live Oral Polio Vaccine Approved By Government"; Apr 30, 1962, "Operation Smooth And Easy"

[592] BC, Sep 26, 1951, "Kern Fair Opens To Throng"

[593] Bates

[594] Bailey. Collector's Choice: The McLeod Basket Collection, p. 8-36; BC, Jun 29, 1951, "Bailey Authors Booklet On History Of McLeod Yokuts Basket Collection"; Edwin Lincoln McLeod and E. L. McLeod Memorial Collection, Hearst Museum Portal, https://portal.hearstmuseum.berkeley.edu/

www.ingramcontent.com/pod-product-compliance
Lightning Source LLC
Chambersburg PA
CBHW060013100426
42740CB00010B/1473